W9-ABY-937

Native Americans and Archaeologists

Stepping Stones to Common Ground

Native Americans and Archaeologists

Stepping Stones to Common Ground

Nina Swidler
Kurt E. Dongoske
Roger Anyon
Alan S. Downer
editors

ALTAMIRA
PRESS

A Division of Sage Publications, Inc.
Walnut Creek ■ London ■ New Delhi

Published in cooperation with the
Society for American Archaeology

For information address:

AltaMira Press
A Division of Sage Publications, Inc.
1630 North Main Street, Suite 367
Walnut Creek, CA 94596

SAGE Publications Ltd.
6 Bonhill Street
London EC2A 4PU
United Kingdom

SAGE Publications India Pvt. Ltd.
M-32 Market
Greater Kailash 1
New Delhi 110 048 India

PRINTED IN THE UNITED STATES OF AMERICA

Library of Congress Cataloging-in-Publication Data

Native Americans and Archaeologists: Stepping Stones to Common Ground / edited by Nina
    Swidler . . . [et al.].
        p.   cm.
    "Published in Cooperation with the Society for American Archaeology."
    Includes index.
    ISBN 0-7619-8900-5 (cloth: acid-free paper). — ISBN 0-7619-8901-3 (pbk: acid-free
    paper)
    1. Indians of North America—Material culture. 2. Indians of North America—
Antiquities—Law and Legislation. 3. Indians of North America—Civil Rights. 4. Human
remains (Archaeologyy)—Law and legislation—United States. 5. Archaeologists—United
States—Attitudes. 6. Cultural property—Repatriation—United States. 7. United States. Native
American Graves Protection and Repatriation Act. 1. Swidler, Nina.
E98.M34N37 1997
973. 1—DC21   97—4593
                                                                              CIP

97   98   99   00   01   02   9   8   7   6   5   4   3   2   1

Editorial Management by Nicole Fountain
Production Services by Carole M. Bernard
Cover Artwork by Gary White Deer
Cover Design by Ravi Balasuriya

Contents

Section VI: Commentary   235

Dedication

William V. Tallbull (1921–1996). Photo courtesy of M. Crummett.

In dedicating this volume to Bill Tallbull, we seek to honor an Elder who has left us with many important memories. By example and story he taught us to recognize and respect the spiritual as well as the physical aspects of the environment. Bill would not care for flowery accolades but he would expect us to be mindful of those who have gone before as we meet our responsibilities to those who will come. As he told us, we are the ancestors of those to come. We serve as their environmental caretakers. We must balance living human values with those of science. To truly honor him, we must continue his work. He has left us a blueprint in his understanding of living human values.

—Sherri Deaver

WILLIAM V. TALLBULL ■

SHERRI DEAVER

Foreword
Living Human Values

Living human values are the network of symbolic relationships that tie people to the land and landscape.

All people have connections to the places where they live, work, and play. People form relationships with these places. People define places as good, powerful, and safe. They find comfort by living in these places. There is a sense of belonging that is valued. This sense of belonging is based on the compatibility between the group's way of life and its environment.

The eastern Montana rancher sees the vast prairie as a sea of grass that sustains his way of life. It is full of forage for his herds, coulees for shelter. Crop Rotation Program fields sustaining the grouse and pheasant and patches of water must be carefully managed and respected in order for life as he knows it to continue. It is the place where three generations of his family have given birth, gone to school, worshipped with their neighbors, and buried their dead. He has a personal relationship with his landscape, he knows the coulee where he found the crippled calf, the butte where the first homesteader is buried, and the two-tracks that swallow four-wheel drives after a spring rain. His landscape is meaningful and cherished because it supports his chosen way of life.

The western North Dakota coal miner sees the prairie as overburden, which must be removed to reach the thick lignite beds. The beds sustain his family, providing the revenue base for his schools, towns, and churches. He names each pit and tells stories about the people who work in them. The drag lines have names and personalities. The historic spoil piles sticking up above the flat prairie provide cover for pheasants and a place to train his spaniel. His children visit the dancing grouse leks, and he schedules his mining activities so as not to disturb the spring dances. After he harvests the coal, he recontours the land, replants the grasses, and puts up fences to corral the Coteau bison herd. Then he expands the mine into a new area, digging, contouring, and naming a new pit. His relationship with the land is a continuing focus of his life.

The Northern Cheyenne of Muddy Creek see this drainage as the place chosen by Little Wolf when he was exiled from the tribe. Another exile had told him it is a good place to live. It has timber, grass, and water—all of the things necessary for a good life. The Northern Cheyenne have developed a relationship to this place. It is marked by the birth bundles they place in the trees to ensure that children will always know their home. To protect the living, they place the powerful medicine bundles and graves in the hills away from the home sites. The spirits living in the hills, springs, and streams provide them a network of meaning that sustain their chosen way of life. These relationships give them guidance in their daily lives.

Preface and Acknowledgments

This book is the result of three sessions organized for the 1996 annual meeting of the Society for American Archaeology[1] (SAA) to examine the relations between Native Americans and archaeologists. Each session was conceived independently. When the organizers of each session became aware of the others, plans were made to coalesce them into a thematic forum. The organizers jointly requested, through the SAA Native American Relations Committee, that the SAA Executive Board sponsor and support the thematic forum at the annual meeting in New Orleans. Following Executive Board approval, the organizers raised more than $16,000 to support the travel, registration, and lodging expenses of the Native American presenters.

The forum, "Exploring the Relations Between Native Americans and Archaeologists," was divided into three parts:

Native Americans and Archaeology: Personal Perspectives from Both Sides, organized by Kurt Dongoske, Hopi Tribe, and Roger Anyon, Pueblo of Zuni

Roles and Relevancy: Native American Perspectives on Archaeology, organized by Nina Swidler and Alan Downer, Navajo Nation

Stepping Stones to Common Ground: Native Americans, Archaeologists, and Consultation, organized by Joe Watkins, Bureau of Indian Affairs, and Lynn Larson, Larson Anthropological/Archaeological Services

The relationship between archaeologists and Native Americans has been lopsided from the inception of American archaeology as a discipline. Although archaeologists study the past and, by doing so, study the history of Native Americans, the opinions and traditional history of Native Americans are often left out of archaeological interpretations. Generally, archaeologists do not consult Native Americans during the development of research designs, and the information gathered is inadequately disseminated to the Native American descendants of our study populations. This lack of communication has only led to further impasses.

Legal issues and economic factors have thrust American archaeology into a period of intellectual and methodological unrest. The archaeological community often speaks of the need to transform American archaeology into a discipline that both appeals to and serves the greater public. From our perspective, this transformation requires opening and establishing a lasting dialogue with Native Americans, one of our most important constituencies. To develop a multicultural focus, it is necessary to move toward an understanding of one another's worldviews.

We have gathered in this volume the views of Native American representatives from tribes throughout the United States, professional archaeologists and anthropologists who work for tribes, federal and state agency representatives, museum specialists, and private archaeological and anthropological consultants (Figure 1). We asked the authors to suggest ways to integrate Native American opinions and needs into the mainstream of American archaeology and to discuss and consider other valid ways to know the past. We also asked them to talk about constructive strategies for what tribes, archaeologists, academic institutions, government agencies, museums, and other members of the public can do to open and maintain mutually beneficial communications. For too long, insufficient effort has been devoted to a humanistic approach integrating Western scientific methods with a non-Western perspective. We hope that these relationships will lead to collaborative efforts that document and interpret the past, producing more holistic and realistic interpretations of the past. To accomplish this, we strongly believe that American archaeologists should have a dynamic relationship with Native Americans.

One of the reasons we sought SAA sponsorship for the forum and this volume was because until very recently the archaeological community had not made a concerted effort to listen to the varied voices of Native Americans. Alternatively, few Native Americans have had an opportunity to present their historical perspectives and opinions to a large audience of archaeologists or anthropologists. Despite these hurdles, archaeologists and Native American groups have established open lines of communication, on a local level, in many parts of the country. The forum was designed to facilitate a national dialogue between Native Americans and

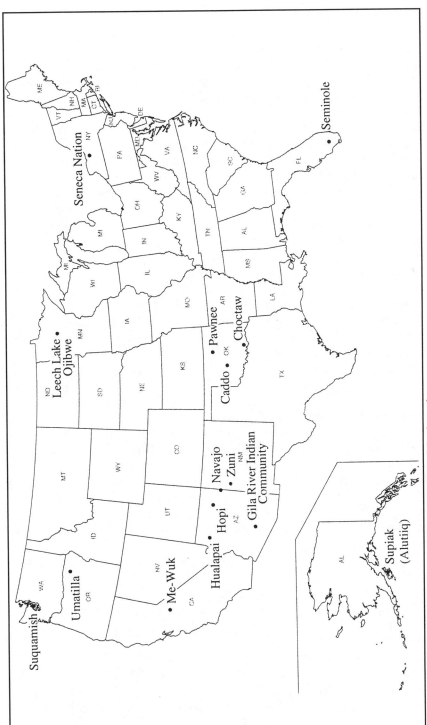

Figure 1. Location of present-day reservations discussed in the volume.

the archaeological community. From the outset, the organizers were committed to publishing the proceedings of the forum to reach the widest audience possible.

We expect this publication will promote further discussion, and perhaps debate, by those involved in the national historic preservation program. In a country composed of diverse cultural and religious traditions, it is imperative that Native American perspectives and cultural values become an equal part of the national historic preservation process. Recent changes in national laws have given Native Americans a stronger voice in how archaeology is conducted; thus, it is now critical that we integrate non-Western values and concepts of historic preservation into the process. As anthropologists, however, we should consult Native Americans not only because the law mandates it, but also because we recognize other groups' intrinsic interests in their past. We also believe that the results of collaborative research will yield major benefits to archaeologists and the archaeological discipline.

Finally, we expect that publishing the results of the forum will contribute to the evolving dialogue of archaeological ethics currently being addressed by the academic and professional communities. We hope that *Native Americans and Archaeologists: Stepping Stones to Common Ground* will help bridge the gap in communication and understanding between the archaeological community and representative organizations such as the Society for American Archaeology, and Native American communities and representative organizations such as the Keepers of the Treasures.[2] Beyond practicing archaeologists and anthropologists, our intended audience includes national, state, local, and avocational archaeological/ anthropological associations; those proposing ethics and other course curricula at colleges and universities; persons working in government agencies and museums; and members of Native American tribes and organizations.

The editors and the organizers of the thematic sessions wish to acknowledge the support of members and staff of the Society for American Archaeology: Catherine M. Cameron, Margaret Nelson, John Rick, Barbara L. Stark, and Julie Stein, members of the Executive Board; William D. Lipe, SAA president; Joe Watkins, chair of the Native American Relations Committee; Tobi Brimsek, executive director; Janet Walker, publications manager; David L. Whitlock, former finance and administration director; and, in particular, Ralph Johnson, former executive director.

Paul Fish and Suzanne K. Fish, program chairs for the 1996 SAA Annual Meeting in New Orleans, were instrumental in providing the venue and arranging a schedule that allowed for presentation of the three sessions that led to this volume.

Individuals and organizations who provided financial support enabling Native American speakers to participate in the forum in New Orleans are Kimball M. Banks, Bureau of Reclamation–South Dakota Region; Francis McManamon, National Park Service–Archeology and Ethnography Program; Ruth E. Lambert,

Office of Navajo-Hopi Indian Relocation; Signa Larralde, Bureau of Reclamation–Upper Colorado Region; Mary Barger, Western Area Power Administration–Colorado; A. Eugene Rogge, Dames and Moore Environmental Consultants–Phoenix Office; David Sabo, Western Area Power Administration–Salt Lake City; Judy Brunson-Hadley, Salt River Project; Steven W. Carothers, SWCA Inc., Environmental Consultants; and John W. Hohmann, Louis Berger and Associates–Phoenix Office.

Two individuals, Tessie Naranjo and Bruce Crespin, participated as presenters in the New Orleans forum but were unable to include their papers in this volume. In addition, Lynn Larson coorganized one of the three sessions.

Finally, we would like to acknowledge the assistance of Audrey Roberts, Sharon Lastyona, and Leigh Kuwanwisiwma, and the support of the Navajo Nation Historic Preservation Department, the Hopi Tribe, and the Pueblo of Zuni. Nicole Price shared memories of William Tallbull and put us in contact with Sherri Deaver, who contributed the dedication to him. Gary White Deer created the cover art, Michael Crummett provided the photograph for the dedication, and Ron Stauber drafted or redrafted the figures. June-el Piper is responsible for the excellent editing despite the heat, the beer, the wine, the lack of sleep, and the politics. Thanks to the peer reviewers, Don D. Fowler, Hartman Lomawaima, and Thomas F. King, for their insightful comments. We would also like to thank Mitch Allen, Erik Hanson, and Nicole Fountain of AltaMira Press for supporting this volume and for the prompt publication of this work. Finally, Michael Yeatts provided a steady hand, always ready with encouragement, support, and upon request, welcomed counsel.

All royalties resulting from this publication will be placed in SAA's Native American Scholarship Fund. We encourage other professional archaeologists to follow this example and donate royalties from their publications to this fund.

NOTES

1. The Society for American Archaeology is an international organization dedicated to the research, interpretation, and protection of the archaeological heritage of the Americas.

2. The Keepers of the Treasures is a cultural council of American Indians, Alaska Natives, and Native Hawaiians who preserve, affirm, and celebrate their cultures through traditions and programs that maintain their native languages and lifeways. The Keepers protects and conserves places that are historic and sacred to indigenous peoples.

Introduction

Many of the papers in this volume present a personal perspective on the relations between archaeologists and Native Americans. This is intentional. All too often, issues of emotional intensity such as those discussed in this volume become watered down because of the perceived imperative to present positions in "objective academic formats." As the authors show, the issues addressed must be approached with a full and clear understanding of just how personal these issues are. Consequently, while some of the papers may not be as formal as one might expect, we believe that their tenor is just as important as the issues being presented.

We feel it is essential to the dialogue that the Native American authors' presentations be as purely in their own voices as possible. As a result, their presentations are often more personal and charged than is typically the case in scholarly works. In our view, part of the communication gap between archaeologists and Native Americans results from the former failing to hear the real concerns of the latter. The key to bridging the gap is understanding that these views are real, not posturing, and that they are deeply held, core beliefs—they cannot be brushed aside, nor can they be changed casually. In fact, it may not be reasonable to expect them to change very much. The key, then, lies in accepting these beliefs at face value and finding ways to make archaeology relevant and useful despite fundamental differences.

A number of themes run throughout the volume. The Native American Graves Protection and Repatriation Act (NAGPRA) is a pervasive issue. As many authors note, NAGPRA has fundamentally changed the way archaeologists and Native Americans interact. Part of this is the issue of ownership: NAGPRA has legislatively redefined ownership of cultural items such as human remains and funerary objects. This new legal reality has forced archaeologists to face the fact that they no longer have total control of the archaeological record.

Consultation is another common concern. Consultation can no longer be perceived as a one-way avenue of communication in which archaeologists inform Native Americans of what will be happening to archaeological, cultural, and heritage resources. Now, any meaningful consultation must be a dialogue between equals: real communication involves listening as much as speaking and ensuring that the message received is the one that was actually sent.

One question that continually arises is just how much, if at all, archaeology is really changing in response to recent legislation and Native American concerns. We find that archaeologists who are tribal employees perceive a great deal more change than is discerned by the majority of practicing archaeologists. Tribal members perceive a change in their status and note that opportunities for their involvement have increased. The traditional relationship between tribes and archaeologists and other non-Indians, however, has probably not fundamentally changed. It is clear from the legislation that Congress intends to force archaeology to become more humanistic. We urge all practicing archaeologists to understand the legally mandated transformations in our discipline and work constructively toward ameliorating relations between archaeologists and Native Americans. The alternative is a long and unproductive fight for control and, ultimately, one that will end unsuccessfully for the archaeological community.

Another topic the authors address is archaeology's relevance to tribes. Many tribal people see a limit to its applicability. When archaeological inquiry is used, it must be conducted with a sense of responsibility to the living communities. Some authors note that archaeology is useful as a tool in establishing land tenure and can assist tribal members to understand and learn about the past by preserving and protecting cultural and heritage resources. Others view archaeology as a source of employment and as a means to educate tribal members in tribal traditions while providing economic security. Still others see it as simply a hoop that must be jumped through in order to comply with federally imposed legislation. In this sense, tribes are in the same boat as most project proponents and development agencies.

The flip side to this topic, the relevance of traditional history to archaeologists, is also explored. It appears that the potential of traditional history to affect archaeological interpretation is much greater than the reverse. However, we often hear tribes express concern that archaeologists will soon be "mining" their oral history, similar to the way in which archaeologists mine the physical evidence of their ancestors. The archaeological community should be sensitive to this heartfelt sentiment. Similarly, the issue of intellectual property rights will affect how archaeologists interact with Native Americans in the future, but it is not the focus here (cf. Greaves 1994).

The issues pertaining to the relationship between archaeologists and indigenous peoples are not unique to the United States, but are being examined worldwide. For example, many of the issues presented in this volume are also being addressed by our Canadian colleagues. Nicholas and Andrews (1997) provide a thorough discussion of these issues in their forthcoming volume, *At a Crossroads: Archaeology and First Peoples in Canada*.

***

This volume consists of six sections, beginning with a historical overview of the relations between Native Americans and archaeologists. Alan S. Downer makes several observations: there is an absence of real communication; the Native American position has not substantially changed through time; and NAGPRA has ushered in a new era of Native American–archaeologist relations. As noted above, these are among the pervasive themes discussed by many of the authors.

Section II focuses on the changes occurring as a result of the new era of Native American–archaeologist relations discussed by Downer. Gary White Deer opens with a poignant statement for a balanced consideration of both science and Native American spiritual sensibilities. Larry J. Zimmerman follows with a provocative discussion of how archaeologists have been reinterpreting the relations between Native Americans and archaeologists with respect to the reburial and repatriation debate. The tenor of this debate, one that remained virtually unchanged until very recently, is well illustrated by G. Peter Jemison. The legal mandates that have forced archaeologists to deal directly with Native Americans are presented by Rebecca Tsosie. Roger Anyon and his colleagues talk about the relevance of oral tradition to archaeology and the value of archaeology to traditional history, emphasizing the differences in the needs of archaeologists and Native Americans. How oral tradition and archaeology can be combined to generate a powerful method to understand the past is the subject of Roger Echo-Hawk's paper. In all of these chapters, NAGPRA is identified as the primary agent of change.

Section III deals with the integration of tradition and science. Leonard A. Forsman provides compelling evidence that traditional and scientific issues can be addressed through mutual respect, communication, and tolerance. How this is manifest on the Leech Lake Reservation is the subject of Rose Kluth and Kathy Munnell. The inherent complexities and cultural paradoxes of a Native American becoming a professional archaeologist within the academic context are insightfully examined by Dorothy Lippert. Rena Martin questions the appropriateness of archaeological practices in a traditional tribal context, a point further explored by Loretta Jackson and Robert H. ("Hank") Stevens. Reba Fuller provides a good example of how one tribe has educated itself about the nature of cultural resource management and archaeology, and how the Me-Wuks are promoting their traditional views as an integral part of archaeological practice.

The subject of Section IV is the relevance of archaeology to tribes. Cecile Elkins Carter opens the discussion with an eloquent statement regarding the need for trust and open communication between archaeologists and Native Americans. Billy L. Cypress discusses the way archaeology can be useful to the Seminole Tribe while respecting the cultural wishes and practices of the tribal members. In contrast, Richard M. Begay examines archaeology as the imposition of foreign cultural values on the Navajo Nation. A program involving both traditional knowledge and archaeology as a means to educate tribal members about their past, their culture, and their natural and cultural resources is the subject of Jeffrey Van Pelt and his colleagues. John C. Ravesloot talks about the use of archaeology as a means to promote tribal self-governance and sovereignty.

Section V is about consultation. Reba Fuller discusses how the attitude of participants can color the outcome of consultations between archaeologists, project sponsors, and Native Americans, often resulting in the success or failure of consultation. Kurt E. Dongoske and Roger Anyon examine the tensions that can arise when professional archaeologists represent and advocate tribal positions to other archaeologists, and to government agencies, and represent the scientific perspective to their tribal employers. Nina Swidler and Janet Cohen address the ramifications of tribal assumption of federal and state compliance responsibilities, and how this change in status can affect intertribal consulting relationships. Robert L. Brooks offers a perspective on the challenges of consultation between state and federal agencies, archaeologists, and federally recognized tribes in Oklahoma. Promoting a humanistic approach to archaeological studies, David G. Rice presents a federal perspective on consultation in the Northwest. As a "tribal-turned-federal" employee, Alexa Roberts articulates an eloquent and balanced perspective on the management requirements of the National Park Service and the very human needs of living communities, both of which require a shared commitment to common values and consistency in the application of policies. Our final section provides a commentary by T.J. Ferguson, Joe Watkins, and Gordon L. Pullar.

SECTION I

Historical Overview

ALAN S. DOWNER ■

One

Archaeologists–Native American Relations

For the past 20 years I have been a participant and observer in the discourse between archaeologists and Native Americans on repatriation/reburial and a number of other matters. During this period, a considerable level of conflict and controversy typified the relationship between the archaeological community and Native Americans. The most striking feature of this conflict was the near total absence of communication.[1]

I watched archaeologists discount most of what they heard from Indians as political rhetoric, repeatedly reassuring themselves that if they could just educate the Indians, then, after an epiphany, the Indians would leave them alone to continue sciencing.[2] The Native Americans, for their part, simply could not believe that scientific curiosity was sufficient justification for the desecration of the graves of their ancestors. Nor could they believe that anyone, let alone archaeologists—who, after all, traced their intellectual lineage to the founders of American anthropology—could be so insensitive to the beliefs of Native Americans. Finally, they could not believe that archaeologists as anthropologists, practitioners of the "most human" of the social sciences, could so thoroughly dehumanize and *objectify* the people they studied. Archaeologists and Native Americans have inherently different perceptions of the past and of archaeological sites (see Downer 1989).[3] These differences in perspective were the fundamental source of the communications breakdown (see Layton 1989).

Although it was never the only issue, repatriation/reburial of Native American human remains was the central and most contentious matter discussed between Indians and archaeologists. No matter what else was on the agenda, reburial almost always came up (see Downer and Klesert 1990). In truth, by comparison all other issues dwindled to the virtual vanishing point (although they rarely actually vanished).

Over the years, meetings were organized between archaeologists and Native Americans. Roundtable discussions and symposia occurred at regional and national professional meetings. These sessions were well attended. No one who wanted to be informed could have missed them. But for all the apparent effort at "dialogue" and education, very little change occurred in the thinking of either Native Americans or archaeologists through most of this period.

Archaeologists and Native Americans were largely talking past one another—did not share a common frame of reference or even, apparently, a common language. A handful of archaeologists did learn from these exchanges (e.g., Zimmerman 1989). And a handful of Indians learned from them as well; some were even motivated by them to learn about archaeology, on their own, through various amateur archaeologist training programs or by pursuing more formal academic training (e.g., Carter, this volume).

Recently things have changed, perhaps not as much as some of us would like, but some real progress in bridging the gap between archaeologists and Native Americans has occurred. Much of that change occurred as a result of the "national dialogue" that led to the language for the Native American Graves Protection and Repatriation Act (NAGPRA) (see Goldstein and Kintigh 1990).

NAGPRA has changed the basic context of discussions among archaeologists, museum people, and physical anthropologists. Before NAGPRA there was no real need, other than politeness to treat Indians as equals. Native Americans were persistent, vocal, and occasionally got their beefs to the media. While the media largely cared very little about the substance of the Indians' complaint, they have always been very good at identifying a story with legs. So archaeologists had "bad press" to deal with. As long as Native Americans were viewed as essentially powerless to affect what archaeologists wanted to do, they were no more than a minor irritant. But their persistence, and the occasional ability to get stories in the media, made them increasingly irritating.

Archaeologists being trained as academics (even if they decreasingly ply their trade in universities) offered the standard solution to their problem—education. If we could just get Indians to see how important our work is and how it has benefited them directly, then they will stop bothering us. This approach, too, relies on the superior status and authority of archaeologists. It assumes that the solution to the reburial problem is for the archaeologist-magister to train the uneducated and uninformed Indians. Education is a one-way street: knowledge flows from top to bottom, and the bottom learns to conform.

NAGPRA changed everything. No longer were archaeologists in a superior position. NAGPRA gives Indians a more than equal status to the other parties to the dialogue. It is certainly true that pro forma compliance with the terms of NAGPRA is probably possible, and it is almost certainly equally true that some agencies will attempt to get by with pro forma compliance—going through the motions without actually consulting. Neither the spirit nor the letter of NAGPRA can be complied with in the absence of dialogues among archaeologists, museum personnel, and Native Americans in which all participants are equals. And while there are instances of archaeologists continuing to attempt to control the dialogue as if they still occupied a privileged position, by and large these situations are atypical. Real discussions are occurring. And real change in attitudes seems to be the result.

The papers in this volume are an early part of the next chapters of this discourse. To understand these papers and where they stand in the development of a real dialogue among archaeologists and Native Americans, it is necessary to have some understanding of both the general history of Native American–archaeologists relations and the history of the repartition/reburial dialogue that provide the context for the largely unsuccessful attempts at communication that occurred prior to the enactment of NAGPRA. The longer history of archaeologist-Indian relations is imbedded in the larger historical context of the overall development of American archaeology.

Antiquarian Researches

Almost from the time they stepped off their boats, the Euroamerican settlers of North America have offered explanations of the archaeological remains they encountered. Some of these explanations, from the very earliest days, accord fairly closely with modern archaeological understanding. Other explanations ranged from the ridiculous, to the self-serving, to the racist, through the plainly fantastic. These latter explanations always discounted the contribution of Native Americans, some-times to the point of denying any relationship between precolumbian archaeology and contemporary Indians.[4]

Ruins in New England have been deemed to be "megalithic" and attributed to European mesolithic settlers. The Vikings were everywhere (including apparently even in the California desert!) with who knows what consequences for the pre-columbian cultures of North America and the archaeological record of that era (cf. Williams 1991). Petroglyphs across North America have variously been read as Norse runes, Egyptian hieroglyphs, Hebrew, Arabic, Phoenician, or Ogam.

The precolumbian archaeological record, or at least some substantial portions of it in North America, also has been attributed to the Lost Tribes of Israel. Other explanations of the archaeological record rely on the influence of the high cultures of the long-since sunken continents of Mu or Atlantis or both. There is even supposed to be a Romano-Jewish settlement in the southeastern United States. Even more fantastic explanations are out there; for example, "high culture" in the pre-columbian Americas has been attributed to direct contact with and intervention by extraterrestrials.

Many of these explanations of the archaeological record have their origins in the antiquarian researches and musings as far back as the work of Spanish scholars in the sixteenth and seventeenth centuries. The late eighteenth and the first half of the nineteenth centuries were, however, the heyday for American natural history and antiquarian research. We owe most of these discounted explanations of the archae-ological record to this era. (In fact, however, none of these explanations is dead; they continue to have vibrant—if, we may hope, marginal—lives in a new anti-quarian literature and the popular press. This literature revives and "validates" nearly every one of these "explanations" of the archaeological record. See Williams [1991] for a thorough discussion.)

Moundbuilders and Cliff Dwellers

Throughout most of the nineteenth century in the Midwest, mid-South, and Southeast, the ancient mound complexes were a source of intense interest. They were identified, explored, mapped, and occasionally test excavated by curious colonists, explorers, and more or less formal natural history/archaeology expeditions. Almost from the earliest sighting, two competing explanations of their origins were offered. One explanation held that the mounds had been built by the ancestors of contemporary Indians. In the scholarly world there was debate, but it was not until the latter half of the nineteenth century that the proponents of this explanation were in the majority.

The other explanation attributed the mounds to "the Moundbuilders." In one ver-sion or another of this view, the mound complexes were attributed to almost any ethnic group other than Native North Americans: for example, the Lost Tribes, Danes, Tartars, Romans, Aztecs, and even Hindoos [sic] (Silverberg 1968; Willey and Sabloff 1980; Williams 1991). In the popular mind, the Moundbuilder view held sway.

Who the Moundbuilders actually were was a subject of lively debate. The mounds could have been the product of almost any ethnic group other than the nineteenth-century Indian occupants of the region. In fact, they could have been the work of the "high-culture" Indians of Mexico or South America. The only Indians they could not have been were the ones who were being actively dispossessed from their occupation of the lands over which the mounds were scattered.

John Wesley Powell captured the essence of this view when he wrote about the myth of the Moundbuilders:

> The ghosts of a vanished nation have ambuscaded in the vast solitude of the continent, and the forest-covered mounds have been usually regarded as the mysterious sepulchers of its kings and nobles. It was an alluring conjecture that a powerful people, superior to the Indians, once occupied the valley of the Ohio and the Appalachian ranges, their empire stretching from Hudson bay to the Gulf [of Mexico], with its flanks on the western prairies and the eastern ocean; a people with a confederated government, a chief ruler, a great central capital, a highly developed religion, with homes and husbandry and advanced textile, fictile and ductile arts, with a language, perhaps with letters, all swept away before an invasion of some copper-hued Huns from some unknown region of the earth, prior to the landing of Columbus (Powell 1894:xli).

The kindest thing that can be said about the myth of the Moundbuilders is that it was self-serving. Williams rightly describes some of its most active proponents as racist. In addition to the general racist attitude toward Indians, some of the foremost scientist-proponents of the Moundbuilder myth revealed both a virulent anti-Indian sentiment and a powerful propensity for rationalizing the European usurpation of Indian lands.

> In the study of American prehistory racism has a long history. The nineteenth-century Myth of the Moundbuilder was for many of its adherents a way of softening the racist notion that Indians were nothing but savages who were residing on lands of greater value to others. It was thought that the Native Americans could not really "own" the lands because it was suggested that they had only recently taken them away from the Moundbuilders, probably a fair-skinned race. It was also evident to many that the Moundbuilders were capable of cultural achievements that no mere Indian could have attained (Williams 1991:23–24).

Archaeological research, including analysis of grave goods and human osteological remains, contributed essential elements for developing the arguments that disposed of the racist Moundbuilder myth explanations of the archaeological record. The Smithsonian Institution and Powell's Bureau of American Ethnology were essential to debunking the myth. Powell set the bureau to work on the question of the Moundbuilders in 1881. Cyrus Thomas's report of these investigations was a painstaking and comprehensive compilation of archaeological research, which thoroughly discredited the Moundbuilder myth (Thomas 1894). And it put the myth to rest, at least for archaeologists and the scholarly community.

In the southwestern United States, as had been the case for the mounds in the east, the complexes of ruins and cliff dwellings that dot the landscape were at first attributed to peoples other than the ancestors of contemporary southwestern Indians. Perhaps the most popular attribution is preserved to this day in the names of several national parks: for example, Aztec Ruin and Montezuma Castle. This myth didn't last long. In the imagination of nineteenth-century archaeologists, the villages of southwestern Indians looked a lot like the ancient ruins. The presence of these villages exerted an overwhelming influence on the interpretation of the archaeological remains (Cordell and Plog 1979). Non-Indian explanations of the origin of these ruins had little real chance to take hold, at least among archaeologists.

Archaeologists and archaeological research had succeeded in returning a bit of Indian heritage to the Indians. Even though there were powerful social reasons undergirding the non-Indian explanations, science had triumphed. Even though the Indians remained dispossessed of their lands in the East and Midwest, their heritage had been validated. Racism had been dealt a blow.

Other Archaeological Contributions

By the third quarter of the twentieth century, archaeological research also provided essential evidence for many tribes in the proceedings they brought before the Indian Claims Commission (and subsequently before the United States Court of Claims). Archaeological evidence established antiquity of occupation. More importantly, it could be used to demonstrate the maximum distribution of material culture associated with a particular tribe at the time when it lost its lands. To a greater or lesser extent, archaeology might provide evidence (necessary to sustain a claim before the Claims Commission and/or Court of Claims) that the tribe had exclusive use of the land it was claiming and for which it was demanding compensation. Here, too, archaeological research was directly beneficial to Indians.

The work of archaeologists led to the enactment of the Antiquities Act of 1906. The Antiquities Act was early legislation that helped to protect archaeological sites from the activities of looters, pot hunters, and museum artifact procurers. The Antiquities Act also provided the legal basis for establishing an entire class of national parks called National Monuments. These actions led to the preservation of many important archaeological sites—sites that were ancestral to contemporary Indians. Furthermore, these efforts preserved the material record of the history of Native Americans.

Much later, archaeologists also pushed for and obtained passage of the Archaeological Resources Protection Act (ARPA). This law had the same general benefits as the Antiquities Act, but brought it up to date. It increased the penalties for violation. Importantly, it acknowledged that tribes owned the cultural resources on their reservations, which is an essential acknowledgment of tribal sovereignty. ARPA also requires consultation with tribes before an ARPA permit can be issued on federal lands, an essential recognition of Indians' interests in and ties to their archaeological heritage.

In the early days of American archaeology, archaeologists sometimes worked closely with Indians. Native American oral traditions were viewed as valid sources of information about at least some aspects of the archaeological records being explored. But throughout the early part of this century this attitude gradually changed. Native American oral traditions were increasingly viewed as, at best, unreliable sources of evidence about the past. In many cases, they were viewed as being nothing more than a collection of "just-so stories" that were often of anthropological (i.e., ethnographic and ethnological) interest in their own right but provided no reliable factual information about the past.

By the 1970s, most archaeologists had few if any contacts with Native Americans. With the exception of an occasional stab at ethnoarchaeology, the most common source of contact probably occurred in the Southwest, where Indians were routinely hired as laborers on excavation projects. In anthropology programs of the major southwestern universities, which include some of the foremost anthropology programs in the United States, students could go from freshman to doctoral degree without ever actually learning anything about the contemporary Indian cultures in the region, even when they proposed to specialize in southwestern prehistory. Indeed, in some of these programs it was (and still is) possible to obtain a Ph.D. in anthropological archaeology without ever taking an ethnography course.

Although the work of archaeologists has directly and indirectly benefited Native Americans, there has been an increasing distance between archaeology as a discipline and Native Americans. This has occurred as archaeology has matured and become more scientific. As archaeology has evolved, there has been an increasing tendency to seek explanation of the archaeological record in the material record itself. Reference to or reliance on other sources of explanation—historical evidence, ethnographic reports, oral traditions—has been increasingly eschewed within the profession. The result is an increasing disconnect between archaeological description, explanation, theory, etc., and the general populace, including the people whose ancestors had left most of the archaeological remains.

The Repatriation/Reburial "Dialogue"

Throughout much of the past century, the work of archaeologists produced benefits both direct and tangible, as well as less tangible, to Native Americans. Archaeologists certainly recognize these contributions. And so, for the most part, do Native

Americans. Archaeologists and Indians don't necessarily see these contributions in the same light, nor do they necessarily value them in the same way, but they generally recognize that there are benefits from archaeology and that, to some extent, Indians have been beneficiaries as well as subjects of archaeological research.

For most of the past 20 years, the principal issue and subject of discussion among archaeologists and Indians has been the curation of Native American human remains in museums, universities, and archaeological laboratories. Indians often called archaeologists grave robbers and/or pot hunters, lumping archaeologists with ghouls and looters. Native Americans often asked archaeologists to justify the ongoing curation of their ancestors' remains. What could possibly justify this desecration of the graves of their ancestors and disturbance of what many Native Americans thought of as the final spiritual journey taken by the spirits of the dead?

Archaeologists, for their part, pointed out that scientific research on human skeletal remains had yielded important insight into past social organization. These studies had also provided data critical to understanding disease patterns in the past. They also stated that their research illuminated the prehistory of American Indians, thereby contributing to the understanding of their past.

With a certain amount of pride, archaeologists could, as noted above, rightly point to research demonstrating that the mid-continent's mound sites or that the cliff dwellings of the Southwest were built by ancestors of contemporary Indians, which had helped to dispel the racist myths about the capacities of Native Americans. Archaeologists also indicated that they had played a critical role in preserving many important archaeological sites and were instrumental in fighting the looting of archaeological sites. And archaeological data had often been crucial in proving tribal land claims (resulting in payment of at least nominal compensation but not recovery of lands that had been taken from the tribes).

Archaeologists were genuinely mystified when they found themselves lumped with ghouls and the looters of the past. After all, they saw themselves as the good guys. In their eyes, their research had directly benefited the people who were attacking them. Their efforts deserved praise, not approbation.

Archaeologists typically dismissed the Indian activists who were in the forefront of dealing with these issues as radicals who had seized on what they hoped would prove to be a hot-button issue. Or, alternatively, they were professional Indians[5] who were motivated purely by the consideration of the political and professional benefits they could milk from the issue. Archaeologists routinely declared, "If we could just educate the Indians about what we are doing, and why, and what the results of our research have been, then they would stop trying to make us rebury Native American skeletal remains."

Over the years, this position was repeated over and over again. Discussion sessions among archaeologists and Native Americans became a fixture at regional and national archaeological meetings. Archaeologists preconceptions were reenforced at these meetings because the Indians kept asking the same questions.

When Indians asked why their ancestors were (under the best of circumstances) in storage boxes in museums,[6] they were told about all of the wonderful science that these remains represented. When archaeologists were asked exactly what remains they had and where the remains were from, they typically replied in so many words that they really did not know—no one had actually looked at the remains since they came out of the ground. When asked why the remains couldn't be studied and then reinterred, the archaeologists replied that new techniques were being developed all of the time—that application of these new techniques yielded vast quantities of new scientific data. They could even cite studies to prove this point (e.g., Buikstra and Gordon 1981).

The archaeologists seemed amazed that Indians would continually ask these same questions. They mostly assumed that they were not making themselves clear. In all of the years I went to these meetings and talked about these issues with archaeologists, I can not recall hearing a proponent of curation admit that there was something amiss when archaeologists told the Native Americans, on the one hand, that they simply *had* to have these human remains because they were invaluable sources of scientific data, but, on the other hand, that they did not really know what remains were in the collection because no one could be bothered to actually look at them.

The Indians I spoke to made it clear that they *did* understand exactly what the archaeologists were saying. They kept asking their questions because they could not believe that what they were hearing was so stupid. They also, I think, hoped that if they forced archaeologists to repeat themselves often enough, the archaeological community might begin to notice that there was something wrong with claiming that Native American human remains were of paramount scientific importance but that they were not really important enough for anyone to actually study.

From the Native American side, matters were complicated by the fact that many of the activists pushing for repatriation *were*, in fact, well established in the radical Indian movement. Other advocates of repatriation *were* "professional" Indians, who occasionally admitted to archaeologists that they were indeed motivated by the fact that they thought this was a fight they could win. But these things just obscured the deeply held beliefs of Native Americans—beliefs about the dead, spirit journeys, the powers of the spirits of the dead, some of which were fervently adhered to by the activists and even by some of the professional Indians. The fact that for the most part it was not the tribal elders, medicine people, and spiritual leaders who were coming forward to demand repatriation served both to "muddy the waters" and to help archaeologists rationalize away any need to come to a settlement with tribes over this matter.

Eventually, the activists took their case to Congress, asking it to rectify the situation. It proved not to be a difficult case to make. Some museums were refusing to return the remains of known individuals, whose remains had come into the possession of the museum as a result of out-and-out grave robbing.

Over a number of years, Congress considered a number of bills that would have required repatriation. The Society for American Archaeology (SAA) steadfastly fought those bills on the grounds that there should be no national policy of repatriation, but that each case should be decided on its individual merits.[7] Each year for seven years the SAA Executive Board made fighting the "national policy" the number one priority for the Government Relations Committee.

Finally, the Government Relations Committee was able to convince the Executive Board that SAA was fighting a battle it could not win. At best, it could hope to delay the inevitable, and the inevitable was that Indian remains would be repatriated. The most that SAA could hope for was to take a seat at the table and attempt to work out the best language it could get. And if it didn't negotiate soon, the opportunity would be lost and the Native Americans would write the law with no real input from the archaeological community. What ensued was the famous "national dialogue" and eventually the Native American Graves Protection and Repatriation Act.

NAGPRA *has* created a "new world order." Archaeologists must deal directly with Native Americans and deal with them as equals. From what I've seen so far, this is having positive effects. Archaeologists and Native Americans are beginning to discuss things and deal forthrightly with repatriation. Museums and curation facilities have not been stripped bare. Indians are seeing that archaeologists can be dealt with on this issue.[8]

Archaeologists and SAA are adjusting to this new world order. One sign of this adjustment is that they are in the process at least editing if not entirely rewriting the recent past (see Zimmerman, this volume). Recall, for example, that SAA never "opposed" reburial. To my knowledge, at least, it is true that SAA never actually issued an official statement (written or otherwise) opposing reburial; it opposed a national policy. But to suggest that SAA and the archaeological community were not opposed to reburial is an outright lie.

This Is Now

NAGPRA has indeed ushered in a new era. By removing a central issue of contention, it has made it possible for communication to occur. Archaeologists and Native Americans have discovered that they can talk about reburial and other issues important to both. They have discovered that it is possible to communicate essential views. They have found a common language. And, as we all knew all along, they have found many common interests and shared goals, all of which disappeared in the fire and smoke of the repatriation discourse. Nevertheless, it is important not to forget that the past 20 years was indeed an era of the reburial/ repatriation *debate.*

The papers in this volume must be seen as the early part of the next era of archaeologists–Native American relations. Reburial is still part of this mix, and it will be for a long, long time to come. But so are other issues. And it is actually possible to bring them into the open for discussion in a rational and reasonable fashion, in a way in which real communication can occur.

It should be clear from the tone of many of the following papers that Native Americans are still wary of archaeologists. We have to prove ourselves with our words and our actions. It is also clear that there are a range of issues on the table, now that NAGPRA has made room for them.

A number of the papers in this volume are written by Native Americans who are professional archaeologists. Some of them adhere to their traditional beliefs, but they can still be archaeologists. They also demonstrate that it is possible to do good science/archaeology, as well as archaeology that is in the service of their people. It should be equally clear that there is ample room in archaeology and cultural resource management for people with traditional beliefs and for the traditional knowledge of those individuals to enrich the efforts of archaeologists. NAGPRA, by ending the fruitless and antagonistic debate over "ownership" of human remains and all that it entailed, has created an environment in which true collaboration between Native Americans and archaeologists can begin. We can only hope that the chapters that follow are just the opening rounds of this collaboration.

NOTES

1. This essay attempts to frame the papers that follow in the context of the history of Native American–archaeologist relations. These relations have recently been quite strained. I do not attempt a general or detailed history of them but simply provide a framework.

2. I use "archaeologist" very loosely in this paper. Except where the context makes it clear that I am referring solely to archaeologists, I use the term to refer to archaeologists, physical anthropologists, and museum curators and administrators. This usage is simpler than attempting to identify a particular profession with a particular position or issue, which simply is not possible in such a brief essay. Furthermore, in the overall context of this discussion, archaeologists, physical anthropologists, and museum curators and administrators have almost always made common cause. Finally, this usage is generally consistent with the Native American usage and point of view. Indians waste little time and effort trying to figure out which one of these is the exact profession of the people they are dealing with and generally assume them all to be archaeologists.

3. In keeping with the overview nature of this essay, I have kept citations to a minimum. Except where I am quoting someone directly, references cited are of two kinds. The first are general works that provide good historical background and good bibliographies; these books

should be familiar to most archaeologists even if they haven't read them. The other works bear generally or specifically on these issues but are not as widely known in the archaeological community as I think they should be.

4. Native Americans rightly object to the blithe characterization of the precolumbian portion of their history as "prehistoric." Almost all tribes retain rich oral histories and traditions, which describe in detail their precolumbian past. History did not begin in the Americas with the arrival of Columbus: Europeans merely began to record it in writing. Accordingly, except where directly quoting someone, throughout this paper I use "precolumbian" to refer to the era archaeologists and scholars typically refer to as prehistoric.

5. "Professional Indian" is a term generally used in a derisive sense in Indian country (mostly by Indians) to describe Indians whose careers are built on promoting their Indianness as essentially a professional qualification. Professional Indians are usually seen as opportunists who advocate Indian positions on sensational topics more for their own careerist purposes than out of any particular commitment to the position being promoted.

6. More often, they were in paper bags and cardboard boxes in the basements of the condemned buildings archaeology programs were routinely consigned to by university administrations.

7. If this sounds like double speak, don't worry, you are not alone. It *is* double speak. It always escaped me how a national policy to consider each case on a case-by-case basis, wasn't a national policy, but never mind.

8. I readily admit that I am most surprised by this. Since the enactment of NAGPRA, many people have said that they thought it would serve as a way to begin bridging the gap between Indians and archaeologists. I thought that they were just mouthing platitudes or attempting to put the situation in the best possible light. But dialogues are occurring and bridges are being built. The prophets of reconciliation have, so far at least, been more right than wrong.

Changing the Paradigms

Two

Return of the Sacred
Spirituality and the Scientific Imperative

> *The communication of the dead*
> *is tongued with fire*
> *beyond the language of the living.*

These words grace a tombstone, somewhere near Dylan Thomas's grave, in Westminster Abbey, London. In that gray place, the paving blocks are, quite literally, tombs. Somewhere between when you pay admission and when your eyes adjust to that dim light, it occurs to you that you are in the middle of an immense burial ground.

Everywhere there are bodies. Graves line the floor, impossible to avoid, endless chiseled names and descriptions, stepping stones to walk upon. Bodies are buried in the walls. Bodies molder between the relics and altar pieces, and under sculpted mausolea on which Byzantine images of their diminutive occupants stare with fixed expressions past endlessly curious lines of tourists.

Over the centuries, this venerable sanctuary has produced a solitary ideal, distilled to a strict taboo, posted—in bold letters: NO PHOTOGRAPHY PLEASE.

The temptation here is to suggest that if science is indeed a religion, then Westminster Abbey could easily qualify as archaeology's Mother Church simply by lifting its ban on photography. Especially apparent to Native American sensibilities, however, is that within this sepulcher of western theology dwells a profound absence of the sacred.

It is this singular absence of the sacred that constitutes the gulf between empiricism and Native American spirituality. If we as particular groups are molded in part by the space between ourselves, then the separation between spirit and science must be a definitive chasm.

Into this void new federal laws have thrown two groups that have, in living form, been for the most part mutually exclusive: archaeologists and Native Americans. There seems to be some tension here. To archaeologists, the idea of consulting with potential specimens must seem annoying. For Native Americans, it's yet another version of this country's oldest and deadliest game: Cowboys and Indians.

Right at this moment it's obvious where both groups are; we're contemplating the void between ourselves, looking for a common ground. At this moment, the space between ourselves is neither sacred nor scientific, neither spirit nor matter. Welcome to the Twilight Zone.

Within this great space there is growing communication. Memos, faxes, formal letters, phone calls, and official visits between tribes and institutions now litter the chasm. Early on, tribal governments received a blizzard of summaries, then inventories, all required by the new federal mandate, from prestigious institutions and agencies that for years had avoided any interaction with Native Americans as living people. Depending on how well various tribal nations understand the new federal mandate, or how seriously its agenda is taken, those required manifests are now either the basis for ongoing consultations or they remain in cardboard containers, somewhere.

In regard to ongoing consultation, tribes, agencies, and institutions are constructing a trail mostly of letters, memos, and faxes. We should always be careful when using such paper trails, lest we make for ourselves and others the worst kind of common ground: an enormous landfill that will be made almost entirely of official communications. Our next task obviously will be to begin the process of crafting a true common ground, one that will in practice bridge the spaces between all concerned parties.

How do we begin to craft a true common ground across the chasm that separates archaeology and tribal nations? I suggest that we start by celebrating the obvious; it's our void, yours and mine. It's a unique tribal/archaeology space—a place we have entered, to be sure, by federal mandate, but ours anyway. Let us reflect on, and appreciate, what we have. Let's celebrate our great space, our common space in order to consider what kind of mutually inclusive landscape we wish to create.

At this moment, we are the ethos of the space between spirituality and the Scientific Imperative. It is for us to realize what sort of notions we may bring into our space, and what we may have to leave behind.

The Scientific Imperative

At University College, London, there is on display the body of Jeremy Bentham, the utilitarian philosopher. Bentham willed his body to the university medical department, and after he died they did the predictable thing any utilitarian could reasonably expect—they promptly stuffed and mounted him. There exists a notion that empiricism has an overriding mandate to do such things, called the Scientific Imperative. It's a notion with which Indian Country has long been familiar.

The Scientific Imperative presumes an unqualified right to suspend social ethics and cultural taboos in the name of a greater social good: objective discovery.

In the name of objective discovery, empiricism distinguishes for us between animal torture and scientific enquiry, corpse mutilation and medical examination, grave robbery and archaeology. Unfortunately, this notion also amounts to an ethical blank check for visits to Indian Country, a blank check that has purchased, among many other things, thousands of Native American grave goods and remains, many of which, like Jeremy Bentham, have been displayed for public consumption.

Public consumption of Indian remains is a long-standing practice that is just now being abandoned by most reputable venues. Not too long ago the University of Memphis sponsored a tour of Chukalissa, a Mississippian site, which featured the viewing of human remains. I can recall a display of skeletal remains at Woolaroc Museum in Oklahoma. The museum also had on exhibit a collection of shrunken heads. For Native America, such public viewings of the dead are only slightly more objectionable than the mass warehousing of hundreds of thousands of Indian skeletons now on shelves and in boxes across the country.

Now that some of those blank checks are bouncing, and remains and objects are starting to be returned, it is clear that the Scientific Imperative no longer has the currency it once did. It is a notion that we may bring to our mutually inclusive landscape only if we are prepared to recognize its limited applications.

The Buried Treasure Syndrome

Many corollaries to the Scientific Imperative exist as reflex cultural notions. One, we might call the Buried Treasure Syndrome. The other is its close companion, Collecting.

The idea that anything old, or otherwise unique and in the ground, is buried treasure is a notion reinforced by American pioneer-styled property rights. There is a loose consideration about such objects; most often they are regarded as part of the public domain and are therefore up for grabs. Of course, certain federal laws prohibit some of this loose regard. Still, the finders-keepers notion of buried objects as being, in effect, "pay dirt" seems to be a cultural reflex that archaeology has enshrined as a basic tenet.

Collecting also apparently requires a certain kind of cultural instinct. Collecting has been explained to me several different ways by archaeologists and others as a simple desire to possess a unique physical object, one that no one else may have. This instinct to possess the unique and unusual accounts for a range of phenomena, including Elvis memorabilia, butterfly collections, antique shops, art museums, and the ongoing reluctance of some archaeologists regarding repatriation and the subsequent reburial of artifacts.

Recently, an Alabama archaeologist citing the Scientific Imperative proposed that a state collection of Native American remains should not be repatriated since they might one day be used for cancer research. Her proposal raises questions as to what other ethnic collections of remains various agencies and institutions may possess. Are there hundreds of thousands of Irish American, Asian American, Jewish American, or any other American remains now on perpetual tap, ready to be studied for, say, cancer research? Of course not. Only collections of Native American remains are warehoused on a scale of grand proportions.

Collecting within certain ethical limits is fine. Collecting Indian remains and grave objects as buried treasure, however, is no longer acceptable. It is a notion that does not deserve a place within our common ground.

Advocacy

In my community a young boy was buried with his Game Boy tapes. His grave was quickly looted, and the tapes were stolen. Some months previous to this event, tribal members had reburied Woodland period remains that a top soiling operation had unearthed. At the reburial site just beyond a tree line, pot hunters waited, hopeful that we were reburying artifacts as well. The top soiling activity occurred on private property and had been the subject of much regional debate and objection. It was only abated, however, when it was discovered that a soil overburden constituted a wetland fill, a clear violation of the Clean Water Act.

A few issues are apparent in these narratives. How much time elapses before science considers it proper to dig up a burial? What about the destruction of graves by industrial development? What about grave looting, now a major growth industry in America? How viable is the notion of cultural affiliation? What about state and federal laws that protect the environment but ignore human rights?

Archaeologists have always been ideologues, since they are followers of the empiricist notion of linear social progression. As a profession, archaeology needs to realize that the federal mandate has widened the proper scope of their concerns. Social issues are no longer abstract ideas. The entry of tribal governments into the general field of historic preservation has politicized those issues for archaeology. Archaeology and Native America need to maintain an ongoing dialogue, to identify basic common interests, and then to agree on strategies to achieve common goals.

Proactive advocacy, both on a political and professional level, is a notion that now is inevitable. We only need to agree on what form it should take within our mutually inclusive landscape.

Tribal Sovereignty

Tribal sovereignty is a notion that predates the contact period. To Native Americans it is a birthright; to European Americans it is a codified concept that stems from two other notions rooted in English Law, the Right of Discovery, and Eminent Domain.

If the Right of Discovery legitimized (for Europeans) land claims in the name of a foreign power, then Eminent Domain legitimized (again, for Europeans) the right of original inhabitants to live on the land being claimed. In order to settle discovered lands, therefore, and assume full title, the foreign power in question was first required to treat or deal with the original occupants, offering (ideally, at least) just compensation.

This mitigating process was codified into a series of treaties between the United States and the original inhabitants of this continent. These original inhabitants were federally recognized in treaty language as sovereign nations. The Native American Graves Protection and Repatriation Act clearly reaffirms the notion of tribal sovereignty by naming federally recognized tribal governments as sole respondents for culturally affiliated, and unidentified objects and human remains.

Historically, the exercise of tribal sovereignty has ebbed and flowed depending on the political, military, and economic strength of Native America. For our purposes, it is important to note that the reason the Scientific Imperative is in question in Indian Country is because of the continuous reaffirmation of tribal sovereignty by the federal government. The notion of tribal sovereignty is one that we must recognize as part of our common ground.

Spirituality

To Native America, the world is composed of both spirit and matter. This, of course, is not a unique concept, as the world is full of variations on this common theme. What is important for our consideration is that to Native America, burials are sacrosanct, certain geographies are counted as holy places, and the earth itself is a living entity.

Certain objects, too, are considered as being imbued with spiritual presence and power. These objects of cultural patrimony are used to mediate between the seen and the unseen. Metaphysical interdiction is a concept long associated with Native American beliefs and practices. Many cultural objects are considered to be instruments that, in association with other understandings, ensure the continuation of good in our world.

The disruption of burials, the desecration of holy places, and the destruction of the environment are considered part of a negative process that has its roots in a fundamental imbalance between spirit and science.

Native American worldviews are mitigated somewhat by the activities of tribal governments. One southeastern tribe, for example, is considering the disinterment of its historic burials to facilitate construction of a bingo facility. Another tribal nation, curiously enough, publicly displays its own grave goods, making them the centerpieces of its small regional museum. On most issues involving federal historic preservation laws, however, the policies of tribal governments do not differ significantly from the traditional beliefs of their constituencies. Those constituencies, on the whole, still retain a spiritual worldview and still value certain original understandings and practices.

While tribal governments may recognize the validity of archaeology, this discipline, in turn, has never seriously considered Native American spirituality as relevant to its own concepts and practices. This lack of consideration can be understood, given the secular basis of empiricism. Now that the void between spirit and science is narrowing somewhat, Native American spirituality is a concept that must be respected and seriously considered. The participation of tribal historic preservation offices in the issues now before us will continue to ensure that Indian spiritual beliefs will remain important to our mutually inclusive landscape.

Balance

From a full, mutually inclusive consideration of these notions a common sensibility can emerge and with this, of course, a true common ground. I would like to suggest a working model for these considerations, one that we use back home. It's a ceremonial model that holds the potential for wider application.

Balance between spirit and matter is the preoccupation of southeastern ceremonialism. Regulation of weather for crops, protection from illness, and continuity of ethos while allowing for change are the special concerns of our ceremonial leaders.

If we were to extend these considerations further, we could easily transpose them into a recognized need for balance between science and Native American spirituality while ensuring the validity of both. As tribal and professional leaders, these particular considerations have now become our particular responsibilities.

For Native Americans, secular science has already been accepted by tribal government. Tribal employees now include medical doctors, physical anthropologists, and, of course, archaeologists. In order to create a balance between our shared responsibilities, archaeology must also accept the validity of Native American spiritual beliefs and practices, especially with regard to burials and sacred objects.

What is needed at this moment is a return of the sacred. Archaeology must allow sacred considerations to influence its practices. It is not necessary for archaeology to desecularize in order for Native American spirituality to be included as a significant component of a common ground.

To better understand how to mediate between spirit and science, and when to introduce either or both, an interdisciplinary approach should be developed that would integrate both science and tribal traditions. On the archaeology side of things, this could mean introducing more ethnographic studies at the university level, as well as developing special courses in tribal studies, using Native American elders, traditional leaders, and professionals. For Native Americans, workshops in Indian Country involving special scientific concerns and considerations might be helpful. For both groups, hands-on field experience engendering shared learning situations could also be beneficial. In real terms, balance means parity of esteem, a consideration that cannot reasonably exist without parity of accountability.

Most importantly, a new paradigm needs to be developed, one that includes a sense both of the sacred and the secular. Increasingly, the use of Native American traditional practices in conjunction with traditional scientific approaches is widening the scope of the work as presently conceived, and it appears that a form of holistic archaeology is beginning to emerge. From this new model that we may develop from our common ground, we should expect a code of ethics, one that professional archaeological societies, federal agencies, and tribal governments will further refine and follow. It will be a benchmark of standards and practices for archaeology that embodies a balanced consideration of notions from both science and Native American spiritual sensibilities.

***

The current mandate guarantees a process whereby both archaeology and Native America will change each other forever. How that change may occur, and whom it will benefit, will be determined by our ability to fashion for ourselves a true common ground. For Native America, this must always include a balanced return of the sacred.

■ LARRY J. ZIMMERMAN

Three

Remythologizing the Relationship Between Indians and Archaeologists

In the aftermath of a disastrous 1982 meeting with the Executive Board of the Society for American Archaeology, Jan Hammil (American Indians Against Desecration) and I were commiserating about how difficult it would be to convince archaeologists to change their views about human remains. We had gone to the meeting to ask that the board not pass an anti-reburial resolution they were to consider.[1] At the meeting, committee members were polite and seemed genuinely concerned, but the next morning we accidentally discovered how patronizing they had been. They still planned to pass the resolution. They were eventually convinced not to by substantial lobbying and protest by many Indian people and some archaeologists (see Zimmerman 1989 for a personal account of the meeting). We knew that passage of the resolution would be a profound setback for many of the already substantial efforts to structure local compromises. We were depressed about the prospects, and we agreed that the attitudes of many archaeologists probably wouldn't change much within our lifetimes. Events since 1989 have proved us very wrong.

In truth, we probably would have considered the enactment of the National Museum of the American Indian Act and the Native American Graves Protection and Repatriation Act to be impossible. Resistance within the anthropological community seemed so very strong. Remarkably, as is well documented by the many papers in this volume, dramatic change has occurred. In hindsight, some shifts of power were probably inevitable.

More important than shifts of power have been recent adjustments of attitudes by both American Indians and archaeologists. These forecast more substantive changes in the actual conduct of archaeology.[2] I have noticed, with no small amount of amusement, that archaeologists are remythologizing their relationships with Indians. To listen to some, you might think there never really had been any problem or that it was just a misunderstanding. Though I find this ironic and somewhat self-delusive, its effects are generally beneficial. There are negatives, and I will be blunt about them, but the positive trends are apparent as archaeologists and Indians find common ground. Part of finding common ground is the development of syncretism of archaeological views to those of Indian people and remythologizing relationships between them.

Syncretism

The trajectory of the reburial issue has been like that of classic syncretism, in which a coalescence or reconciliation of differing beliefs occurs. In the anthropological experience this most often happens when a belief system, usually of a dominant group, imposes itself on a less powerful group. The result is an amalgamation, a hybrid structure in which each party can feel some comfort about sacrificing some basic principles, or if not sacrificing them, at least couching them in terms acceptable to the other. The structure helps both groups adjust to the other with conflicts eventually losing intensity as the syncretism expands. A process similar to this seems to be at work between American Indians and archaeology.

The reburial issue is profoundly complex and has never just been about the return of human remains and grave goods. Much of the problem stems from the fact that archaeology is part of the scientific tradition of the West, placing great faith in science as a way to know and understand the past. As part of colonialism, archaeological constructions have been superimposed on indigenous peoples' views about their pasts. As part of this process, the remains of indigenous peoples' ancestors, important to archaeologists as a source of information about the past, and already important to indigenous people as being sacred, also became important as yet another symbol of exploitation and repression. McGuire (1992) has documented the history of the relationship between Indians and archaeologists well, and its impact is strongly evident in Deloria's (1995) scathing attack on science, including archaeology, in *Red Earth, White Lies: Native Americans and the Myth of Scientific Fact.*

Because there was little apparent resistance until the late 1960s, many archaeologists erroneously assumed that indigenous people agreed with scientific constructions of the past or at least acquiesced to archaeological authority on the matter. In what became a truism, many archaeologists believed that the Indian past was lost unless archaeologists reconstructed it. The past quarter-century has demonstrated just how wrong archaeology has been.

Since about 1970, contention over human remains has ranged from acrimonious confrontation to legislative wrangling. The debates have demonstrated that archaeologists and indigenous peoples hold a wide range of positions about the value and treatment of human remains. But by the very process of the confrontation and debate, syncretism began to develop. The parties began reconciling their beliefs, each incorporating some views of the other, from the moment they started to recognize the intensity of the other's beliefs.

For North America, the question of just who has been dominant in the reburial issue might be raised. At the beginning of the debates, archaeology was certainly dominant, even to the point of archaeologists wondering why or if Indians cared at all. Archaeologists also believed that the high value most Americans place on science would somehow hold sway in the public arena.

Archaeologists, however, underestimated the intensity of Indian sentiment and overestimated their own power and the amount of support they had for their work. When the Nebraska State Historical Society came up against the Pawnee in 1989, for example, the *Omaha World Herald* conducted a scientific poll, revealing that 69 percent of Nebraskans supported the return of remains and grave goods held by the historical society (Peregoy 1992:160). At numerous times, other papers carried editorials in favor of repatriation, and even *NBC Nightly News* and *CBS Sunday Morning* aired segments very much in favor of returning remains. Certainly, this was all happening at a time when general public sentiment favoring science was declining, further eroding archaeological standing.

Public sentiment definitely favored Indian positions as soon as the debate became more widely known. The argument thus could be made that Indian views actually dominated the views of archaeologists, forcing the latter to become more accommodating to Indian views. Even in the U.S. Senate hearings on repatriation laws, the archaeological community was rumored to have been warned by a senator that if archaeologists couldn't come to grips with the issue, Congress would solve the problem for them! By late 1989, the handwriting was on the wall and compromise was forced, first in the National Museum of the American Indian Act (Public Law 101-185 or NMAIA) of 1989 and then in the Native American Graves Protection and Repatriation Act (Public Law 101-601 or NAGPRA) of 1990.

With repatriation laws now in place, syncretism will be accelerated. Looking back and seeing the issue from this perspective allows to me to say that many archaeologists really did understand some of the Indian concerns and perhaps even the "rightness" of many of their demands. Vested interest in the important archaeological information contained in the remains, however, compelled many of them to speak forcibly against reburial. At the same time, I know that many Indians did understand the importance of archaeology to their "history." Issues of sacredness and of control over their own past were more important to them than benefits gained from an archaeology that, in fact, might have complemented and strengthened their own versions of their past gained from oral tradition. Because of the need for control, some adopted rhetorical positions that initially demanded rejection of *all* archaeology. Thus, there was tension, but with an underlying realization that compromise could be mutually beneficial.

Uneasy Compromise

Transcripts of debates on the reburial issue show both the tension and the wish to compromise. For example, at the 1989 World Archaeological Congress (WAC) Inter-Congress on Archaeological Ethics and the Treatment of the Dead, the debate was sometimes nasty but in the end, passage of the Vermillion Accord (Hubert 1989a:18) showed that the parties to the issue recognized the legitimacy of the other's concerns and that those concerns were to be respected.

As the syncretic process was developing, some Indian people, some arch-aeologists, and most media reporters seemed intent on seeing and portraying the issue as bipolar, thinking that such a portrayal would be helpful. For Indian people, it kept the attention of Congress and the media; for archaeologists it helped suggest that they spoke with one voice; for the media, it kept the public interest so they could "sell papers." Such characterizations simply were and are erroneous as well as damaging. As more people learned that inaccurate char-acterizations of a vastly more complex situation caused tension and conflict, they began to reject them.

NAGPRA actually helped some archaeologists come to terms with the com-plexity of their own circumstances. As a colleague suggested to me, being forced by law to consult and cooperate with Indians would help some archaeologists to save face. NAGPRA allowed those who were sympathetic to Indian demands, but who felt compelled to speak forcibly in "defense" of archaeology, to "give in" honorably. Archaeologists also benefited in that collections ignored for decades were finally analyzed, forced by the need to complete NAGPRA inventories. NAGPRA also brought a feeling of control to the situation and a sense of "victory" in that some archaeological interests would still be protected.

NAGPRA has claimed the spotlight, as perhaps it should, but both Indians and archaeologists have had nagging doubts. Many suspected that implementation of federal law could undercut local or regional solutions. NAGPRA became law after many states already had reburial laws in place. Many of these had been enacted after sometimes torturous negotiations. How would it affect these laws? How would NAGPRA mesh with the proposed, but currently stalled, amendments to the American Indian Freedom of Religion Act?

Considering the complexity of the situation, it is no wonder that NAGPRA regulations took six years to develop, and that length of time has worked in some ways to increase paranoia. Very recently, on the NAGPRA-L listserv on the Internet, one correspondent proposed that NAGPRA was a scheme to divest Indians of the information necessary to back up future land claims and treaty rights! It wasn't altogether clear if this was some sort of convoluted rearguard action against reburial or genuine concern, but it shows the level of worry that still exists. For the current NAGPRA regulations, fine tuning, if not major amendment to the law, will be necessary as problems inevitably develop.

Many Indian people remain suspicious (see Echo-Hawk, this volume). Although the Repatriation Office at the Smithsonian and staff at other museums and repositories work with tribes to do so, many Native Americans feel that demonstration of genetic and cultural affiliation of contemporary groups to skeletal remains is largely an Indian task. They also feel that when they compile the evidence, it isn't trusted. For example, to push for repatriation of remains from the Central Plains tradition, the Pawnee, Arikara, and Wichita, through the Native American Rights Fund, commissioned their own study of archaeological and oral tradition evidence about the origin of Caddoan speakers on the Plains. The Repatriation Office did not accept the results of that study and commissioned an independent reanalysis of the information. The result was largely the same.

Although the kinds of acceptable evidence have been broadened to include oral history, a kind of information many archaeologists consider unscientific, many Indians feel it is used and will continue to be used in delaying tactics by archaeologists. Although hearsay and rumor by some may not be considered appropriate in a paper such as this one, it would be profoundly naive to think that they don't affect opinion and, sometimes, policy. For instance, rumors have been floating around Indian country that the Smithsonian thinks it will only have to return about 10 percent of the remains in its collections because Indians will be unable to demonstrate affiliation. Whether these rumors are true or fabricated through paranoia, they have a real impact. For example, Congress is taking notice. Several recent calls to Indians from congressional offices indicate that Congress will not allow regulation or technicality to impede the spirit of the law.

Some archaeologists still remain angry or at least suspicious about NAGPRA. In fact, at a session on the draft NAGPRA regulations held at the 56th Society for American Archaeology (SAA) Annual Meeting in New Orleans in 1991, some indicated extreme dissatisfaction, with one past president of SAA saying: "We've been hoodwinked!" Clement Meighan (1996) considers NAGPRA to be anathema to archaeology, suggesting that it disowns a common past and may be even be a violation of the Constitution. Complex problems such as the demand for repatriation of human hair from the Mammoth Meadow site (Center for the Study of the First Americans 1995), material that could provide extremely valuable DNA information, seem to violate the intent of NAGPRA and cause great consternation, even for those generally supportive of the law. Whatever the many causes, the delays in both drafting and implementing NAGPRA and proposed amendments to the American Indian Religious Freedom Act, as well as complex problems such as Mammoth Meadow, leave many archaeologists and Indians uneasy. Many frankly believe that, in the end, making NAGPRA work will still come down to local, case-by-case solutions (cf. Powell, Garza, and Hendricks 1993:2). If problems and reactions to the National Museum of the American Indian Act can be seen as a precedent, this trend is already well demonstrated by Smithsonian responses, although the situation seems to be improving.[3]

Remythologizing Relationships Between Indians and Archaeologists

As is important in syncretism, both sides are in the process of *remythologizing,* that is, making their belief systems seem as if they were not exactly what they earlier seemed to be. This is an important and *positive* process that is generally neither intentional, nor conspiratorial, nor planned. It is a necessary step toward reconciliation. Although some will see this paper as a criticism of archaeology, that is not my intent. Rather, my interest is in exploring how people process the past and trying to understand what seem to be ironical and sometimes paradoxical actions and statements of archaeologists.

For example, to maintain the notion that the discipline was speaking with one voice, no views from archaeologists favoring reburial appeared in mainstream literature, that is, in the key journals or major series, until very recently, but the remythologizing process was nonetheless operating to make the profession *seem* more reasonable. The best example of this is a sequence of commentaries appearing early in the 1990s in *American Antiquity,* the flagship journal of the Society for American Archaeology, where the important, mainstream theoretical, methodological, and ethical issues are presented and discussed.

Although the controversy had raged since the early 1980s, little of significance about repatriation had appeared in the journal except for the "fine print" appearance of the SAA's reburial policy in business meeting minutes. Finally, *American Antiquity* published a commentary by Goldstein and Kintigh (1990) on "Ethics and the Reburial Controversy." The authors took a "middle-of-the-road" position suggesting that while archaeologists must be more attentive to Indian concerns, they also must "address our various constituencies, educate all of the publics about the past, and make certain that we don't alienate or disenfranchise past, present, or future generations" (Goldstein and Kintigh 1990:590).

The authors were writing as individuals, but many took this to be a softening of the SAA position, given that Goldstein had been SAA secretary and that Kintigh had been head of the SAA ad hoc Committee on Reburial, involved in negotiations on NAGPRA. Klesert and Powell, two archaeologists who had worked closely with Indians, submitted a critique of this commentary to the journal but were rejected. Soon thereafter, the journal editor, J. Jefferson Reid, noted that his attendance at the Third Southwest Symposium included a plenary session of Native Americans commenting on archaeology and archaeologists where he was astounded by "new and rather startling" realizations that Indians didn't trust archaeology or its accounts of the Indian past and that the latter were seen as a threat. He concluded that "[a] North American prehistory irrelevant to North American Indians would seem to be in jeopardy or, minimally, in serious need of epistemological adjustment" (Reid 1992:195). Two issues later, Reid published a very negative critique of Goldstein and Kintigh by Clement Meighan (1992), one of the more "vocal" archaeologists against reburial. Meighan's critique clearly put archaeologists against reburial on the radical conservative fringe while bolstering Goldstein and Kintigh—the perceived SAA representatives—by making them seem very, very reasonable, and by implication, though perhaps not intentionally, made the SAA seem forward looking. In mid-1993, the commentary by Klesert and Powell (1993) finally appeared, but with its criticisms of Goldstein and Kintigh dramatically toned down.

Remythologizing among archaeologists was most apparent at the 1995 SAA annual meeting in Minneapolis. On the opening night, a past SAA president, identified by some Indians a few years ago as being obstructionist to reburial, gave a major address that sounded as if everything had not been as bad as it had seemed at the time. He had recently begun training programs at his university on how to work with Indian people and how to deal with NAGPRA's consultation clauses. During the sessions, with the SAA Executive Board's blessing, a group of First Nation archaeologists held an organizational meeting. At the closing plenary, an archaeologist from a major museum—who had quietly supported reburial all along—pointed out, to loud applause, the promise of working closely with Indian people.

In a related matter, SAA also began to work on revision of its ethics code. Its accountability principle proposes that archaeologists be more aware of and responsible toward the interests of nonarchaeologists with interests in archaeology. Supporting statements specifically dealt with Native Americans and reburial. Although they will not be in the actual principles, they were at least part of the formulation of the code and were published (Watkins et al. 1995). The final principles, as accepted by the SAA Executive Board at the 1996 annual meeting, only mention Indians in the public education section.

In 1995 I had the opportunity to address the annual meeting of Keepers of the Treasures, a national organization developed to protect and promote the living traditions of American Indians, Alaska Natives, and Native Hawaiians. I explained this remythologizing process to them. I suggested that on our part as archaeologists, we will sound like we have always been your strongest supporters and friends. We will say that we have always been willing to work closely with you. We will develop new and cooperative programs that will offer to train Indian people in archaeology. I was pleased when Northern Cheyenne elder Bill Tallbull, who had attended my archaeological field school in 1988 for two weeks, said to me afterward, "You know, I have seen this happening already." One can predict that this remythologizing will continue, probably to the point where it seems that archaeology was always in favor of reburial and really was just trying to seek clarification of certain points.

The remythologizing process among Indians with respect to their relationships with archaeologists is not as clear, but it is happening. In their recent dispute with the Nebraska State Historical Society, the Pawnee relied heavily on very traditional archaeological views of Pawnee origins to bolster their case for cultural affiliation of remains. A Pawnee tribal historian involved in that case, Roger Echo-Hawk, has recently had to defend his acceptance of this and other archaeology to a mixed-nation group of Native Americans in Colorado where he acted as a monitor for archaeology on construction of the new Denver airport (also see Echo-Hawk, this volume). The fundamental problem for Indians is that many have gone to great lengths to distance themselves from archaeology. Many others, however, recognize the contribution that archaeologists have made on such issues as land claims and that when it comes to preservation of important cultural sites, Indians and archaeologists could be almost natural allies. Indians will probably not have to go as far in their remythologizing because their position is more understood by the public as being "right." Nonetheless, if they choose to deal with archaeology, they must go through the process.

Professional Ethics

While the remythologizing process has been going on, some groups have tried to cement relationships between indigenous peoples and archaeologists. Certainly the Society of Professional Archaeologists (SOPA) took into account the early 1970s rumblings about reburial and included in their ethics code a statement that archaeologists be "sensitive to, and respect the legitimate concerns of, groups whose culture histories are the subject of archaeological investigations" (SOPA 1981). Another group has recently been more decisive, not by remythologizing but by going directly to archaeology's indigenous constituents for solutions.

Invited to the World Archaeological Congress II in Venezuela, a group of indigenous people developed a draft ethics code with a single goal: indigenous control over indigenous heritage. They recognized openly that some nonindigenous heritage specialists (archaeologists, cultural resource management, and museums specialists) understood their obligations to others. Some of these specialists, they agreed, knew that freedom to pursue academic and scientific studies is not sacrosanct, but must be infused with humanity toward the aspirations of others (Matunga 1991:53). The indigenous committee was concerned with how the archaeological community would react to the code and worried that their code might be overly demanding. The very idea that they would have such concerns suggests that the remythologizing process was in operation for them.

Codes of ethics are no panacea. They are meant only to apprise people of key issues. The World Archaeological Congress (WAC) code is unique, however, because it demonstrates a shift of power and, most importantly, because it was drafted by indigenous people in terms of how *they* would like archaeologists to behave, rather than by archaeologists in terms of archaeologists' views of ethical obligations. The power shift is a crucial element here as well in that it portends an increasing transition toward what Powell, Garza, and Hendricks (1993:29) eloquently label "covenantal archaeology."

Covenantal Archaeology

Among the major Native American complaints about archaeology is that it has benefited only itself and its practitioners. Whatever the truth of this complaint, many archaeologists have worked closely with Indian people on land claims and in very successful heritage preservation programs. The exemplary, well-developed, and relatively long-term programs of the Navajo, Zuni, and Hopi in the Southwest have been extremely successful. Though no program is perfect, and some cannot incorporate even the entire range of Indian views or concerns, nonetheless the programs are at least administratively under Indian control, dealing with Indian concerns first and those of archaeology later.

As many archaeologists who have worked closely with Indian people have discovered, archaeology need not come to a screeching halt when it accedes to Indian demands. Many have discovered that if a relationship of trust can be built, archaeology may gain increased access to materials and sites. At the same time, control of the archaeology transfers to Indian hands, and they can see it as a benefit; their own questions about their own pasts receive primary attention. The kind of work done is essentially a covenant between archaeologists and Indians; this is fundamentally what indigenous peoples have asked for in the WAC ethics code. The approach *will* work, and I agree with Powell, Garza, and Hendricks that it will flourish as soon as its benefits are more widely realized.

The covenants will include not only research, but education. At first many archaeologists believed that if they could just educate Indians about what archaeology does, then Indians would come to appreciate it more. Many archaeologists still do not understand, however, that supposedly beneficial educational programs, such as the proposed scholarships offered by SAA and the Plains Anthropological Society, can be seen as an effort to co-opt Indian people and are viewed with suspicion by some. If the attitude, on the contrary, is to train Indian people in archaeology theory and method to apply these tools to their own research questions and *not* necessarily to get them to buy into archaeological interpretation, then these programs have a good chance of success. As an aside, I now chair the SAA's Native American Scholarship Committee, which has been slow to get off the ground due to lack of funds. Initially, I objected to the whole concept of an SAA Indian scholarship until I figured out that it was part of the remythologizing process.

If covenantal archaeology works, archaeological interpretation will change to better meet Indian interpretations of the past. This is a profoundly complex matter. As one editor of this volume pointed out, there may well be no pan-Indian interpretations of the past. There may even be conflicts, as in the case of the Hopi and Navajo differences of the settlement of the Southwest. Asked if archaeology could be made to meet both histories, which could grate on some Native sensibilities and draw archaeologists into the explosive political arena, I might counter by saying that archaeology as a profession is already there.

One might also point out that there is a substantive difference between archaeology as a profession and archaeology as a way of knowing. If one views archaeology as the former, then no, archaeology cannot meet both histories. If one sees archaeology as the latter, then the answer is absolutely yes. As a way of knowing, all archaeology provides is a basis of interpretation from material remains from a past. Archaeology does not seek or determine truth about the past; whether done by non-Indians or Indians, archaeology is a tool that helps people construct— not reconstruct—the past. In one sense this question betrays a fundamental epistemological issue in archaeology: that there is one correct view of the past and that it can only be known archaeologically. That view causes no end of problems in the archaeological profession's relationship with Indians.

On the other hand, if archaeology as a way of knowing is under the control of Indian people, then archaeology as a profession can change. What archaeologists teach the non-Indian public about Indians, for example, will perhaps downplay such solid archaeological dogma as the Bering land bridge migration route to the Americas and the like. Of course, this grates on archaeological sensibilities because archaeology *must* find grounding for interpretation in the material record from the past, not in peoples' belief systems about themselves and their origins. Some archaeologists suggest that this issue is akin to debates between scientists and creationists, but there is a major difference, because in archaeology and the associated issues of repatriation and reburial we are dealing with "archaeological colonialism." Pasts created by archaeologists have been imposed on Indian pasts without a chance for debate. There is, in other words, a major power relationship difference in the two issues. They are analogues, not homologues.

Ethnocritical Archaeology

So where does this leave us? Archaeology as a profession and Indian nations must both have their own stories from their own bases of knowledge. They need not be the same stories even if they are discussing the same past(s). To reiterate, however, power relationships are crucial. Archaeology has been a dominant society tool, viewed by Native Americans as part of the western tradition's repression of the "Other," the "Rest" of humanity. The reburial issue has been and remains a forum for Indian declarations of their victimization by the West, and they have a right to complain loudly about that treatment by the profession of archaeology. Although archaeology has a right to its own stories, if archaeology and Indian relations have a chance to improve, then archaeology must be the one to change the most. An approach like that suggested by Arnold Krupat (1992) might be beneficial.

Krupat writes from the perspective of literary criticism, especially of Native American literature. He is suspicious of any scientific theory or position that looks like a metaphor of social ideology or that can be construed as contributing to the alienation of any class or group, which is exactly what archaeology has done.

In essence, if Indians and archaeologists view all issues as oppositional sets, bipolar and black or white, we are bound to fail to change very much. Any compromises between archaeology and Indians still reflect the positions of the opposing sides. For archaeology, this has meant simply another way of telling "our" own story, of "turning 'their' [Indian] incoherent jabber into an eloquence of use only to ourselves" (Krupat 1992:6). As an alternative, however, archaeology could apply what Krupat calls "ethnocriticism," which suggests that scholars work at the boundaries of their usual ways of knowing. In this intellectual frontier,

> oppositional sets like West/Rest, Us/Them, anthropological/biological, historical/ mythical, and so on, often tend to break down. On the one hand, cultural contact can indeed produce mutual rejections, the reification of differences, and defensive retreats into celebrations of what each group regards as distinctly its own. . . . On the other hand, it may also frequently be the case that interaction leads to interchange . . . and transculturalization (Krupat 1992:15).

Oppositional views are simply useless. As they once justified imperial domination, they now serve to justify postcolonial revisionist "victimist history." One can acknowledge that some people have been hurt by others in the colonial context and that they have every right to complain about their treatment, but to where does that lead except more rhetoric? Ethnocriticism is concerned with differences rather than oppositions; it seeks to replace oppositional with dialogical models where cultural differences are explored and where interpretations are negotiated rather than declared. Claims to accuracy, systematicity, and knowledge would reside in their capacity to take more into context, that is, to be more flexible and open to new ideas and approaches that deal with differences. Thus, if ethnocritical archaeology is a way of knowing, even two Indian nations such as the Hopi and Navajo might come to terms with their differences over origins and settlement of the Southwest.

The result is a relative truth, but one that does have rules. Archaeologists can still be scientific, but in ways meaningful to Indians, by negotiating the methods and procedures to be followed and by indicating the empirical and logical components of reasoning. How might this work? In truth, we hardly know yet because so little of it has been tried, but there are indications. One example from the Southwest is discussed in the thoughtful and provocative position paper by Anyon, Ferguson, Jackson, and Lane (1996) that looks at how oral tradition and archaeology can be coalesced (also see Anyon et al., this volume). What happens in ethnocritical archaeology is that the science is clearly articulated and is placed fully into an explicit social context. This is the essence of a covenantal archaeology, where research questions and methods are negotiated and support a mutually agreed upon agenda. As this approach becomes more commonplace, archaeological science will become more modest and very different from what it has been. It will be the end product of the syncretism begun with the reburial issue.

Conclusions

Some, both Indian and archaeologist, may see these changes as an evil and will fight them, but I see them as doing nothing but good. I am optimistic about the future of relationships between archaeologists and Indians. At the same time, I am not as naive as I once was. I used to have an ideal view about my profession and its concern for humanity; we were "studying the past for the future." I felt that archaeology as a profession would change if we found that what we did actually might be hurting people. But I learned that we can be both self-protective and self-delusive. I've come to understand that power and control are an important part of the reburial issue and they are not easy for the profession to relinquish.

Let me summarize my ideas about what is and will be happening regarding the reburial issue, American Indians, and archaeology. Both archaeologists and Indians are undergoing a process of reconciliation akin to syncretism. This process will continue, with each group remythologizing its position in relation to the other, but with archaeology changing the most, making it seem more sympathetic to Indian concerns. In this context, the profession of archaeology must change the most because it stands to lose the most. Change will include implementing standards of ethical practice, revising theory and method, and scrutinizing power relationships. As both groups realize mutual benefit, archaeologists and Indians will develop more covenantal programs.

NAGPRA will cause problems and many battles will be fought over it. The law and its implementing regulations will be refined, but new laws probably will not be necessary. NAGPRA and any new versions or successors will speed along the process of reconciliation.

Archaeology needs to see the reburial issue as potential rather than threat, and it needs to start examining the bases of the real worldview differences between archaeology and American Indians. Reliance on law, historical precedent, or arguments of science vs. religion are poor substitutes for direct recognition of the problems or for real understanding. If it follows this more enlightened path, archaeology may realize the humanistic potential of which it is certainly capable. I truly believe that an ethnocritical archaeology can be of benefit to Indian people; I hope that we archaeologists can show good faith in demonstrating this benefit. I hope that Indian people will continue to be patient with us and give us the chance to do so.

This paper has benefited from discussions with many people including Brian Molyneaux, Roger Echo-Hawk, Tristine Smart, Elizabeth Prine, Maria Pearson, Randy McGuire, Tony Klesert, and Jan Hammil.

NOTES

1. In this paper I often use the term reburial to incorporate repatriation. Generally to archaeologists and Indians alike, the whole issue has been known as the reburial issue. Certainly repatriation and reburial are not synonyms. Laws that have been enacted technically are repatriation laws. However, reburial, especially of human remains and grave goods, seems to be assumed by both parties as the likely disposition of repatriated materials.

2. I will use "archaeology" for the remainder of this paper for the sake of simplicity, but I actually mean archaeology, physical anthropology, human osteology, museum studies, and those related fields dealing with human remains and grave goods.

3. See Knecht and Hausler-Knecht (1992) for an example of problems. Their paper, presented at the American Anthropological Association meetings on the problems with the Larsen Bay repatriation, was withdrawn for unstated reasons from the final volume on the project (Bray and Killion 1994).

G. PETER JEMISON ■

Four

Who Owns the Past?

[Editors' note: In discussions over the past 20 years or so between Native Americans and archaeologists, two issues have emerged as central: (1) Who owns the past? and (2) Who should control the disposition of Native American human remains? Over the years, many meetings have been held at the local, regional, and national levels. As anyone who attended those meetings can attest, they were characterized by discussions that were fairly stylized. The same questions were raised, and pretty much the same answers were offered.

Here, Jemison summarizes one such meeting conducted in 1989, prior to the enactment of NAGPRA. The statements Jemison reports are very typical. This dialogue provides a basis for examining if, how, and to what degree NAGPRA has (or has not) altered the dialogue.]

In 1989, before NAGPRA became law, I organized a symposium entitled "Who Owns the Past." The symposium was held at the State University of New York (SUNY) at Buffalo during my graduate work in American Studies. Invited discussants included Native Americans and museum personnel from the Rochester

Museum and Science Center, Rochester, New York. The Native Americans included Chief Irving Powless Jr., Onondaga Nation; John Mohawk, Seneca Nation of Indians, an assistant professor at SUNY Buffalo; and Geraldine Green, Seneca Nation of Indians, a Longhouse elder. Charles Hayes, III, the director of research, Lorraine Saunders, a physical anthropologist and a research fellow, and Martha Sempowski, an archaeologist and a research fellow, all from the Rochester Museum and Science Center, represented the scientific and museum communities.

The symposium was organized to examine our differing views of human remains and sacred objects. Participants were each given 10 minutes to present a statement that outlined their points of view. They were then given an opportunity to interact and answer questions from fellow participants or audience members: a lively debate ensued.

I have excerpted portions of their statements to give an idea of each individual's point of view. For example, Charles Hayes made two initial points: "increasing sensitivity to the proper treatment of human remains from archaeological contexts, no matter what group is involved, appears to be gaining momentum and acceptance throughout the world. . . . Secondly, all of us are anxious to combat the ever-increasing looting and destruction of archaeological sites." Hayes further commented, "Those of us in museums in particular are vitally interested in documenting, preserving, and interpreting Native American heritage as part of our concern for the overall history of North America. Never has the general public been so enthused or better informed about Indians." Hayes was concerned that repatriation could have negative effects: "I do not believe any of us would want to have our descendants feel that we made irrational decisions with profound effects on human history."

John Mohawk looked at the history of Native American and white relations as it pertains to the display of human remains. He cited the case of Metacom, the Wampanoag Chief (also known as King Philip) who was beheaded in 1676 in the town of Plymouth, Massachusetts, at the conclusion of King Philip's War.

> He [Metacom] was an Indian. His people were attacked by the New England colonists. He was killed. His head was cut off and it was placed on top of a pointed stake, to be left there on display for some nearly two decades. And at the time the way it was explained by the religious leaders of the Colony was that the Indians were the handmaidens of the devil, and they needed to be dealt with thus. So our first exhibits had what you might call a spiritual explanation for a political end.

In the nineteenth century, this type of exhibit and interpretation was replaced by the work of Lewis Henry Morgan, the father of modern anthropology. According to Professor Mohawk,

> Lewis Henry Morgan, who I believe had some Rochester connections, and some Iroquois connections, really made a call. He called for the study of disappearing peoples as a way of preserving for all time what I would best describe as man's price

to civilization, as it were—the Social-Darwinist theory that people started out in extreme primitivism and then from primitivism they evolved socially through stages. He called for more study of people who were at that hour in some stage of this evolution. And what arose during this period in the nineteenth century was a lot of stuff that was at that time supposed to be science; it was going to be the science of how peoples were distributed along a curve or a graph of worthiness, if you will, arising from primitive peoples to the people who were going to do the study, to civilized peoples . . . a period that was called the period of scientific racism, science was used to explain a political end.

Mohawk listed the negative results of this line of reasoning and concluded:

> We want the sciences that are supposed to serve humanity to serve all of humanity equally, and to serve the dignity of all people equally. We can't have some people's heads stuck up on pikes outside the village, and we can't have some people's sacred objects stuck on display under glass when that's offensive to the people who hold those objects sacred. We can't have some people's remains in cardboard boxes in the bottom of brick buildings while other groups of people are not in cardboard boxes in the building—and we can't call it science; it's politics that does that.

Lorraine Saunders, a physical anthropologist, contended that her work, which involves the study of human osteology, provides direct testimony from deceased individuals about themselves and their lives. "There are written histories of the early days after the arrival of Europeans on this continent. But they were the observations of people of another culture who did not understand and often judged harshly the different and, to them, alien societies that they were seeing." Continuing, she stated, "The sort of study that I do involves direct contact with these people individual by individual. The information comes directly from each person. In that way, it seems to me that I am giving them the opportunity to have some say in what is known about them today." She concluded, "The insights gained from the research of today, and future improvements in methods and technology, will allow an increasingly better understanding of the lives of the earlier inhabitants of this continent. Therefore, reburial, the destruction of the only means they have to be the informants, would be silencing them forever before the whole story has been told."

Geraldine Green, Seneca, and a Longhouse elder, spoke next. She began,

> I'm not used to speaking in lecture halls, or in front of students. As a matter of fact, this is the first time I have gone out, so people know what is going on. All this museum stuff, archaeology, the digging up of human remains, or why we have to prove that they were, and who owns it, all this is strange for me and I have to do quite a bit of rethinking and examining of our way of life because there is more to us than what you see here, believe me. There has to be; otherwise, we wouldn't be here as survivors. And those ancestors who they want information from, I just don't understand that, and am not even going to begin to address that for that is not our way of life. . . .

In our way of life when a person dies, there is a certain funeral address which tells us what to do. We leave them alone, they are through. They have given what information they want. They have done their jobs; we need not bother them anymore. That is why they go to their rest; they have finished their job here, and it is very important to us that we do not disturb them anymore.

Martha Sempowski, an archaeologist, offered this explanation:

Archaeology, then, from my point of view, offers you and your descendants the hope of more accurate treatment in history through its potential for more objective documentation of specific events and interactions that took place during that critical interaction between Europeans and Native Americans. . . . Oral traditions are a very important source of information, but can you be certain that oral traditions will meet all the needs of your children? Your grandchildren? Or generations that will follow them? Can you really be certain? Can you be sure that they won't have new questions about the past that none of us here today has even conceived of? Questions so specific as to time and place that really the best way to answer them is through the archaeological record, if not the only way. . . . If effected on a national scale, the reburial program that's being proposed, however nobly intended and emotionally satisfying it is, would destroy a very substantial portion of this record of the past for Native Americans.

Sempowski made a second point:

Right now there happen to be two large Seneca sites that are under threat from modern development. In both cases we were asked by Native Americans and by local planning boards to make representations concerning the significance or importance of those particular sites. What allowed us to make those statements and recommendations was reference to existing collections of archaeological materials. Finally, one of my greatest fears about the proposed mass reburial of museum collections is that it would unwittingly contribute to further site looting by making the artifacts existing in private collections extremely rare, and thus inflate their monetary value.

The last presenter was Chief Irving Powless. Speaking of sacred objects in museum collections, he said:

We are the ones that know how to use them, how to utilize them, and the purpose of these sacred objects. You do not know what their purpose is. You don't know the songs that go with these sacred objects. You don't know the speeches that go with these sacred objects. You don't know the purpose of these sacred objects. Those sacred objects obviously are for our people. They do not belong in a box in a museum or some art show. There is a definite purpose for these sacred objects, and these sacred objects should be in our possession, not in the possession of some anthropologist, archaeologist, or some museum or private collector.

Chief Powless gave examples of sacred objects and their power. One involved Hopi Kachinas in a plastic bag stored in a drawer at a museum in Washington, D.C., and the apparent consequences of their release from this insensitive treatment. He reflected on the inherent power which sacred objects have and the general lack of recognition or the disbelief with which most museologists and anthropologists approach them.

During the session that followed, the participants raised issues with one another, and then the audience got into the act. Typical of that discussion were the following exchanges:

John Mohawk stated, "First I am personally in favor of more archaeological research and not less. In fact, there's not enough money being spent on serious research. What I'm opposed to is the continuation of museums as monuments to ethnocentrism in our culture." Later, he added,

Where is the Seneca country? Crazy Horse, when they asked him about that, he pointed to the east and he said, "[My land . . . Oglala Teton land . . . is] There where lie the bones of my ancestors. That is our land." And the Seneca country, where lie the bones of our ancestors, that's our land. Now somebody else got this land, and after they got this land, they claimed these were nonconsecrated graves. You can dig a nonconsecrated grave like you dig up the grave of a dog or cat. They're not sacred; they weren't sacred to the first people that came after they got the land.

John continued,

It's not about graves and bones and studying bones. It's about respect for the living. It's about respect for other people. . . . When you argue that the bones that our people left there are useful, more useful for scientific purposes than they are necessary for reburial to maintain the heart and essence of the culture, the continuity of the generations, you're making an ethnocentric argument. . . . I haven't been able to get an accurate count, but there looks like there might be millions of skeletons, two million skeletons, in museum. Who's studying these?

Lorraine Saunders responded,

As far as ethnocentrism goes, in the study of human remains I can give a specific example to show that that is hardly true anymore. In 1984 I was codirector of an excavation in Rochester called the Highland Park excavation. It was a cemetery for several public institutions. When I first became involved, all they knew was that human bones had been found. They were asking what the demography was. In other words, were there males and females? Were there children? . . . Then the real question finally came up. What race are they? Okay. And I said they were white, and the engineers went oh, great, thanks. They were afraid they were going to be Native American but since it was an abandoned white cemetery, there are laws that cover that. . . . In fact, you can take out these burials with a backhoe, with heavy equipment, if it's classified as an abandoned cemetery, which this was.

In the end, the archaeologists did excavate the remains, but Saunders wanted to illustrate a point. She continued, "We are interested in all people. That's what anthropology is, the study of mankind, not just of one group over another group. And when there is missing information, if there is more that we can learn, that's what we want to do. And we do that by studying human remains."

Charles Hayes asked this question,

> . . . I'm talking about the sacred objects in the collections; if all these are taken out of our current museums, and the volume as just alluded to is tremendous, we can realistically think that this material is, or should it be all reburied? Some of the greatest art will be lost forever except for pictures, and this is what bothers me as a museologist as well. . . . is the Native American community prepared to lose this material?

Irving Powless spoke of Art Gerber (an "ethnographic art dealer") and his views of Native American art, "I am preserving the art of the Native American people, and I sell these objects for five hundred, six hundred, depending on how much I can get for them." [Again quoting Gerber he said] "I think we should be able to continue to go into these 'art farms' [grave sites] and get these objects from the Native Americans." Chief Powless questioned how we reach this point when an individual like Gerber refers to Native American burial grounds as art farms. "Where do we come to when we, in the study of man, put these objects that come out of these 'art farms' on display, either in the museum or in collections, private or otherwise?"

Early in the presentations Martha Sempowski had stated, "I'm not talking about the excavation of graves, the digging of burial grounds. Archaeologists do not any longer in New York dig human graves." I shared the following:

> In the spring of 1988 we attended the annual meeting of the New York Archaeological Association (avocational and professional archaeologists), which is also a conference for the New York Archaeological Council (professional archaeologists). The meeting was held in Norwich, New York. Geraldine Green and I attended the meeting and heard the statement made that, in fact, the moratorium was something that the individual archaeologist could choose to follow and abide by or choose to ignore, but it really was up to the individual—it's voluntary. This statement was made by a well-known, professional archaeologist, and I might be overstating the concern I have, but not one individual at the conference rebuked him publicly when he made the statement, and it is that code of silence which still protects avocational and professional archaeologists who excavate human remains.

Recently, the Haudenosaunee Standing Committee on Burial Rules and Regulations, a committee of representatives from the Six Nations Iroquois Confederacy, of which I am the chairman, visited the Rochester Museum and Science Center. The meeting was a preliminary response to a full visit on NAGPRA-related matters. We were pleased to learn from Richard Shultz, director of the museum, that they did not intend to block our request for the return of our ancestors' human remains. They listened carefully to our concerns about contract archaeology that the museum carries out and our concerns that Senecas not be left out of, or barred from, on-site observance when there is a potential for the disturbance of human remains. They promised to look at their contractual agreements and add language to allow for Native American observers. With regard to removing sacred objects from exhibits at the museum, they promised to revisit the question. I have heard, although I can't confirm it, that our medicine masks will be removed from display cases in the museum.

Perhaps a new era has begun with this one institution that has major Seneca and other Haudenosaunee holdings—we earnestly hope so. However, I recently received a letter from a staff person at the Rochester Museum looking for a letter of support for a NAGPRA grant application to fund the museum to study the human remains in the collection. I found this ironic, considering that the museum needed an extension of the November 1995 deadline to complete the inventory of human remains in their collection.

The question of who owns the past, in this case, may have been decided by the federal government because NAGPRA mandates that museums must *study* our remains to be able to return them to us for reburial and their final resting place, a bitter irony in the 200-year-old history between American Indians and the imposition of United States Indian Law on sovereign Nations.

Who Owns the Past? is the title of an unpublished manuscript edited by the author and transcribed from a symposium with the same title. The symposium was supported in part by a grant from the New York State Council on the Humanities.

Five

Indigenous Rights and Archaeology

America wanted museums. But they would be different from European ones. They would not, for instance, be stores of imperial plunder, like the British Museum or the Louvre. (Actually immense quantities of stuff were ripped off from the native Indians and the cultures south of the Rio Grande, but we call this anthropology, not plunder.) (Hughes 1992:23)[1]

The current dialogue between Native Americans and archaeologists concerning the appropriate treatment of Native American human remains and ancestral sites has many dimensions: ethical, moral, and legal. As a law professor, I would like to discuss the legal issues that surround this relationship and explain how those issues are interpreted by Native Americans. It would be ludicrous, however, to pretend that there is one Native American interpretation. There are as many interpretations as there are tribal governments, religious groups within tribes, and political movements among tribes. This chapter adopts one of those interpretations, which I shall call an indigenous rights perspective.

The indigenous rights perspective is founded on the contemporary political movement to reassert tribal sovereignty and self-determination and demand respect for indigenous rights to cultural survival (Morris 1992).[2] This political movement is national and international in scope, and is a response to several centuries of

European domination and forcible assimilation of indigenous peoples. In the international law context, indigenous rights, such as the right to cultural survival, are understood as normative precepts that are derivative of generally applicable human rights principles, such as the right to self-determination (Anaya 1996). However, as James Anaya notes, those broadly applicable human rights principles are "in themselves relevant to indigenous peoples' efforts to survive and flourish under conditions of equality" (Anaya 1996:73).

One important aspect of the fight for cultural survival is the issue of who has control over the past. As Rennard Strickland has noted, federal Indian policy has, with very few exceptions, "been premised on the assumption that the future for the Native American required the destruction of the past" (Strickland and Supernaw 1993:161). Thus, assimilationist federal policies have focused on erasing sacred tribal traditions and religions and inculcating Euroamerican Christian traditions. As Indian nations strive to overcome the legacy of these assimilationist policies, their future survival as distinct cultures rests to some extent on their ability to understand and protect their ancestral past.[3]

Thus, critical issues arise as we consider who has the right to control the past. Are the material remains of past cultures a "common good" or "public resource" for the people of the nation-state where they are found? Or do they represent cultural resources that belong to the descended cultures of contemporary indigenous America? In many ways, the federal cultural preservation statutes treat indigenous human remains and ancestral sites as public resources. This chapter will discuss the complex web of federal statutes that governs cultural preservation, including the Archaeological Resources Protection Act (ARPA), the National Historic Preservation Act (NHPA), and the Native American Graves Protection and Repatriation Act (NAGPRA). Before examining these statutes in detail, however, I will examine the values and legal concepts that are triggered by these statutes and explain how these statutes can be interpreted from an indigenous rights perspective.

Native Americans and Archaeologists: The Duality of Values and Interests

Attitudes within archaeology are starting to reflect the postmodern influences of academia, including the commitment to understanding diverse perspectives and viewpoints through a dialogical process with others. Although there have been many changes in professional ethics and attitudes as a result of this process, Indian people's perceptions of archaeologists tend to be driven by their past experiences, which have been quite unpleasant for the most part. In particular, the relationship between Native Americans and archaeologists has been problematic because of the different values that each group holds about the past.

Archaeologists research the past, as do historians. However, the methodology of the archaeologist is much more invasive. Not content to study tribal oral histories or traditions, the archaeologist will often seek to excavate and appropriate the material remains of the past. Other times, the archaeologist will probe the spiritual and intangible aspects of the past in the quest for knowledge. The values that archaeologists seek to protect are those of science, of documenting "facts" about the past for the sake of knowing (Bowman 1989; Meighan 1993). Archaeologists argue that knowledge and research benefit all people. Until the relatively recent change in professional attitudes, archaeologists perceived ancient peoples as research specimens, like dinosaurs or fossils, and claimed that the codes of ethical behavior that governed European burials did not pertain to the treatment of ancient peoples.

Thus, archaeologists have often faced vehement opposition from Native Americans, who, for the most part, do not agree with any of these views. Although they believe in the importance of the past, most Native American peoples see the past as connected to the present in an unbroken continuum. The past is very real to contemporary Indian people and is preserved in oral histories and ongoing ceremonial practices and beliefs. Many native people dispute that science can tell them where they came from—they already know this from their origin stories, and they honor their ancestors regardless of how long ago they passed away (Bowman 1989). Furthermore, native people often see care of the past as a duty and responsibility; they have firm ideas as to what behavior is appropriate and believe that they should have the right to stop others from desecrating their ancestors.

I imagine that many would assert that the central legal issue at the heart of this debate between Native Americans and archaeologists is one of property law: that is, "who owns the past?" After all, legal scholars use the concept of "ownership" to designate legal rights to specific objects—such as the rights to possess, to control, to exclude, to include, and to alienate. To the extent that archaeologists assert a right to control and use material remains in their quest for knowledge, they are acting as property owners. Moreover, federal statutes, such as ARPA and NAGPRA, are largely phrased in the language of property rights. However, at a more fundamental level, the idea of human remains and funerary objects as "property" is odious, both to non-Indians and to Indians.

Under English common law, for example, dead bodies cannot be owned, and the removal of funerary objects from a burial site is considered a dreadful and abhorrent crime. In the old Anglo-Saxon tongue, a burial ground was referred to as "God's Acre," a sanctified resting place for the deceased (Trope and Echo-Hawk 1992). Because of these strong spiritual beliefs about the dead, English common law regards the next of kin as having only a limited or "quasi-property" interest in the body that entitles them to control the disposition of the deceased and allows them to obtain compensation in tort for any misconduct toward the remains (Bowman 1989). However, even the next of kin cannot "own" the dead. Therefore, property law is, in many ways, completely unsuitable to address the legal rights of Indian people with regard to their ancestors.

From an indigenous rights perspective, it may be more accurate to argue that in seeking to protect their ancestors, Native Americans are attempting to secure recognition of basic human rights such as the right to religious and spiritual fulfillment, and the right to control burial sites on ancestral lands, which have been removed from native "ownership" through colonization and appropriation (Harjo 1992; Riding-In 1992; Trope and Echo-Hawk 1992).[4] The outrageous conduct that Euroamericans have displayed toward Native American remains, funerary objects, and sacred objects exemplifies a basic and ongoing disregard for Native American human rights. After all, the very first Pilgrim exploring party returned to the *Mayflower* with items taken from a very recent grave: "We brought sundry of the prettiest things away with us and covered up the corpse again," one member of the party later recalled (Trope and Echo-Hawk 1992:40). And this callous disregard turned into calculated evil with the genocidal military campaign conducted against Indians, which culminated with an 1868 U.S. Surgeon General's order directing army personnel to collect Indian crania and other body parts for the Army Medical Museum. Over the next few decades, that order resulted in the collection of more than 4,000 Indian heads from battlefields, burial grounds, hospitals, and POW camps (Trope and Echo-Hawk 1992). Importantly, this policy was accomplished in the name of "scientific research."

Professor James Riding-In links the rise of archaeology in the 1800s as a science to the spread of colonialism and the belief that Christianity and civilization offered justification for the study of "inferior" cultures, such as those of Africa and the Americas (Riding-In 1992). Riding-In points to the fact that the early science of "craniology" that inspired the infamous 1868 order was developed precisely to prove that inferiority. Thus, for Indian people the designation of "science" does not immunize a practice from pointed moral scrutiny. Nor, as amply shown by federal Indian policy as well as the history of slavery in America, does the designation of "law" insulate governmental policy from moral scrutiny, a scrutiny that examines whose values the law seeks to protect and how those values are enforced. Not surprisingly, both science and the law have come under attack as Indian people struggle to overcome the bitter legacy of colonialism and its disrespectful practices and to preserve their past in the ways that they see fit.

The Effect of Federal Historic and Cultural Preservation Statutes

Largely as a result of official policies encouraging the pursuit of "knowledge" about indigenous peoples through the study of anthropology and archaeology, which in turn inspired a popular fascination with Native American "artifacts," artifact collecting and archaeological site desecration have been long-standing practices. The problems caused by artifact collecting and site desecration have been severe on both public lands and private lands, although for the most part federal regulation has attached to public lands (Hutt, Jones, and McAllister 1992).

Notably, however, the law as it relates to historical preservation and archaeological excavation has been consistent with the popular perception of Indian people as "historical resources" and as appropriate objects of scientific study. Thus, there is no real argument between the amateur pot hunter and the professional archaeologist as to the underlying values at stake; both agree that Indian remains are objects for non-Indian study and excavation. There is merely the argument of who is the appropriate party to conduct the investigation, and perhaps one as to the ultimate disposition of the remains: that is, are they to reside on permanent display in a museum or are they to be bought and sold on the market. The federal statutes attempt to define rights of access and control in a way that authorizes the activities of the professional archaeologist and attempts to punish the activities of the amateur pot hunter.

Antiquities Act of 1906

The Antiquities Act of 1906, which was intended to protect archaeological sites on federal and tribal lands from looters, defined dead Indians interred on federal lands as "archaeological resources," as "objects of historic or scientific interest," and treated these deceased persons as "federal property" (16 U.S.C. §§ 431–433). Thus, under federal law it was entirely permissible to disinter Indian bodies—provided that the necessary permits were secured—and deposit the bodies in permanent museum collections. The act recognized federal agencies as having the authority for the proper care and management of all archaeological resources on federal and tribal lands. Indeed, as of 1990, at least 14,500 Native American bodies were in the possession of various federal agencies, such as the National Park Service, the Bureau of Land Management, and the Fish and Wildlife Service (Trope and Echo-Hawk 1992).

Importantly, the Antiquities Act does not speak of tribal interests at all, nor does it give effect to tribal laws, customs, or beliefs as to the appropriate care of such sites. The act is thus completely unresponsive to tribal concerns and merely furthers the interests of professional archaeologists in having access to the sites unimpeded by amateur pot hunters and looters. For most purposes, of course, the Antiquities Act has been replaced by the Archaeological Resources Protection Act (16 U.S.C. § 470aa–mm).[5] However, ARPA does not represent a significant departure in terms of the values and interests it protects.

Archaeological Resources Protection Act of 1979

The stated purpose of ARPA is to protect irreplaceable archaeological resources on federal and Indian lands from individual and commercial interests and to foster the professional gathering of information for future benefit. ARPA considers "archaeological resources on public lands and Indian lands" to be "an accessible and irreplaceable part of the Nation's heritage." Thus, like the Antiquities Act, ARPA considers Native American remains and cultural items to be "archaeological resources"—provided that they are more than 100 years old. If they are excavated on federal lands, they are considered "federal property" of historic and scientific interest to the public at large. Only if they are excavated on tribal lands are such remains and objects considered the property of the tribe.

There are many problems with ARPA, and it can be fairly said that the statute epitomizes the essential differences in values and beliefs about the past between Native Americans and Euroamericans. ARPA allows desecration of ancestral and sacred sites, although it requires a permit to undertake such desecration. ARPA considers research on Indian remains to be "in the public interest." ARPA treats human remains and funerary objects as "property" and directs that ultimate management and control of the excavated objects reside with the landowner—whether federal or tribal. Thus, to the extent that tribes have control over the excavation and disposition of such objects, it is because they are property owners and not because they have a recognized legal interest in their ancestors' remains.

Although ARPA pays lip-service to Native American interests by specifying certain notification and consultation requirements whenever excavation of a site could result in harm to or destruction of a religious or cultural site, the statute does not give a tribe the right to veto excavation on public lands. And the responsibility to mitigate damage is merely an option, not a requirement, for the federal land manager. Moreover, although the excavated remains ultimately may have to be repatriated under NAGPRA, the remains and objects can be legally excavated and studied prior to such repatriation.

Thus, ARPA's only value may lie in deterrence of illegal excavation of archaeological sites and illegal trafficking in the excavated objects. Through enforcement of ARPA's criminal and civil provisions, some site desecration may be stopped. However, ARPA does not disallow *all* site desecration. And the fact that the statute legalizes excavation, which many native peoples regard as site desecration, is testament to the fact that old attitudes still remain: Indian bodies and sacred objects are not treated the same as non-Indian bodies and "church property."

The Antiquities Act and ARPA are weighted heavily toward the interests of archaeologists in obtaining knowledge about the past. The permit requirements of the statutes ensure that only "qualified" people will excavate, but the statutes definitely support excavation and scientific study as a "public benefit."

Native American Graves Protection and Repatriation Act of 1990

Unlike ARPA or the Antiquities Act, NAGPRA is primarily "human rights legislation" designed to remedy the inequality in treatment between Caucasian remains and Native American remains: a history of inequality that, as Senator Daniel Inouye pointed out, carries the message of racism—that "Indians are culturally and physically different from and inferior to non-Indians" (136 Cong. Rec. S17174-75 [daily ed. Oct. 26, 1990]). NAGPRA thus governs the treatment of Indian remains, funerary objects, sacred objects, and objects of cultural patrimony by imposing certain requirements when such objects are excavated, and by specifying when objects that are in museum or agency collections must be repatriated to descendant tribes and individuals (25 U.S.C. §§ 3001-3013).

NAGPRA has been heavily criticized by some archaeologists who fear that the statute will impair their ability to research past cultures, and who assert that repatriation of remains and objects to contemporary Indians is unjustified because the connections between ancient and modern Indian cultures are too tenuous (e.g., Meighan 1993). Grossman, for example, asserts that NAGPRA is merely a response to the pressures of militant Indian groups that share the "same political orientation and multiculturalist agenda" as other ethnic rights advocates (Grossman 1993:9). Grossman claims that science has become a tool of ideology and that statutes such as NAGPRA prevent the exploration of "objective knowledge," which, she asserts "should be treasured for its own sake . . . and should be made available to all" (Grossman 1993:12).

Grossman's comments marginalize native perspectives on repatriation as being merely a politicized movement to gain "ethnic rights." This designation denies legitimacy to Native American values and interests. In accordance with recent attacks on notions of "group rights" (e.g., Graff 1994), native interests are considered "preferences," attempts to assert "victim" status to gain *special* rights.[6] In fact, NAGPRA *is* built around the notion of separate tribal governmental status and the federal government's unique trust relationship with the tribes (25 U.S.C. § 3010). Thus, NAGPRA requires that requests for repatriation come from the tribal community and makes the interpretation of ownership and alienability dependent upon tribal concepts of property (Strickland and Supernaw 1993).

Importantly, however, the native interests in gaining repatriation of ancestral remains and objects recognized by NAGPRA are largely an effort to obtain the *same* rights that Euroamericans have always had to *their* past, which is largely consecrated in Christian, marked cemeteries along with the bones of their ancestors. In this way, NAGPRA seeks to recognize indigenous human rights, which are inherent rights of all peoples that command international support and recognition. As Edward Halealoha Ayau comments: "NAGPRA recognizes the cultural right of living . . . Native Americans to speak on behalf of their ancestors and to determine proper treatment of ancestral remains. Such recognition is a basic human right, the exercise of which is a long standing attribute of native sovereignty and self-determination" (Ayau 1992:216).

In fact, some Indian people would assert that NAGPRA does not go far enough in acknowledging indigenous human rights. For example, NAGPRA applies only to excavations on federal or tribal lands and to repatriation of objects in federal or federally funded institutions. This leaves out many excavations undertaken on private lands or state lands (if not federally funded projects); and for the most part, unless the objects were illegally acquired and are commercially traded in interstate commerce, NAGPRA leaves private collections of Native American remains intact. Moreover, NAGPRA authorizes the intentional excavation of human remains, funerary objects, sacred objects, and objects of cultural patrimony if these objects are removed in accordance with all permit requirements (such as those under ARPA), and so long as notification and consultation with the affected Indian tribes occurs prior to excavation.

Thus, although NAGPRA represents an important recognition of indigenous cultural rights, the statute provides only limited protection for Native American interests in preventing desecration of ancestral sites. The objects may ultimately be repatriated to the tribe under NAGPRA, but they may still be unearthed and the subject of scientific testing before being returned to the tribe. Both activities constitute desecration under the belief systems of many indigenous peoples.[7]

National Historic Preservation Act of 1966

The NHPA serves as the basic charter for America's national historic preservation program (16 U.S.C. §§ 470–470w-6). As early as 1896, the Supreme Court had acknowledged the federal government's authority to designate and preserve "historic sites," finding that this was a "public purpose" within the meaning of the Fifth Amendment takings clause when accomplished by condemnation of private property (*United States v. Gettysburg Electric Railroad Company*, 160 U.S. 668, 681–682 [1896]). The NHPA accomplishes this "public purpose" through several means. First of all, the statute establishes a National Register of Historic Places and dictates the criteria for eligibility. Secondly, the statute mandates a review process (the "Section 106" process) for federal undertakings that might have an effect on any "district, site, building, structure, or object that is included in or eligible for inclusion in the National Register."

Although the NHPA was originally interpreted as being fairly consistent with Euroamerican practices in terms of defining a historic site, the 1992 amendments clarified that "traditional cultural properties" are included. Significantly, Native

American sacred sites may be considered traditional cultural properties, even absent evidence of human occupation, provided that they meet the appropriate criteria (Parker and King 1990). Moreover, the Section 106 process mandates notice and consultation with Native American tribes if a proposed federal undertaking might affect a sacred site or ancestral site that is eligible for listing on the National Register.

As with the other federal statutes, however, the NHPA is only marginally protective of tribal interests that involve sites off the reservation. Under the 1992 amendments, the tribal historic preservation officer has significant authority with respect to tribal lands; however, the tribes' role in the Section 106 process on other lands is much more limited. The NHPA is first and foremost a procedural statute, designed to ensure that there are no inadvertent impacts on historic properties. The statute, however, does not forbid adverse impacts on historic properties when no other measure is deemed adequate. Indeed, "establishing that a property is eligible for inclusion in the National Register does not necessarily mean that the property must be protected from disturbance or damage" (Parker and King 1990:4).

In fact, the very requirement that an ancestral or sacred site be documented as "eligible" for protected status is problematic for Native American people. Rather than being accorded respect as a matter of right, Indian people have to "prove" that their ancestral sites are "worthy" of preservation. Although this requirement is thought to be necessary to differentiate genuine from spurious claims, what counts as adequate proof is determined by the dominant society's legal structure. Native American people must generally enlist the services of professional archaeologists and anthropologists, who are seen as credible by the outside world. This process raises concerns for Native American people, who are often held to norms of secrecy and confidentiality when dealing with sacred information. While NHPA regulations counsel confidentiality, the mere act of revelation to an outsider can constitute a violation of traditional religious and cultural norms. Moreover, all expert testimony is subject to contradictory testimony from opposing experts, and to ultimate adjudication by non-Indian courts.[8]

National Environmental Policy Act of 1969

The National Environmental Policy Act is intended to serve as America's "basic national charter for protection of the environment" (42 U.S.C. §§ 4321–4370d). NEPA requires an analysis of major federal actions that may significantly affect human health and the environment. As the courts have held, this includes not only traditional environmental concerns of air and water quality, but also the "historic, cultural and national aspects of our heritage" (*Havasupai Tribe v. United States,* 752 F. Supp. 1471, 1493 [D. Ariz. 1990]). Thus, NEPA is an umbrella statute that generally mandates inclusion of environmental impact analyses under other relevant statutes as well, such as the NHPA, ARPA, and arguably, the American Indian Religious Freedom Act (AIRFA), although the courts have been less than charitable in assessing impacts on Native American religious interests under AIRFA.

However, NEPA is also purely a procedural statute, designed to ensure that agencies make informed decisions when engaging in development projects. NEPA does not require any particular substantive result, and, indeed, a project may go forward even if it will have some adverse impact on human health or the environment. Moreover, some courts have held that where Indian tribes fail to make full disclosure of religious interests, including the specific location of sacred sites and a detailed description of practices affected, the statute will not protect these interests (*Havasupai Tribe,* 752 F. Supp. 1498–1500). Even where the tribe does disclose this information, it is subject to analysis and criticism by other "experts," such as anthropologists or archaeologists.

In short, NEPA, like NHPA, provides limited protection for Native American interests. While both statutes require studies to document historic and cultural sites, neither precludes subsequent development that would negatively impact these sites or the living cultures that treasure them. All of these statutes, however, require some kind of relationship between the professionals who document the sites for the government studies and the Native Americans who oppose desecration of the sites. To the extent that the statutes require the disclosure of sensitive information by Native Americans to the professionals, a fiduciary relationship may arise. I leave for others the discussion of what that relationship should look like and the extent to which the professional must honor constraints on the disclosure of information and refrain from using it inappropriately. Like it or not, however, the federal statutes render Native American cultural preservation to some extent dependent on an accurate translation by archaeologists and anthropologists. Because of this, the ethical boundaries of this relationship must be articulated.

Conclusion

Although my discussion has focused on the federal cultural and historic preservation statutes, I should acknowledge that state and tribal statutes also play important roles in detailing applicable values and interests and defining the appropriate role of the archaeologist. While archaeologists continue to assert that scientific goals benefit society as a whole, and yield an understanding of the past that is a common good, these assumptions are clearly challenged by many Native Americans. Native Americans regard their ancestors and their past as belonging to the living descendants of these cultures and believe that they must be honored and respected according to tribal customs and traditions. These customs may specify that knowledge should remain exclusively within the indigenous culture. Thus, for many

Native Americans, knowledge of the past is not a common good; it is a legacy of past generations that must be respected and treated with care by this generation.

Many Native Americans do not distinguish appropriation of their ancestors for commercial gain from appropriation for scientific benefit. A looter of archaeological sites desecrates burial grounds for commercial gain. A scientific excavation of archaeological sites desecrates burial grounds for the sake of gaining knowledge about the past. Indeed, knowledge of the past which becomes the property of the public at large (through, for example, publication in national magazines) encourages the idea that Native American people are historic resources that belong to the American public. In fact, from an indigenous rights perspective, nothing could be more offensive or less grounded in reality.

The federal statutes encourage controlled access to Native American ancestral sites, which can be problematic. Although recent efforts to recognize tribal governments as the primary decision makers for cultural preservation issues on tribal lands are a step in the right direction, an ethic of respect mandates similar control over sites on ancestral lands that have been removed from tribal ownership. The idea that Native American remains and cultural objects can serve some common good must become a relic of a dying colonialism. The future relationship between archaeologists and Native Americans depends on the ability of the archaeologist to understand the cultural values that drive indigenous cultural preservation efforts. NAGPRA is a positive step toward recognition of basic human rights for Native Americans, but there is still significant work to be done. Perhaps no one can really "own" the past, but we need to acknowledge the special responsibilities of those Native American people who are caretakers of an ancestral past that lives on.

I would like to thank Kurt Dongoske, Nina Swidler, and the other organizers of the SAA forum on Native Americans and Archaeology for inviting me to participate. I benefited from their remarks as well as those of the other participants. I would also like to thank Professor Robert N. Clinton (University of Iowa) and Professor Jeffrie G. Murphy (Arizona State University) for their thoughtful comments on earlier versions of this chapter.

NOTES

1. I am indebted to my colleague, Jeffrie Murphy, for calling this quotation to my attention. Hughes's acerbic comment makes an important point: whether the collection of artifacts is called anthropology or plunder can depend on one's position as the researcher or the subject. I would argue that similar problems attach to the designation of "scientific benefit" as it is understood within the discipline of archaeology.

2. An indigenous rights perspective has been taken by a number of Native American rights organizations in relation to protection of indigenous human remains and ancestral sites and was a major impetus for the Native American Graves Protection and Repatriation Act

(Riding-In 1992:25). Professor Riding-In details the history of the reburial movement and efforts of groups such as American Indians Against Desecration, the National Congress of American Indians, the Association of American Indian Affairs, the American Indian Science and Engineering Society, the Native American Rights Fund, and the International Indian Treaty Council. As another scholar notes, the reburial issue has become "a political issue of respect—respect not only for the dead, but also for the Native American people" (Bowman 1989:150).

3. For example, as James Anaya points out, issues of indigenous cultural integrity, encompassing "indigenous peoples' works of art, scientific knowledge, . . . songs, stories, human remains, funerary objects and other such tangible and intangible aspects of indigenous cultural heritage" are the subject of a study sponsored by the U.N. Subcommission on Prevention of Discrimination and Protection of Minorities (Anaya 1996:103). The 1993 *Study on the Protection of the Cultural and Intellectual Property of Indigenous Peoples* "identifies widespread historical and continuing practices that have unjustly deprived indigenous peoples of the enjoyment of the tangible and intangible objects that comprise their cultural heritage" (Anaya 1996:103–104).

4. I should note that property has been affirmed as an international human right (Anaya 1996:105), and in that sense, a distinction between "property rights" and "human rights" is nonsensical. However, indigenous property rights have long suffered from a lack of equal recognition according to international law constructs of property, and it is only now, "where modern notions of cultural integrity and self-determination join property precepts," that indigenous rights are beginning to receive equal respect and recognition, at least in theory (Anaya 1996:105).

5. The Ninth Circuit's opinion in *United States v. Diaz,* which held the Antiquities Act to be unconstitutionally vague because it fails to specify the age of the objects to be protected, has cast doubt on the legality of the Act: 449 F.2d 113 (9th Cir. 1974); cf. *United States v. Smyer,* 596 F.2d 939 (10th Cir. 1979) (upholding constitutionality of the act as applied to protection of Mimbres jars that were up to 900 years old). However, the Antiquities Act remains valid as a means to establish historic and scientific sites, and it may be used to gain permission to excavate sites that are less than 100 years old.

6. For example, Graff attacks the notion of "ethnocultural nationalism" as "a metaphor designed to serve ideological or political objectives" (Graff 1994:209–210).

7. It is important to acknowledge that there is no uniform view among Native Americans as to the propriety of scientific testing of ancestral remains. Some Native Americans believe that this is permissible when there is a "specific purpose to the study and a definitive time period for the study" (S. Rep. 101-473, 101st Cong., 2d Sess., Sept. 26, 1990, "Providing for the Protection of Native American Graves and the Repatriation of Native American Remains and Cultural Patrimony," pp. 4–5). Some Native Americans object to museum retention of human remains with only a general intent to research at some future time period, and some Native Americans question the scientific value of unidentified human remains altogether (Bowman 1989). In a 1993 article, for example, Vine Deloria rejected the standard arguments regarding the scientific value of research on Native American remains and said that if this is true, then archaeologists should also be unearthing old non-Indian bodies in towns across

the nation "to uncover information regarding malnutrition, premature deaths, and other human afflictions" (Riding-In 1992:26–27) (citing Vine Deloria, Jr., "A Simple Question of Humanity: The Moral Dimensions of the Reburial Issue," *Native American Rights Fund Legal Review,* Fall 1989, p. 5). Finally, it should be noted that under some tribal religious views, scientific testing of human remains is considered inappropriate behavior (Marsh 1992:92).

8. A recent case illustrates the potential problems for Indian tribes seeking to protect sacred ancestral sites under the NHPA. In *Pueblo of Sandia v. United States,* the Pueblo of Sandia and various environmental groups brought an action against the United States and a National Forest Service supervisor, alleging that the Forest Service failed to comply with the National Historic Preservation Act in its evaluation of Las Huertas Canyon in the Cibola National Forest. The Forest Service had concluded that the canyon did not constitute a traditional cultural property and it promulgated a new management strategy for the area. The Forest Service relied on a report by one expert, although there were conflicting opinions by experts testifying on behalf of the Pueblo that indicated that the canyon was a traditional cultural property. The District Court upheld the conclusion of the Forest Service, although it was later overruled by the Tenth Circuit, which held that the Forest Service's efforts "were neither reasonable nor in good faith." See *Pueblo of Sandia v. United States,* 50 F.3d 856 (10th Cir. 1995). On remand, the experts will most likely develop their reports and a final determination will be made as to the legal status of Las Huertas Canyon.

ROGER ANYON ■
T.J. FERGUSON
LORETTA JACKSON
LILLIE LANE
PHILIP VICENTI

Six

Native American Oral Tradition and Archaeology
Issues of Structure, Relevance, and Respect

After decades of archaeological research during which Native American oral traditions were virtually ignored as a source of information about the past, archaeologists are once again turning to oral traditions as a means of enhancing scientific interpretations of the past. Much of this change is a result of recent legislation, at the federal and state levels, mandating repatriation and the inclusion of Native American traditional cultural properties as an integral part of historic preservation activities. This change has immense potential for positive collaborations between archaeologists and Native Americans, as well as for developing more comprehensive and inclusive interpretations of the past. At the same time, it is fraught with problems of misuse and misunderstanding.

In this paper we briefly address some of the issues that underlie the process of collaboration between archaeologists and Native Americans. Assumptions, methods, relevancy, and expectations differ for both groups. Collaboration requires mutual understanding and respect, and it is with this in mind that we outline some similarities and differences that should be considered by archaeologists when using oral traditions in research. First, we discuss the nature of knowledge in oral tradition and archaeology, followed by the structures of Native American oral tradition and the archaeological record that are in some ways similar and in others different. We then address the issue of relevance that archaeology may or may not have to Native American oral tradition and the relevance of oral tradition to archaeology. Time and space, which provide a fundamental framework in archaeology, often have different meanings in oral traditions, and this can be difficult to reconcile in a scientific framework. We discuss research methodologies and the uses of oral tradition in archaeological research. We conclude with a statement concerning the need for respect and sensitivity in the research of oral traditions.

Nature of Knowledge in Oral Tradition and Archaeology

As archaeologists begin to incorporate Native American oral traditions into archaeological research once again, it is important to recognize that oral traditions and archaeology represent two separate but overlapping ways of knowing the past. There is no doubt that a real history is embedded in Native American oral traditions, and that this is the same history archaeologists study. Oral traditions contain cultural information about the past, carefully preserved and handed down from generation to generation within a tribe. The archaeological record contains material remains of past human behavior that provide physical evidence for many of the same events and processes referred to in oral traditions. Oral traditions and archaeology both have inherent but different limitations, which is why combining them in research can create knowledge that goes beyond what is possible using either source by itself. In this respect, oral traditions have a potential to assist archaeologists in the interpretation of the archaeological record, and archaeology can be useful in the corroboration of oral tradition, such as in court cases regarding land claims or water rights. However, the utility of archaeology to enhance Native American oral tradition in traditional cultural contexts is limited and often irrelevant.

Oral traditions are narrative statements about the world as known by the group that maintains and transmits that knowledge from person to person. For scientists, including archaeologists, theory does the same thing; it is a statement about how the world works. In many ways, oral tradition is akin to scientific theory. Both oral traditions and theory are subject to change when circumstances warrant. Oral tradition incorporates new experiences by layering new information into existing oral narratives. In this way, the new collective experience becomes incorporated into knowledge about how the world works. In science, a theory is modified as a result of the learned experience from research.

One of the fundamental differences between oral tradition and science is how observations and measurements are made and interpreted. There is really no way to adequately translate and interpret into English, for example, how Zuni observations lead to conclusions about the world. English simply lacks the critical concepts needed to characterize Zuni thought processes in this regard. Suffice it to say that Zuni observations and measurements are based on the workings of a group of people operating within a holistic environmental and societal framework. Western science, on the other hand, breaks things down into discrete observational units and measurable variables that can then be recombined for analysis even in cross-cultural contexts.

Despite differences in the way archaeologists and Native Americans observe and interpret the world, they both value the archaeological record as preserved in sites. This does not, however, automatically translate into Native Americans valuing the interpretations of the archaeological record by scientists.

Structures of the Archaeological Record and Oral Tradition

Oral traditions and archaeology are both palimpsests of history, analogous to a piece of parchment written on one or more times after the initial writing was erased, but where traces of the earlier uses remain to the present day. Oral traditions incorporate the cultural knowledge of many ancestors at multiple levels of signification. Similarly, archaeological sites incorporate a stratigraphic record of past human behavior embedded in artifacts and archaeological deposits. In many ways, the structures of the archaeological record and oral tradition are remarkably similar; both exist in the present and contain information about the past.

The archaeological record has these characteristics. While traces of earlier land use and the features on the landscape are difficult to read, they offer insight into the past and societal changes that have occurred over the centuries (Crawford 1953). Except under exceptional circumstances, the archaeological record is a cumulative and compressed record of both past events and the natural and cultural forces that shaped the world. In most instances, this record is a naturally and culturally modified version of the combined events that produced the present-day landscape.

Oral tradition is also a palimpsest relating knowledge transmitted in the present to earlier times, expressing the collective remembrance of generations. These are memories of past natural and cultural events and the deeds of people. Memories relevant to present-day life are compressed into oral tradition. As the stock of memories increases, some may be forgotten, discarded, or modified as new memories are added and circumstances warrant. The end result of this process is a palimpsest—a record in which traces of earlier events show through into the present.

Whereas the archaeological record reflects the material remains of past inhabitants, oral tradition reflects the way in which a specific culture defines itself through its past and the way it relates to the world in its present form. The archaeological record, as interpreted by archaeologists, depends on fixed and known space and time referents. Oral tradition, on the other hand, conjoins many events where a fixed time and space are often neither implied nor necessary. As a record relevant to the present, oral tradition need not be embedded in specific and linear time frames, nor need places and events be firmly fixed at the precise location they occurred.

Despite the structural similarities between the archaeological record and Native American oral tradition, they are two separate ways of knowing the past. Because oral traditions and archaeology derive from two different sources of knowledge about the past, different standards apply to how information is collected, evaluated, and used. The two sources of knowledge do converge in a broad sense on certain issues and themes, however, such as migrations, warfare, residential mobility, land use, and ethnic coresidence. Both oral traditions and archaeology have inherent limitations, which is why combining them in research can create knowledge that goes beyond what is possible using either source by itself.

Issue of Relevance

It strikes us that there are numerous examples of archaeologists using oral tradition to enhance archaeological interpretations of the past, but few examples of the reverse. While oral tradition can be very illuminating for archaeologists, most arch-aeology has little meaning to Indians as a way to enhance oral tradition itself within a traditional cultural context. Archaeology's relevance to Native Americans has very practical aspects to it. It is useful as an adjunct to oral tradition and can be used to support tribal rights litigation, such as land or water claims, where scientific information can corroborate a tribal claim in the western context of a courtroom (Ferguson 1995a, 1995b; Hart 1995). In addition, tribes use archaeology as a means to help establish cultural affiliation under the provisions of the Native American Graves Protection and Repatriation Act and other repatriation legislation when they are making claims for the return of cultural items from museums (Bray and Killion 1994; Zedeno and Stoffle 1995), and protecting religious freedom (Anyon 1996). In some cases, archaeology can also be used by tribes to correct history. Perhaps one of the best examples of archaeology supporting the Native American view of a historical event is the archaeology of the Little Big Horn battlefield (Fox 1993). In this case, archaeology not only supports the tribal oral tradition, it clearly debunks the western historical tradition about this battle. In most cases, however, the ability to link a specific event in this way is not possible because of the nature of the archaeological record and oral tradition.

Recently, there has been a renewal of interest by scholars in the historicity of Native American oral traditions (e.g., Wiget 1982; Teague 1993; Bahr et al. 1994). Indicative of this work is Lynne Teague's analysis of O'odham and Hopi oral traditions, oriented toward increasing our understanding of the cultural events and processes of the period before documentary history in southern Arizona. Teague (1993:436) concludes that "oral histories can be shown to conform to . . . archaeological evidence to an extent not easily attributed to after-the-fact explanation for the presence of numerous ruins in the region. These histories reflect direct knowledge of events in prehistoric Arizona." Her article represents the renewed respect archaeologists are beginning to afford Indian accounts of traditional history.

This juxtapositioning of archaeology and oral tradition, as well as the great difference in the interpretations of archaeology and oral tradition, reminds us that, as Tesse Naranjo (1995) has recently pointed out, Native American oral traditions are often axiomatic rather than hypothetical. Whereas scientists search for exclusive and universal truths, Native Americans use their oral traditions to attain a multi-versal understanding of the past that simultaneously operates on many different levels of meaning. In this regard, we return to the observation that oral traditions and archaeology are both palimpsests of history in that oral tradition incorporates the cultural knowledge of many ancestors at multiple levels of signification and the archaeological record incorporates a stratigraphic record of past human behavior embedded in artifacts and deposits. Both oral traditions and archaeology thus constitute sources of knowledge that have intricate structures that must be systematically and carefully analyzed in terms of their own internal logic in order to use them in scholarly research.

The difference between Indian and archaeological views of an archaeological site is very apparent in the case of a site in west-central New Mexico. This site illustrates the links between archaeology and oral tradition. It is also illustrative of the relevance of oral tradition to archaeology but the lack of relevance of archaeology to the oral tradition itself.

For Zunis, this site is known as Kia'ma:kya. It was here that the Zunis fought a people called the Kia'na:kwe. The battle is said to have lasted for four days, with the fight being joined each day until the Zuni were victorious. It is also where Cha'kwena had corralled all the world's game animals, and from where, each day, she would let the animals out to graze, only to corral them each night within the enclosure at Kia'ma:kya. After the last great battle between the Zunis and the Kia'na:kwe, the gates of the enclosure were opened and since that day game animals have freely roamed the earth.

The Kia'na:kwe and Kia'ma:kya have an important place in Zuni oral traditions. The Zuni celebrate the Kia'na:kwe in a quadrennial ceremony. Although this ceremony has not been performed in recent years, some members of the group responsible for it continue to have fond memories of the dance and have discussed revitalizing it. Approximately five years ago a group of religious leaders, at least one of whom has responsibilities for the Kia'na:kwe, visited the site as part of a larger tour of the area. When they reached Kia'ma:kya, they immediately identified it as the site of the Kia'na:kwe and began to discuss these stories in detail.

To archaeologists, this site is known as Fort Atarque. It is described as a basalt masonry pueblo, measuring approximately 160 by 80 m, with rows of rooms surrounding a large central plaza and a number of depressions reminiscent of kivas. The outer wall is continuous except for a gap in the west side. Ceramics date the occupation to sometime in the A.D. 1200s and perhaps the early 1300s (Fowler, Stein, and Anyon 1987:145–146). It has not been excavated.

Some points of the Zuni oral tradition about this site are of interest to arch-aeologists. Kia'ma:kya appears to have been one of the most recently occupied pueblos in the area, an area in which at least one other nearby contemporary site has evidence of violence and where burned rooms with fully intact assemblages on the floor were excavated (McGimsey 1980:38–42). Such archaeological deposits have been interpreted as evidence of warfare. According to LeBlanc (1996), Zuni became the preeminent Puebloan group in the area by the A.D. mid-1300s. Here, arch-aeology and oral tradition relate the history of the area to similar events such as warfare and residential abandonment, but describe these events in quite different ways. Here, oral tradition can be used by archaeologists as corroborating evidence for the archaeological record and thus has relevance for archaeologists. The Zuni, however, have made no use of the archaeology to corroborate their oral traditions. It simply is not necessary because archaeology has no relevance in this aspect of Zuni oral tradition. While few archaeologists would argue the interpretation that this site is ancestral Zuni, there is no known way for archaeologists to derive the oral tradition of the Kia'na:kwe and Cha'kwena from the archaeological record. Because of their different approaches to understanding the past, the meaning of this site is radically different to the Zuni and to archaeologists.

Issues of Time and Place

For archaeologists, time is a fundamental measure of the antiquity of archaeological remains set along an inflexible linear projection. As such, it can be used to measure rates of organizational and technological change in times past, topics of great interest and relevance to archaeologists. In oral tradition, however, such a strict measure of time has little relevance. For some Native Americans, the past is a way to know the present, and, as such, something that happened centuries ago can have as much or more relevance to present-day issues as an event that happened last year. The length of time separating these events is not as important as the relevance of these events to present-day identity and life. As a record of relevance to the present, oral tradition need not have specific time referents.

Similarly, places and events in oral tradition need not always be firmly fixed at the precise location they occurred. As knowledge becomes incorporated into oral tradition, it is sometimes associated with a place or places that are within the current land use area of a tribe, whether or not the placement is "accurate" in a western historical or scientific sense. Although precise location and temporal placement are sometimes critical in oral traditions, at other times spatio-temporal frames of reference are less important than the didactic relevance of an account to modern people. In contrast, in archaeology temporal ordering and accurate provenience are always critical to developing an understanding of past behavior.

Methodologies for Using Oral Traditions in Scholarly Research

Studies by Pendergast and Meighan (1959), Eggan (1967), Wiget (1982), and Echo-Hawk (1994) have unequivocally demonstrated that real history is embedded in Native American oral traditions. As Eggan (1967) pointed out, anthropologists now have more data and better historical controls than earlier generations. Consequently, it should now be possible to analyze social and cultural data in a more sophisticated manner to develop the means to segregate history from other aspects of oral traditions. Vansina (1985) presents a rigorous methodology for incorporating oral traditions in historical research. Such methodologies need to be more fully incorporated into archaeological method and theory to establish the scholarly basis for using oral traditions in historical research.

Good scientific research proceeds using a methodology based on the falsification of hypotheses. The whole is broken down into analytically meaningful parts, which are then quantitatively reconstituted in ways that provide meaning to the archaeological record. In essence, archaeologists disprove what they can and then try to explain the residual hypotheses. This scientific methodology may not be appropriate for the research of oral traditions, where more humanistic, holistic, and qualitative approaches are sometimes warranted. Applying a humanistic rather than a scientific methodology in the use of oral traditions should be done in a manner that meets high scholarly standards while maintaining the integrity and context of the subject matter.

Uses of Oral Tradition and Archaeological Research

Archaeologists are interested in learning about the past. Native Americans are interested in maintaining the cultural traditions they inherited from their ancestors who lived in the past. For Native American tribes with strong oral traditions, the primary sense of history comes from narratives, stories, and accounts as told by tribal elders. In this context, archaeology constitutes a potential secondary source of supplemental information about tribal heritage, albeit one that may be limited in its relevance.

Archaeology can also be used by tribes to achieve their own political and legal goals in relation to the larger United States society. Archaeological data can be used to help document land claims and water rights and to manage tribal cultural resources on state and federal lands. A small but increasing number of Native Americans are coming to believe that archaeology can be used constructively to validate tribal history.

In recent years, archaeologists have been called on to expand their professional activities with respect to historic preservation. They have been asked to collect information about traditional cultural properties and sacred places as well as historic archaeological sites of interest to particular tribes. Native American oral traditions contain essential information about cultural values and beliefs pertaining to traditional cultural places, natural features, specific sites, and landscapes that are important cultural resources for Native Americans (e.g., Kelley and Francis 1994; Roberts, Begay, and Kelley 1995). In order to meet the legal mandates for historic preservation, contemporary archaeologists must either work with oral traditions or coordinate their work with other researchers who are working with this source of information. This creates an ethical and methodological imperative for archaeologists to work closely with Native Americans so that the information needed to manage tribal cultural resources properly can be collected and reported in an appropriate manner.

Need for Respect and Sensitive Issues in the Research of Oral Traditions

Indiscriminate references to oral traditions as "myths and legends" are demeaning to Native Americans. Such references perpetuate a false dichotomy that implies that oral traditions are less valid than scientifically based knowledge. Oral traditions and scientific knowledge both have validity in their own cultural context. Scientific knowledge does not constitute a privileged view of the past that in and of itself makes it better than oral traditions. It is simply another way of knowing the past.

Archaeologists need to have respect for sources of knowledge about the past that are unique to Native Americans. Even in situations where oral traditions are not used in archaeological research, archaeologists should be more sensitive to both the inherent limitations of scientific knowledge and the ways that oral traditions can transcend scientific knowledge with respect to cultural heritage.

Sometimes archaeologists publish findings that contradict Native American oral traditions (Deloria 1995). This need not be done in a belligerent manner that directly challenges oral traditions. Rather, archaeologists should strive to place their conclusions in a cultural and intellectual context that will help Native Americans better understand the nature of scientific knowledge and other archaeologists better understand the nature of oral traditions. By respecting the values of Native American oral traditions, archaeologists will lay a foundation for Native Americans to respect the values of scientific knowledge and for scientists to respect the values of oral traditions in ways that do not demean either approach to understanding the past.

Oral traditions are intimately connected with Native American religious beliefs and knowledge, much of which are esoteric in nature. For this reason, it is essential for archaeologists to collaborate with tribal cultural advisers regarding the use of oral traditions in archaeological research. Tribal cultural advisers are needed to determine what aspects of oral traditions are appropriate for use in scholarly research, to help interpret the results of research, and to guide decisions about what information from oral traditions is appropriate for publication. Reducing oral traditions to a written form has a cultural impact that needs to be considered in research. As Whitely (1988:xvi) has observed, written texts turn oral traditions into fixed literary images widely disseminated in the larger American society in a manner that Native Americans cannot control. This is a critical concern when sacred knowledge is misappropriated for scholarly research, and a dynamic oral tradition is reduced to a static point of reference.

The preferences of each tribe regarding the use of oral traditions in archaeological research should be respected. Some tribes encourage the use of oral traditions in archaeological research. The Hopi Tribe is one of these, especially when this research is done by researchers working in collaboration with Hopi cultural advisors (Dongoske, Ferguson, and Jenkins 1993). Hopi cultural advisers are the best judge of what aspects of oral traditions constitute historical information and what aspects constitute esoteric religious knowledge that should remain confidential.

The Navajo people have an abundance of oral traditions that coincide with and complement contemporary archaeological research. The store of Navajo traditional knowledge can enhance archaeology and the Navajo Nation by furthering our understanding of the past. Many Navajo people are fascinated by the oral traditions that ground historical stories in the context of places that can still be seen in contemporary landscapes. An important part of the physical counterpart of stories are the ruins studied by archaeologists. The Navajo Nation therefore recommends that archaeologists augment their scientific conclusions with Navajo oral traditions. To facilitate this approach, the Navajo Nation Historic Preservation Department is developing ways for the Navajo people to interface with the science of archaeology.

The Hualapai Tribe places great value on the oral traditions of its elders. These oral traditions constitute an important part of the cultural heritage of the Hualapai people. When Hualapai culture is the subject of research, it is the Hualapai people who are the experts. Consequently, the Hualapai Tribe prefers that research using oral traditions be conducted by tribal members so that sensitive information can be controlled and the tribe can be sure it is used for appropriate purposes.

Others tribes, such as the Zuni, are reticent about the use of oral traditions in scholarly research. At present, the Zuni Tribe does not encourage the use of oral traditions in scholarly research, except in a very limited fashion by researchers employed by the tribe and for purposes Zuni cultural advisers feel are acceptable to tribal cultural sensitivities. This makes it imperative for scholars researching oral traditions to consult with the tribe.

Conclusion

We have briefly examined the nature of knowledge and the structures of Native American oral traditions and the archaeological record, the relevance of archaeology to Native Americans, the relevance of Native American oral traditions to archaeology, and the need for mutual respect and sensitivity. Remarkably, the structures of oral tradition and the archaeological record are in some ways quite similar. Both are palimpsests: archaeology, of material remains, and oral tradition, of the collective memory of generations. Although their structures are similar, their uses and the contexts of their use are quite different. It is here that the issue of relevance becomes acute, since it is the contextual relevance of oral traditions and archaeology that is most likely to expose the differences between Native Americans and archaeologists. American archaeology, inherently relevant to archaeologists, is often assumed by them as being relevant to Native Americans. This may or may not be the case, and it certainly cannot be assumed. Archaeology may have use as a means to bolster a tribal claims case or help establish cultural affiliation, but it rarely if ever has any relevancy in oral tradition used in its traditional cultural context. On the other hand, the relevance of oral tradition, inherent to many Native Americans, often has relevancy to an archaeologist only as corroborative information. This is a serious issue for archaeologists to consider.

Some Native Americans think that in the past archaeologists have mined archaeological sites to collect the artifacts that form the basis of archaeological research. There is an increasing concern that archaeologists now want to mine oral traditions to interpret the archaeological record. There is also growing anxiety that unless tribal members fully collaborate in the research process, this approach will result in continued cultural exploitation.

To allay these fears, and to create a positive working relationship between archaeologists and Native Americans in the use of oral traditions, we recommend that the following suggestions be implemented by archaeologists. First determine, by asking tribal officials, whether or not a tribe wants its oral traditions used in archaeological research. If a tribe wants its oral traditions used in archaeological research, then archaeologists need to establish the parameters of that use with Native American cultural advisers and tribal officials at the outset of the research. Tribal cultural advisers are subject specialists who should be compensated for their time and expertise, as are other professional researchers. If a tribe does not want oral tradition used in archaeological research, then archaeologists should acknowledge this in the scientific report. Finally, archaeologists should encourage tribal review of archaeological research, especially if it uses oral traditions.

This paper is a compilation of two previous papers; the authors are listed alphabetically. The first is "Native American Oral Traditions and Archaeology," by Roger Anyon, T. J. Ferguson, Loretta Jackson, and Lillie Lane, SAA Bulletin 14(2):14–16. The second is a paper by Roger Anyon and Philip Vicenti entitled "Oral Tradition and Archaeology: History, Science, and Knowledge," presented at the annual meeting of the American Anthropological Association in San Francisco, 1992.

■ ROGER ECHO-HAWK

Seven

Forging a New Ancient History for Native America

Some observers fear that "repatriation" will scorch our ability to investigate the ancient past, but I am intrigued with the possibility of harnessing the flames ignited by this issue in order to shed significant new light on human history. Whatever use we choose to make of this particular fire, it is clear that the landscape of relations between Native America and the American archaeological community has undergone dramatic changes since the 1980s—changes favoring the development of what might be termed a "partnership ecology." The character of this growing national environment of interaction between Indians and archaeologists has been shaped by the passage of the Native American Graves Protection and Repatriation Act of 1990 (NAGPRA). This federal law creates a role for native communities in asserting some administrative authority over archaeology, and, in terms of the practice of archaeology in the United States, this may well emerge as the primary result of NAGPRA's intent to foster cooperative relations. But important questions have yet to be answered. Are mutually rewarding partnerships possible, since many Native American leaders are fundamentally unsympathetic toward the discipline and some archaeologists are unsympathetic toward Indian political agendas? Is it accurate to assume that Native Americans can only serve as administrators over archaeology, and that they have no other legitimate contribution to make as partners in the quest to understand the ancient past? Until these questions are addressed, few archaeologists will be enthusiastic about the idea of becoming "partners" with Indian people in the study of ancient America. Significant answers to these questions, however, may emerge from the study of oral documents.

Interest in the contribution of oral traditions to ancient historical settings has long been an aspect of scholarship on Native America. The vast majority of academic researchers, however, reject oral traditions as a source of historical information about events dating back more than two or three centuries, and the complexity of verbal literature has served to discourage further scholarly interest. In addition, the American academic community has a well-established history of viewing the intellectual and cultural heritage of nonwhite societies as inferior. Therefore, native specialists in the preservation of oral traditions are not treated as peers, colleagues, and intellectual equals. Even when racist paradigms have been successfully challenged and defused, one lingering legacy has been that legitimate insights into the human past are viewed as the sole prerogative of Euroamerican scholarship—simply because no convincing alternative exists. Finally, scholars are hesitant to defer to Indian experts on oral traditions since most such experts are religious leaders who emphasize the spiritual aspects of oral traditions and who typically see academic analysis as inappropriate. A religious approach accepts oral texts as the source of holistic truths rather than as documents that require evaluation for historicity, and this clashes with the Euroamerican academic heritage of disqualifying religious belief as a basis for verifying constructions of human history.

The entrance of NAGPRA onto this stage has created a special problem, since it lists oral information as a permissible source of evidence in evaluating the cultural affiliations between ancient and modern Indian societies. Relying on oral information, Indians can now assert claims for the return of human remains and funerary objects dating back centuries or millennia, and academic institutions must evaluate evidence with which they have little experience. Most typically, the vast literature authored by "prehistorians" offers little convenient guidance for administrators who must decide whether oral traditions can serve as a reliable source of evidence about the past. It is therefore important to give some attention to instances in which oral traditions have been offered as evidence in repatriation negotiations. In this chapter, I discuss the reception given to Pawnee oral traditions in such settings and I suggest that the current trend in American archaeology favors changes not only in how archaeology is administered but also in creating exciting new avenues of research on ancient Indian history. First, however, it is necessary to outline my approach to what I call "ancient Indian history," and to justify my opinions and arguments regarding historicity in oral texts.

Flight of the Bookworms

Attorneys for the Pawnee Tribe began to consult with me during the 1980s on historical issues related to Pawnee efforts to repatriate human remains in Kansas and Nebraska. In 1988, when I began to investigate the evidence pertaining to the identity of Pawnee ancestors, I made the decision to treat archaeology *and* oral traditions as valid sources of information. My research benefited from the existence of an extensive literature on Pawnee oral traditions created through the efforts of James R. Murie, a Skidi Pawnee scholar who wrote down stories from virtually all of the Pawnee storytellers alive around 1900. I began by sorting this literature into stories presumed to be fictional and those presumed to be nonfictional; the nonfictional stories I further separated into three subgroups: (1) stories that displayed indicators—such as references to firearms and horses—for recent historical settings; (2) stories that could be usefully compared to archaeological data relating to Pawnee ancestors or possible ancestors; and (3) stories that did not fit either of the first two categories and were presumed to articulate historical landscapes of the most distant human antiquity. Information from stories contained in the third subgroup ultimately served as the focus of my master's thesis (Echo-Hawk 1994), in which I argue for the transmission of historical information from the late Pleistocene.

Several general categories of oral data can be presumed to have traveled into the present from the distant past. The first such category involves the transmission of oral information relating to physical processes, such as the very useful insight that sexual intercourse leads to pregnancy in human females, or the knowledge that every person will eventually die. These simple ideas may represent the most ancient topics of unbroken transgenerational human conversation. We can only speculate as to how long humans have been talking about the concepts of procreation and mortality, but it would be unreasonable to presume that, at any point during the last 40,000 years or more, some people somewhere engaged in sexual relations, left descendants, and died without holding any discussions about death and sex.

A second category of enduring information is inherent in archaeological research but is rarely an area of explicit interest: the implied coexistence of technology *and orally transmitted awareness of technology*, such as the awareness that clothing is useful as a means of insulating humans from environmental conditions and as a focus of cultural identity. The concept of clothing can be conveyed nonverbally, but it stretches my sense of credibility to presume that it is rarely, or only intermittently, a topic of discussion among succeeding generations of humans. It is possible to estimate the length of time that the idea of clothing has been a topic of human conversation in any region of the world by examining the archaeological record for pertinent evidence. Indirect evidence might also be considered, such as evidence that humans dwelt in places where the use of clothing might be reasonably inferred. Where the archaeological record suggests long-term continuity in technology—even where the superficial form of such technology undergoes change—we ought to presume the coexistence of human discourse about that technology. Too often, we are encouraged to picture humans producing technology for thousands of years without ever once commenting to one another about this activity.

These represent instances in which a given topic of conversation can be presumed to survive over great spans of time. In both areas, however, the endurance of topical data offers little potential for concurrent preservation of historical information about ancient times, but the perseverance of *any* information over millennia through oral means implies that it is at least possible for historical data to survive long transmission periods. This implication is further strengthened by the fact that folklorists accept the proposition that it is possible to preserve fictional narratives for thousands of years, and it is not difficult to find statements conveying such opinions (Thompson 1966:xxi–xxiii; Wiget 1985:6; Lankford 1987:243). If it is possible not only to imagine a continuing human discussion on topics of interest, but also to acknowledge the likelihood that specific verbal texts have been passed along for thousands of years, then it is reasonable to wonder whether any useful historical data have persisted from the distant past.

A real debate and serious discussion needs to be opened on the analysis of information that has conceivably been handed down from our distant Pleistocene ancestors. I have identified a spectrum of oral traditions with potential for shedding light on Pleistocene worldscapes (Echo-Hawk 1994). These include memories of Arctic Circle patterns of solar behavior, the transition (from the perspective of settlers moving southward) to lower latitude diurnal/nocturnal cycles, descriptions of permafrost thawing/freezing patterns, Pleistocene weather phenomena involving powerful atmospheric disturbances, discussions of European and New World glacial ice sheets, Pleistocene sea level changes, human relationships with New World megafauna, memories of the initiation of complex intergenerational social settings, references to glacial lakes, and the onset of Holocene seasonality. The possibility that these oral traditions have a relationship to the Pleistocene requires serious investigation and informed discussion.

Such a discussion would also motivate scholars of more recent time periods to investigate oral traditions for information relevant to their studies, particularly since two categories of orally maintained information are gaining acceptance for transmissibility over time periods involving centuries—though, generally speaking, not millennia. These categories involve the movement of cultural concepts over many centuries (Hall 1989; Bacon 1993) and the endurance of historical information over the past 1,000 years (Pendergast and Meighan 1959; Moodie, Catchpole, and Abel 1992; Teague 1993). My research cited above would extend the durability of actual historical data in verbal records back to the Pleistocene. At least one scholar has advocated a similar position for cultural concepts (Hall 1983).

It is unfortunate that scholarship in recent decades has led to conceptualizations of past peoples as if they were actors in silent movies. This implication, reinforced by heavy reliance on the term "prehistory," has become ingrained in bibliocentric academia. I advocate the treatment of verbal records as documents that ought to be accorded the same regard given written records, and from this perspective it may be appropriate to view prehistorians as simply incipient historians. With proper attention to oral documents, they may someday be historians; but for the present, they are merely prehistorians: voracious bookworms refusing to metamorphose and take flight into a world that is filled with the echoes of human voices. It should be surprising (but it is not, somehow) that any serious scholar would be skeptical of a "talkies" version of the human past, in which the actors actually have speaking roles. I hold the opinion that every living human on Planet Earth contributes to an unbroken chain of conversations with roots extending back in time to the Pleistocene, and we do not need to rely wholly on speculation or imaginative reconstruction in order to hear the content of at least some portions of those conversations.

An important obstacle to the development of scholarly inquiry into verbal records is the well-established literature demonstrating the malleability of oral documents (see Vansina 1985). For good reasons, serious researchers ought to hesitate to blithely embrace the sort of claims that I have made, particularly since writings that advocate uncritical acceptance of oral traditions as literal characterizations of past events continue to appear in print and are very popular with the general public (see, for example, Deloria 1995; Hancock 1995). These works generally require readers to dispense with the findings of geologists, physicists, archaeologists, and Euroamerican Enlightenment science and substitute a faith-based reliance on oral information—a substitute typically bolstered by selective use of science. A consumerist approach to science permits the modeling of wildly diverse, irreconcilable versions of ancient human history and is therefore an approach that cannot be subject to any form of verification other than faith.

Advocates of literalism in oral traditions often liberally exploit instances in which scholars have been overly autocratic. This strategy takes clever advantage of the insight that inconvenient science need not be discredited through careful study and analysis when it can more easily be dismissed as scientific dogma imposed by totalitarian scholars. It is not difficult to find oppressive behavior in the academic world, but few researchers whose work has unfairly been the target of acts of oppression would agree with the notion that it is reasonable to respond by rejecting the basic precepts of science and scholarship.

One practical effect of the strategy of promoting unverifiable literalism in verbal documents is to create highly polarized landscapes that serve as fertile ground for the formation of cultlike groups of "Velikovskians" and "Von Dänikenites" whose members unhesitatingly accept even the most astounding pronouncements. This "fringe" literature has great popular appeal because it presents fascinating and highly entertaining depictions of the human past that are very accessible to a wide readership. Scholars who take pains to denounce these popular cults may not recognize that such groups thrive best under circumstances of confrontational polarization, particularly because literalism based on selective science is not, by its nature, subject to critical challenge in any manner familiar to science-based scholars. For this reason, any confrontational "debate" essentially empowers and authorizes an unresolvable conflict. My treatment of oral traditions relies on a paradigm that does not lend itself easily to such warfare.

Since the known inherent malleability of verbal literature provides a rather sandy foundation for constructions of human history, my approach to oral traditions requires acceptance of science-based models of past world settings. We should acknowledge that the spoken word is indeed a pliable substance, but we also need to develop analytical procedures to identify the presence of durable information in verbal messages. I have proposed such procedures (Echo-Hawk 1994), and it is my hope that this work will become generally available in some form. For the moment, it is important that archaeologists and Indians understand how recent efforts to use oral traditions may point to future developments in the study of what I call "ancient Indian history"—that is, the creation of historical models based on the integration of archaeology and oral traditions. As detailed below, repatriation negotiations have opened a new forum for oral traditions, but one which currently invites collisions between conflicting perspectives rather than productive discourse. In my view, however, this is a short-term situation rather than a permanent condition.

Battlefields of Ancient Indian History

While conducting repatriation research for the Pawnee Tribe on the collections of the Nebraska State Historical Society (NSHS), I was asked in the summer of 1990 to provide the tribal attorneys with an affidavit communicating the results of my research on ancient Pawnee history. I asserted that Caddoan oral traditions were compatible with archaeological evidence supporting the presence of Pawnee ancestors in the Central Plains during the past 1,000 years or more. In December 1990, the Pawnee Tribe released my report (Echo-Hawk 1990) as evidence attached to a petition filed in support of the Pawnee claim to human remains associated with the Central Plains tradition, dating from A.D. 950 to 1400. This paper, entitled "Ancient Pawnee History," identified more than 40 Caddoan oral traditions that, in my view, have some connection to historical settings predating the sixteenth century.

The response of the NSHS archaeologists followed in January 1991 (Ludwickson et al. 1991).

This response included letters solicited during the fall of 1990 from various scholars, several of whom commented on my affidavit. One archaeologist expressed the view that connecting Pawnee oral traditions "to the specifics of the available archeological record is impossible" (Peter Bleed to Terry Steinacher, September 13, 1990, correspondence appended to Ludwickson et al. 1991). The National Park Service's Midwest Archeological Center weighed in with a letter expressing amusement at my credentials as an "expert witness" and wondering whether I had "lifted" the list of sources attached to my affidavit (F. A. Calabrese to Terry Steinacher, September 7, 1990). This letter from a federal agency advised the NSHS that my professors at the University of Colorado should be informed of my misdeeds, presumably to encourage that institution to silence me through academic censure. I am uncertain as to why such stark hostility emerged from the NPS Midwest Archeological Center, but it is clear that this form of academic critique is not designed to promote productive and informed discussion. For Indians who see archaeologists in terms of a homogenous, oppressive stereotype, it is relevant to note at this point that letters provided to the NSHS by several other archaeologists contained brief comments responding more favorably to my affidavit, but all of these responses— both pro and con—were formulated before the release of "Ancient Pawnee History."

The NSHS archaeologists prepared a reply to "Ancient Pawnee History" and contacted Melburn Thurman, an ethnohistorian, for an additional assessment of my work. Both appraisals rejected my approach. Thurman characterized my paper as an "ideosyncratic" [sic] expression of "belief" and claimed that "few Plain [sic] anthropology specialists, whether archaeologists or ethnohistorians, would care to argue that Indian traditions provide any kind of useful historical information beyond the living memory" (evaluation by Thurman dated December 31, 1990). The NSHS archaeologists adopted a more sophisticated strategy. They argued that reconciliation of the archaeological record with written documents and Pawnee oral traditions favors a scenario in which the Spanish drove the Pawnees out of the Southwest into the Central Plains sometime around A.D. 1600. Whether or not these scholars actually supported this theory, their fundamental point was to question oral traditions as a source of useful information, and their views have since received wide and influential circulation among other specialists in Plains archaeology.

None of my suggestions on connecting specific oral documents to the archaeological record were directly refuted by any of these appraisals; rather, their strategies centered on efforts to cast doubt on my basic assumption that oral records can be reliably integrated with archaeological evidence. This approach was remarkably effective in undermining serious consideration of my work. Up to this point, I had occasionally indulged a naive expectation that the NSHS archaeologists would be intrigued at the implications of my research, and I looked forward to the possibility of working with and learning from these experts on Central Plains arch-aeology. I recall thinking that by working together, we could more effectively address questions surrounding Pawnee ancestry on the basis of cooperative scholar-ship; but as it turned out, the mediation of lawyers, judges, legislators, the attorney general of Nebraska, the governor of Nebraska, and the president of the United States proved far more essential to Pawnee repatriation efforts than any of my ideas on oral traditions.

As of 1996, not a single set of human remains had been repatriated and reburied as a result of my work on oral traditions. This is an important symbolic victory for those scholars and institutions who have conscientiously labored as a matter of academic politics to protect their prerogatives in the practice of traditional American archaeology. It is, moreover, a source of amazement to me that some scholars unself-consciously deplore Indian repatriation efforts as politically motivated, par-ticularly since my experiences in dealing with archaeopoliticians have starkly clarified for me some of the personal costs that my research might entail—including the unambiguous threat to destroy any aspirations I might have for an academic career. Though my efforts to investigate oral documents in the context of repatri-ation claims have borne discouraging results, I am convinced, nevertheless, that many Indians and archaeologists are open to these explorations, and I am encour-aged by the favorable interest that I have received from individuals in both communities. My experiences with the Smithsonian's National Museum of Natural History (NMNH) underscore this point.

The Pawnee Tribe discovered that the NMNH also held Central Plains tradition human remains, and in 1992 the tribal attorneys submitted various research papers supporting a Pawnee claim for these persons. A meeting in 1994 with the NMNH Repatriation Office produced a somewhat dismaying result. In the course of this meeting I mentioned some of my ideas on oral traditions and was invited to prepare a report containing this evidence. The Smithsonian representatives were surprised to hear that this information had already been provided in the form of *two* reports: my 1990 paper and a more detailed 1992 version (Echo-Hawk 1990, 1992). Unfortunately, neither paper had been circulated to two scholars—Donna Roper and Richard Jantz—who had been hired by the Smithsonian to help evaluate the Pawnee claim.

Roper's subsequent report (1993) on archaeological evidence offered some consideration of evidence from oral traditions, but it simply responded to a conference paper presenting the views of the Nebraska State Historical Society (NSHS) archaeologists. Though she took a position that challenged their perspective, she made little effort to assess the oral traditions for relevant information. Physical anthropologist Richard Jantz took pains in his report to emphasize research results that he believed contradicted the "Pawnee position" (Jantz 1993). Nevertheless, Roper and Jantz both provided research conclusions that conformed in very interesting ways to my evidence from oral traditions, but this circumstance did little to attract the curiosity of the NMNH Repatriation Office.

Roper's treatment of oral traditions illustrates the fact that even when the findings of archaeologists support Indian repatriation efforts, such support need not reflect any sympathy for investigating the contribution of verbal literature to ancient historical settings. In Roper's case, the difficulty of assessing the contribution of Pawnee oral traditions may have been unnecessarily magnified by her ignorance of my research. For this reason, I volunteered to assist the NMNH in assessing the oral evidence, but I was given no opportunity to contribute to this process, and though the NMNH ultimately affirmed a cultural affiliation between the Pawnee Tribe and the Central Plains tradition, oral traditions were dismissed as a factor. William Billeck, the NMNH case officer who handled the Pawnee claim, later defended his approach with the assertion that he saw no need to assess oral documents since the archaeological and biological evidence proved sufficient. It is notable, however, that the NMNH cited and relied on the NSHS position on Pawnee oral traditions in declining to accept such evidence (Billeck et al. 1995:17).

The Pawnee Tribe continued negotiations with the Smithsonian for the repatriation of human remains associated with the Steed-Kisker phase—contemporaries and neighbors of the Central Plains tradition. This effort led to a stalemate of conflicting opinions in 1995, and the matter was brought before the Smithsonian's Native American Repatriation Review Committee for resolution. In a hearing held in September 1995, I was given an opportunity to discuss at some length the contribution of Pawnee oral traditions to the question of Steed-Kisker cultural affiliations. The committee subsequently issued findings that favored the position of the Pawnee Tribe, giving credence to Pawnee oral traditions as a source of historical information about the ancient past (Thornton et al. 1995). It is also highly significant that in two separate publications in 1995, one NSHS archaeologist has acknowledged that Pawnee oral traditions might be of some use to archaeologists studying the ancient Central Plains (Bozell 1995a, 1995b). These recent developments offer important and encouraging signs of change.

Animal Architects

It may be useful to suggest how it is possible to integrate oral traditions and archaeology in an effort to clarify cultural affiliations between the Pawnee people and the Central Plains tradition. As mentioned earlier, I have identified a variety of Caddoan oral traditions concerning ancient historical settings, and in my opinion some of these stories can be connected to the time of the Central Plains tradition (A.D. 950 to 1400). A particularly strong area for productive analysis is found in the topic of architecture.

At least three separate statements and stories concerning the origins of earthlodge architectural structures were collected and recorded by James R. Murie and George Dorsey from Pawnees alive at the end of the nineteenth century (Dorsey and Murie 1906:19-21; Linton 1923; Murie 1981:158-162). This group of statements and stories was told as historical observations, rather than as fictional tales or speculation, and I presume that these stories are not only derived from actual historical circumstances, but that they concern a variety of separate events. One South Band Pawnee story begins with the statement that the first people were placed near Nemaha, Nebraska, where they constructed an earthlodge facing west (Dorsey and Murie 1906:19-21). This story—told by a Kitkahahki Pawnee about the Kawarakis ancestors of the South Band Pawnees—is not a detailed narrative about earthlodges, but it conveys the impression that the first use of such structures occurred while the Kawarakis Caddoans dwelt in southeastern Nebraska at some point in time prior to extensive reliance on corn cultivation and bison hunting.

Two Skidi Pawnee narratives contain detailed information about the circumstances under which the ancestors of the Skidi first adopted earthlodge architecture. One story (Murie 1981:158-162) is set on the Elkhorn River in northeastern Nebraska and concerns the development of earthlodges with circular floor plans, implying that circular earthlodges first appeared in some region beyond the central Nebraska Loup River homeland of the Skidi Pawnees. According to the narrative, this architectural innovation is associated with animal lodge ceremonialism.

The second Skidi oral tradition (Linton 1923) differs in significant ways from the Elkhorn River story and makes no mention of the earthlodge floor plan shape. This narrative describes the origin of the Skidi "Medicine Lodge"—a formal expression of animal lodge ceremonialism. The story reports that a "man who lived alone, and did not mingle with the rest of the tribe" traveled "for many days" toward the east until he arrived at the Missouri River, where he was inducted into an animal lodge beneath the water. Speaking for these animals, a "water monster" explained that it had been sent by Tirawahut from the "Big Waters" in order to "tell these animals to instruct you in their mysteries." After a time, the man returned home, and sometime later, he was told to embark on another journey eastward "to the place where Freemont [*sic*], Nebraska, now is." At an animal lodge located on an island in the Platte River, the man received instructions on building "a new kind of house," which was to be a gift to the Skidi people; the animals then took the man to a nearby hill where they constructed the first earthlodge for him. Until this time, "the Skidi did not know how to build earth lodges." Though this structure is associated with animal lodge ceremonialism, it is also clear that earthlodges were intended to have both ceremonial and residential purposes.

Available literature on the archaeology of the Central Plains often touches on earthlodge architecture but typically makes no mention of these Pawnee oral traditions. Archaeologists have been reluctant to treat these verbal documents as a useful source of information about the historical past, presumably due to elements in the narratives that sound nonhistorical. In other words, few scholars would give serious attention to any colleague who may embrace the "fact" that the Skidi Pawnees received knowledge of earthlodges from spirit animals in eastern Nebraska —animals that actually built the first such structure. For both archaeologists and Indians, therefore, this situation must be written off as yet another frustrating example of a collision between science and religion. An additional problem presents itself to those scholars who wish to understand "the Pawnee" account of the origin of earthlodges, and then find that they must contend with three separate and conflicting stories describing how the Pawnee acquired such buildings. These two problems probably account for the fact that no scholar who has written about Pawnee earthlodges has ever assessed the potential for integrating these oral traditions with the archaeological record.

Insights from the archaeological record are essential in reconciling the three extant Pawnee perspectives on the origins of earthlodges. Two broad classes of earthlodge structures can be distinguished in the archaeological record: a form with a circular floor plan, found in sites dating after A.D. 1500, and an older form featuring a square floor plan, associated with the Central Plains tradition. The Skidi oral tradition that discusses the origin of circular earthlodges (the Elkhorn River story) most likely concerns a historical setting that follows the time period of the Central Plains tradition, while the other Skidi story (the Missouri River/Fremont story) must describe the adoption of the square structures associated with Central Plains tradition sites. Thus, it is my view that we have Skidi Pawnee oral traditions that discuss not only the historical origin of earthlodge architecture but also its later modification from square to circular. This implies that both forms are expressions of a single continuous architectural legacy and that certain features ought to be present in both square and circular earthlodges. In fact, similarities between these two differing structures served as the primary basis for Donna Roper's finding of cultural affiliation between the Central Plains tradition and the later Pawnees (Roper 1993).

The Kitkahahki story bears no resemblance to either of the Skidi stories. My explanation for this situation is that the Kawarakis ancestors of the South Band Pawnee tribes are derived from a group distinguishable from the ancestors of the Skidi Pawnees—an idea that is further aided by a number of other Pawnee oral traditions that are beyond the scope of this limited review. The reference in the Kitkahahki story to the Nemaha region suggests that the folk who dwelt in this region at the time that earthlodges first appeared were probably more directly ancestral to the South Band Pawnee than to the Skidi Pawnee. On the basis of craniometric evidence, Jantz (1993) suggested that the Central Plains tradition may be divisible into two subgroups: a western group comprising Upper Republican phase and Itskari phase populations and an eastern group including the Nebraska and Steed-Kisker phases. On the basis of my study of Pawnee and Arikara oral traditions, I am in general agreement with this division.

A recent analysis of radiocarbon dates by Roper (1995) also suggests that Central Plains tradition lifeways appeared earlier in the east and spread westward, a model that conforms to the Skidi account of a man who traveled from somewhere west of the Missouri River to eastern Nebraska to learn of earthlodge construction. It is my suggestion that the eastern Central Plains tradition groups became engaged in cultural activities that included some form of ceremonialism involving animal impersonation and the associated utilization of earthlodges as ceremonial structures, and that this religious complex was subsequently transmitted to the ancestors of the Skidi in the west. Modern forms of this ceremonialism clearly did involve animal impersonation (see Murie 1981). Thus, the following description in the Skidi story takes on a meaning that has little to do with literal animals, and everything to do with humans who are engaged in a specific form of religious life:

> In the lodge he saw the beaver, the owl, the otter, the ermine, the bear, the buffalo, the wolf, the mountain lion, the wild cat, and all sorts of birds. He stayed with them for many days, and they taught him more mysteries. At last they told him to go to a nearby hill where they had cleared a site for a medicine lodge. The deer led him from the animals' lodge and put him safe on dry land. When he came to the place for the medicine lodge, he found everything ready. All the animals had cleared away the grass. The badgers had dug the holes for the posts, the beavers had cut them down and peeled them, and the bears and mountain lions had carried them up the hill. The animals helped him to raise the framework and told him how to lay on the willows and grass and cover the whole with earth. They then told him to return to his village and to tell the chiefs to bring the people to the new place, which had been selected for them by the animals (Linton 1923).

I regard this scene—preserved in the form of a highly memorable verbal narrative—as a credible record of an important event in ancient Pawnee history. A more complete review of Pawnee and Arikara oral traditions and a fuller consideration of the archaeological record will, I believe, eventually provide a convincing argument to most specialists in Central Plains archaeology as to the utility of seeking to integrate these data from two different sources.

A variety of significant observations can be made about the oral traditions reviewed here:

1. The historical chronology of the stories cannot be understood without reference to archaeological data.
2. The presence of earthlodges in the archaeological record is a manifestation of some form of animal lodge ceremonialism, and it may be possible to identify specific Central Plains tradition earthlodge structures that were built to accommodate such ceremonialism.

3. Oral traditions point to the appearance of lifeways utilizing earthlodges in the eastern Central Plains and a subsequent diffusion westward, and this is compatible with archaeological evidence.
4. The archaeological record for the Central Plains and adjacent regions should be reviewed to identify sites that date to the general period of A.D. 1300–1600 and feature both square and circular earthlodges.
5. The modern Pawnee people have cultural roots extending very unambiguously into the period of the Central Plains tradition, and this connection is effectively clarified through the integration of the archaeological record with oral traditions.

It is unfortunate that my research, forged in the fires of bitter disputes over repatriation, has moved some very powerful Central Plains archaeopoliticians to attempt to extinguish rather than encourage the light that "ancient Pawnee history" can shed on the prehistory of the Central Plains. In terms of my personal aspirations for an academic career, mine is certainly not a glowing success story; but my research has enabled me to assure the leaders of the Pawnee Tribe that in reburying Central Plains tradition human remains, they are laying to rest the bones of persons who are ancestors of the Pawnee and Arikara people. It is also important to observe that the Pawnee Tribe has relied on the advice and hard work of archaeologists like Larry Zimmerman and Tom Witty in seeking (and accomplishing) the reburial of nearly 400 persons who lived and died during the Central Plains tradition period.

The End of Conquest Anthropology

If the spirit of NAGPRA is to ever have a reasonable chance for fulfillment, then attitudes must change on the part of both archaeologists and Indians. For archaeologists, the building of partnerships can focus on the contribution of Indian knowledge to our understanding of human history. For Indians, the opportunity to address long-standing grievances from a position of power should create new settings in which the contribution of archaeology to Indian historical self-awareness can be explored and embraced. The successful integration of oral evidence with evidence from archaeology and physical anthropology holds forth great potential for reshaping the essential character of academic constructions of ancient human history.

The circumstances under which my research first became available in 1990 offered fertile ground for hostility on the part of archaeologists intent on defending important collections of human remains from repatriation, and it is understandable that my work was not simply rejected, but effectively quashed. From this inauspicious beginning, we need to move forward into more productive interactions. Although I cannot ignore the personal costs of these experiences, I have little sympathy for Indians who may seek to extract from my story some justification for dismissing archaeology as a tool for understanding ancient Native America.

Despite the current trend favoring a new "partnership ecology," some Indians will continue to advocate the view that it is reasonable to dispense with archaeology and elevate oral traditions as the only source of legitimate information about ancient human history, but such advocacy will find no support in NAGPRA. This advocacy is not simply an expression of cultural pride, since—as I have touched on earlier—the politics of polarity are also useful in bringing together like-minded persons whose unified opinions can serve as a basis for the wielding of power. While I personally support Indian efforts to control the quality of Indian lifeways through the manipulation of social power, I am unwilling to conduct inquiry into ancient human history on the basis of a racialist paradigm that treats "Indian" knowledge (oral traditions) as inherently superior to "white" knowledge (archaeology).

NAGPRA gives no standing to religious belief as a source of evidence about the past, and many Indian religious leaders will be hesitant to submit their knowledge to analysis for historical content. In dealing with the concerns of Indian religious leaders, it is the responsibility of scholars to find a course offering maximum sensitivity to religious perspectives while conducting research that meets acceptable standards of academic scholarship. Even in those cases where tribal authorities support such research, few Indian communities have the financial resources to take advantage of the opportunity under NAGPRA to explore the use of oral evidence in elucidating the cultural affiliations of persons who lived and died long ago. As a practical matter, these conditions therefore shift the burden for conducting this research onto the academic community.

Not every archaeologist will be interested in pursuing partnerships with Indians. At least some archaeologists and physical anthropologists will continue to promote their spheres of inquiry as the only valid means of investigating the ancient past. At present, the assertion that archaeology and physical anthropology together hold an inviolable intellectual copyright to the ancient past pervades anthropological literature and is frequently pressed into service as a powerful tool for uniting scholars who are opposed to Indian repatriation efforts. An implication of my research is that such claims will become increasingly recognized as questionable, narcissistic, and as diagnostic artifacts of a time when paternalistic scholars felt that only they held the power to open windows on so-called prehistoric Native America.

As one result of my experiences, I have learned that archaeopolitics, rather than any interest in scholarship, can dominate the responses of some archaeologists to claims for historicity in oral traditions. The current interest of archaeologists in the contribution of oral traditions to the study of ancient Native America is a matter of some guesswork, but no major archaeology journal has yet made such inquiry a prominent (or even minor) topic of research. I am doubtful that change in this area will come swiftly. I have little doubt, however, that what I call "ancient Indian history"—the integration of oral traditions with the archaeological record—will become a major feature of archaeology in the twenty-first century.

Researchers who wish to investigate oral traditions about ancient times would be wise to expect a certain amount of skeptical rejection. More positive environments are gradually emerging for such scholarship, though my personal optimism on this point is, as I have mentioned, somewhat speculative. It is certainly appropriate for any academic interpretation of oral literature to be subjected to careful scrutiny and reasoned criticism, and Indians should expect such treatment for any claims made for historicity in oral traditions. Research associated with repatriation, however, enters a highly confrontational political realm, and efforts to bring oral traditions into this setting may provoke an initial response of automatic dismissal from the classroom rather than a fair evaluation according to academic standards.

For scholars, institutions, journal editors, and publishers who are committed to encouraging the growth of partnerships with Indian communities, every archaeological research project involving ancient Native America ought to be evaluated for the potential contribution of oral traditions. A recent article in the *SAA Bulletin* offers excellent advice to archaeologists interested in practical guidelines for exploring this topic (Anyon et al. 1996; also see Anyon et al., this volume). Indians must also be prepared, in the short term, to encounter research that is rudimentary, naive, or less than sensitive to major concerns. It will take time to create mutual trust and productive relationships, and more sophisticated analysis of oral literature will necessarily require a period of development since few archaeologists or other scholars have spent time working in this area. The setting of high standards and demands for faithful adherence may, for the moment, be unrealistic and simply serve to inhibit the growth of interest in oral traditions and interfere with the cultivation of meaningful partnerships.

In conclusion, I sincerely hope that Indians and archaeologists who prefer to reject opportunities to explore common ground will find themselves increasingly marginalized in a world that recognizes the desirability of a true partnership ecology. The short-term benefits of pursuing cooperative relations mostly revolve around the practical recognition that both groups must now work together on projects involving archaeological inquiry. Long-term relationships between Indians and archaeologists will only flourish when both groups can view each other as colleagues with legitimate interests and contributions. The key goal, thus, is to seek engagement in processes that can enhance *mutual* respect. Indians and archaeologists face great challenges in the commitment to find common ground, but the exploration of the ancient past can bring us all forward into an exciting future—a future in which genuine partnerships will open a whole new world of insights for us all.

My thanks to Kurt Dongoske and Roger Anyon for inviting me to participate in the forum in New Orleans and to SAA for making it possible for me to attend. This paper has also benefited from comments offered by Nancy Blomberg and Carolyn McArthur.

The Integration of Tradition and Science

Eight

Straddling the Current
A View From the Bridge Over
Clear Salt Water

My experiences as a member of the Suquamish Indian Tribe (a federally recognized group of nearly 800 Indian people living on the western shores of the Puget Sound opposite Seattle), as a member of the tribal council, as a former director of the tribal cultural center and museum, and as an archaeologist have allowed me to be on many sides of issues of contention within the world of cultural resource management. This has enabled me to observe the issues, if not as clearly as the title of this chapter would suggest, at least from several angles, perhaps affording an objective view that a bridge might offer when the person on the riverbank is seeking clarity in murky conditions.

The background presented in this chapter is not intended as another history lesson that shames the archaeologist and solicits more empathy for the native people; rather, I hope the background will give a basis for better understanding and cooperation between the two interest groups.

Distrust between Indian tribes and archaeologists has existed in the United States for many years, and the residue from the unfortunate incidents of the past remains with us today. Excavation of Indian burial places by archaeologists from academic institutions, government agencies, private consulting firms, or amateur societies is a blight on the reputation of the archaeological community. Fortunately, this negative perception of archaeology has nearly become an inaccurate portrayal of archaeologists today. This legacy of desecration precedes every archaeologist (including me and probably other native archaeologists) working in consultation with Indian people and their governments, no matter how sensitive we are to Indian concerns. The study of archaeological material, including human remains, grave goods, and artifacts, has brought a sense of injustice to add to the old feelings of intolerance toward archaeologists.

One layer of the barrier that has precluded a positive working relationship with the Indian community in the past has been the professional archaeologist's academic background. A professional education can affect how an individual is perceived in the Indian community and can also affect the individual's perspective or opinion on sensitive issues. The growing numbers of Indian college students and graduates on the reservations have softened the resentment toward college-educated professionals from outside the community, and often from their own tribe, that Indian communities have demonstrated previously. In the past, Indian students were encouraged to attend college, but many were not accepted or were treated differently on their return home. I am an example of this situation and am often the subject of teasing and sometimes distrust because of my academic background. My college education is often seen as threatening to some members of my community, as if it somehow places me above them. I try to explain to my people that I have not become less Suquamish, but that I have just learned more about the other world. A nonnative academic seeking cooperation from the tribal community can expect to be treated at least as I am by my own people—as a person who lives and succeeds in the other world who might be trusted, but with a watchful eye.

I think that Indian people have been suspicious of traditional academic education for two reasons. First, educated people, mostly from government agencies, historically have made decisions in the "best interest" of Indian tribes that have harmed them, or made promises on behalf of the federal government that were not fulfilled. Second, as a result of these experiences, Indian people have come to regard higher education as a method that dehumanizes the individual, creating a person with a rigid view of the world and its resources, including its inhabitants. This perception is not without justification; traditional anthropology and archaeology programs emphasize the negative impact that organized religion had and still has on the pursuit of evolutionary and other scientific theories. This wariness toward religious intervention has been extended to native people and their concerns about desecration of sacred sites and places. I believe Indian people see this callousness toward their spiritual beliefs by some professional archaeologists as a byproduct of academic training. This makes the qualifications for which many archaeologists have worked and sacrificed of little value to a relationship with Indian people who have traditional values. Respect and trust from the Indian community are earned through understanding Indian values and traditions and by a commitment to honor native interests through actions.

Members of the academic and cultural resource management communities seeking a working relationship with Indian communities need to communicate their motives openly with the tribal community. These motives must be described and must demonstrate some benefit to the Indian community without harming elders and other informants through breach of confidentiality, disrespectful behavior, or deceit. Honesty and commitment to honoring native values is important and can transcend distrust of college-educated nonnative individuals. Indian tribes are becoming more sophisticated, and if cultural representatives can see that a project may benefit the tribal community and not just the career or finances of the archaeologist or anthropologist, then a successful consultation is possible. In simpler terms, let your work speak for itself. If it's worthwhile to the resource, necessary for the public good, and not overly invasive, it will probably be accepted by the tribal community.

This academic rigidity is also brought into the field by archaeologists who apply the rules and values learned at the university to site excavation, testing, and survey. Sometimes these methods clash with the desires of the native community, creating conflict requiring mediation. This situation has created revulsion in some toward the tribal consultation process and has resulted in a backlash against increased Indian participation in cultural resource management. Conversely, in some instances this disagreement has created new relationships between Indians and archaeologists after views were exchanged and differences settled. Some of these cooperative settlements have resulted in better treatment of the resource and the aboriginal descendants, while meeting the professional needs of the archaeologist.

Cultural values are another aspect of the relationship between tribes and the archaeological community that need to be recognized by both groups to foster a good working relationship. In my opinion, the most divisive issue in the entire consultation process is the concept of ownership. The value that Americans place on personal property rights is obvious and is greatly treasured by most of its citizens. Americans are raised with the concept of "finders, keepers" and apply it to their discoveries, whether it be a gold claim or an arrowhead. This sense of "ownership," usually expressed as control of site excavation, dissemination of data, and enhancement of professional reputation, is often extended to archaeological sites by the archaeologists who locate them. Sometimes the sites are loosely considered their "property," at least on an intellectual basis. Sharing the management of these sites with Indian tribes is often considered "troublesome to the work of the archaeologist." In a cultural way, many Suquamish see archaeological sites as belonging to past, present, and future generations; there is no way to own the sites or the material within them. They are a testimony to our past, and the excavation and study of them for knowledge is a commentary on our future. Will the

Suquamish ever return to this way of life and begin leaving similar cultural features on the land? It does not seem likely, and this is difficult for them to accept.

The concept of property ownership is not foreign to my people; the Suquamish acquired wealth and status just as they do today. The difference is that property was amassed to distribute to others in a ceremonial manner, the ultimate demonstration of true wealth in our culture. Those who acquired wealth were expected to share it; this was the only way to acquire status and respect.

The ownership of archaeological sites has become a complex issue. Archaeologists make claims of ownership through discovery and their interpretive qualifications. The Indian tribe has rights through descendancy and cultural connection. To ensure appropriate resource management, a cooperative relationship needs to be cultivated that recognizes the scientists and their instinct to control "their" site and the Indians' need to be acknowledged as the heirs to the site and be treated accordingly. I feel that a cooperative effort at "coownership" of cultural resources can be achieved with open communication and acknowledgment of cultural differences. I think our tradition of giving as a demonstration of wealth and status may be useful in negotiating site "ownership" issues. I feel that it is possible for the scientific values of the archaeologist to coexist with native interpretive needs and desires if differences between the parties are explained and understood. The comparison of native and scientific interpretation of archaeological sites would also be more interesting and therefore better for public education purposes than pure science or independent native perspectives.

Philosophical and spiritual values are another aspect of this relationship. The native philosophy to which I have been exposed in my community is one that conveys responsibility upon my generation to serve our ancestors, who love us dearly, and to provide a good place on earth for future generations, who are depending on us to pass these values on to them. The role of caretaker is extended by tribal leaders and representatives to archaeological sites, burial grounds, and sacred places, and it is our responsibility to protect and care for these places during our time in this world. In this context, it is easy to see why Indian people are adamant about respecting archaeological resources; they are the homes of our ancestors and we would be doing them great harm, and therefore injuring ourselves and our children, by not protecting them.

Scientists are usually sympathetic to native values and beliefs, but many have had difficulty in understanding how these values can outweigh the potential for acquiring data from the material, which could be used by the native people to learn more about their cultural history. From a western philosophical perspective, this might appear to be a reasonable scenario, even considered beneficial to the tribes, and in some cases it has been acceptable. However, many tribes are not interested in learning about their past from archaeology; many are quite secure with knowledge that has been handed down to them from their elders.

History and politics play a major role in shaping the positions taken by native people in cultural resource management. The long history of deceit, lies, violence, and theft that characterized the settlement of the American West are well documented. The federal policies of assimilation that produced the allotment act, boarding schools, and termination are also a part of our history. The effect of these events is ingrained into many Indian people's minds; the Suquamish face it every day when they leave their homes and see themselves as a minority on their own reservation (as a result of the General Allotment Act of 1887, two-thirds of our reservation is owned and inhabited by non-Indians).

Today, many Americans question why they should be held responsible for the actions of their ancestors. Of course, Indian people ask why Indians should have to suffer the consequences of those actions. Archaeologists might also wonder why they are held responsible for these past injustices. They might wonder why they are being restrained from pursuing their valuable scientific research just because Indian tribes insist that they must have meaningful involvement in management decisions. In the case of the Suquamish, and I believe many other tribes, archaeological sites may be the only pristine resource remaining from the aboriginal world that has not been encroached upon by non-Indians. Therefore, Indians see archaeology as a "last stand" in their struggle to maintain their land base, identity, and sovereignty. Tribal councils are sworn to uphold the sovereignty of their people, and sometimes this requires them to act in ways that appear unreasonable to outsiders. We must learn to understand this philosophy, to find ways to work with the tribal governments that acknowledge their sovereign status, and to treat them on a government-to-government basis whenever appropriate.

In my experience as a native archaeologist I have had the opportunity to discuss issues of tribal consultation and the role of Indian tribes in cultural resource management with tribal representatives and with my professional colleagues. I have been involved in two roundtable discussions about Indian views on archaeology. In both of these forums Indian people have expressed their desire to avoid disturbance of archaeological sites in their territory because of spiritual concerns and sovereign rights, showing no interest in acquiring knowledge through site excavation and study. In each case an archaeologist has stated that Indians need to consider the global perspective, to recognize their responsibility to contribute to the development of a worldwide human settlement model. It is difficult to expect Indian people to sacrifice their beliefs, their last remaining resource, to satisfy the human desire for more knowledge. The American Indian people know their history, their creation, their ancestors, and how they arrived in their homeland; they have given enough and should not be expected to give more.

It should be acknowledged that many tribes in the Puget Sound are active in cultural resource management, and many have chosen to support site excavation as an acceptable mitigation measure. I believe that tribes should reserve the right to require avoidance of sites when appropriate and possible. However, some tribal leaders, including some at Suquamish, have supported site excavation over avoidance in some cases. One reason is that most of the sites in our territory are threatened by development, and we feel that opportunities to excavate should be seized now to save the material and the associated data. This is based on the perception that urbanization in Puget Sound will eventually destroy existing sites, and they should be excavated before they are lost forever. This information is valuable to many tribes for public education, especially in our region where Indian fishing rights are a controversial issue that has created a public backlash against tribes. Presentation of the cultural history of the Puget Sound tribes, supplemented by archaeological data, has been effective in changing public opinion about treaty rights to salmon, shellfish, and other resources. This was recently demonstrated in the *U.S. v. Washington* shellfish proceeding in which the Puget Sound tribes' right to half of the harvestable shellfish in western Washington was reaffirmed. Archaeological evidence was used by the tribes to demonstrate their long reliance on shellfish for their livelihood. There are other tribes that would rather see sites left alone and kept private. They are willing to risk the destruction of these sites during land use activities.

Some suggestions to the archaeology community are presented here for consideration and discussion. Through public education efforts, tribal representatives and archaeologists need to cooperate to battle stereotypes that portray archaeologists as professional pot hunters or grave robbers. Cooperative advertising through public media outlets and working together in the schools would be a good, effective start.

As for academic training acting as an obstacle to relationships with the Indian community, I believe we should make an effort to be less technical and more personal. This might necessitate placing more priority on people and their beliefs and understanding of the world than on our scientific goals and values.

In regard to site ownership and control, sites need to be shared. The landowner, whether public or private, may legally own the archaeological site, but it really belongs to the affected tribe. The archaeologist should serve both landowner and tribe equally.

It is vital that the archaeologist not attempt to force archaeology, especially from a global perspective, on Indian tribes in attempts to gain support for treatment plans, research designs, and other proposed agreements. The Indian people and their traditional vision of their territory need to be respected and preserved. We should not attempt to separate the Indian, his or her spirituality, the ancestors, and the land; they are a whole and cannot survive apart.

In conclusion, we must recognize that archaeology is political and that tribes are going to continue to insist on being players in the decisions affecting the resource. Tribal consultation is also a political process, and archaeologists must not only formulate strategies on how to consult, but in Puget Sound, it is necessary to determine with whom to consult on specific projects. The process can be complex, especially with the presence of federally recognized and nonrecognized groups and territorial disputes between tribes over fishing, clamming, and hunting areas. Today's archaeologists working with hunter-fisher-gatherer sites in North America will face numerous challenges in their pursuit of effective and scholarly management of these resources. One of these challenges will be tribal consultation because Indian tribes have been and will continue to be intimately involved in archaeology at a political, spiritual, and physical level. However, if approached and consulted in a respectful manner, with knowledge of our past, our spiritual values, and our cultural ways, Indian people can contribute greatly to the interpretation of archaeological and cultural sites.

■ ROSE KLUTH
KATHY MUNNELL

Nine

The Integration of Tradition and Scientific Knowledge on the Leech Lake Reservation

Integrating scientific and traditional knowledge on archaeological projects is an attainable goal. There are inherent challenges in combining these approaches. In this paper we discuss how we have incorporated traditional and modern scientific research in the Leech Lake Heritage Sites Program. We are not advocating this approach for all tribes, because tribal perspectives on archaeology vary, but we feel that our program has met with success. We also want to encourage communication between archaeologists and Native Americans in a manner that is appropriate and respectful to tribes and approachable by archaeologists.

The first section of this paper is a discussion of the mission and objectives of the Leech Lake Heritage Sites Program by Rose Kluth, offering examples of integrating traditional knowledge into Section 106 compliance and tribal archaeology projects. The second section is a discussion by Kathy Munnell, Leech Lake traditional cultural resources specialist. She presents the views of an Anishinabe woman involved in an archaeology program on her reservation. She discusses the role of Native Americans in the future of American archaeology, as well as why she believes that the knowledge to be gained from scientifically collected and analyzed archaeological data can be useful to her people.

Leech Lake Heritage Sites Program

The Leech Lake Heritage Sites Program is incorporated in the Division of Resource Management on Leech Lake Reservation in north-central Minnesota. The objective of our program is to provide cultural resource management services from a Native American perspective. Archaeological services are provided to several federal and state agencies and include all facets of Section 106 compliance. We exclusively hire Native Americans to participate in this program and we provide training supplemented with on-the-job education. We feel that this is what sets our program apart from others—the employees provide the program with a unique perspective about prehistoric cultural materials, as well as how to deal with sensitive sites and objects in a manner that is acceptable to their cultural beliefs.

Typically, Native Americans have not been encouraged to participate in the preservation process. Traditional beliefs have led some Native American people to avoid the field entirely. In the past, most archaeological fieldwork was performed by non–Native Americans, and the resulting reports were reviewed by non–Native Americans, even if the project involved tribal lands. At no point in the process was there a mechanism for Native American review or consultation, even if burials were involved. This process has changed dramatically within the past decade, with the implementation of federal legislation such as the Native American Graves Protection and Repatriation Act (NAGPRA) and the 1992 amendments to the National Historic Preservation Act. At last, the time has arrived for Native Americans to play a primary role in the preservation process.

Before we discuss the integration of traditional and scientific archaeology, we must define them. *Traditional knowledge* is a compilation of the knowledge of tribal culture history, past and present lifeways, language, spirituality, rituals, and ceremonies. This knowledge is gained by living the culture and by listening to the stories and oral histories of elders, parents, and grandparents. *Scientific knowledge* is knowledge obtained through testable and reproducible data. Archaeological data, and the means employed to obtain those data, are, for the purposes of this discussion, an example of scientific knowledge.

Incorporating Traditional Knowledge in Section 106 Compliance Work

In order to convey the process of integrating traditional and scientific knowledge within our program, we first discuss the incorporation of tradition in our program on a daily basis. Following this, four projects will be discussed. Each project is an example of the successful integration of traditional and scientific knowledge.

Daily Traditions

When the Leech Lake Heritage Sites Program was created, our employees were consulted about their concerns regarding archaeological fieldwork. Several individuals mentioned that their grandmothers had told them never to work on or near burial sites and that they should smudge themselves with sage or cedar every morning before work. They were instructed to place tobacco on the ground before beginning any excavations. This was to be done as a sign of respect to Mother Earth for the disturbance that was about to take place. They were warned that if they did not do these things, they or their families might be hurt. Also, they expressed concern about the use of alcohol on the job—this must be avoided to maintain respect with the spirit world and Mother Earth. After hearing their concerns, we assured them that an ample supply of cedar, sage, and tobacco would be on hand for them to complete these necessary actions prior to beginning fieldwork. Finally, if anyone came to work under the influence of alcohol, they were not permitted to work.

Ogema Geshik Site

In the summer of 1993, the Leech Lake Heritage Sites Program was asked to investigate possible disturbance to an archaeological site in the northwestern corner of the reservation. A survey was initiated to determine the limits of the site, as was an evaluation of the level of disturbance.

Shovel tests were placed every 10 m to determine the horizontal and vertical extent of the site. During shovel testing, four bear claws were found in a single shovel test. The bear claws were removed and bagged for transport back to the lab, along with the other artifacts that were located that day. Later in the day, one of the crew members spoke with the field director. He said that he was a member of the Bear Clan and requested that the field director place the bear claws back where they were found. The field director complied, and the bear claws were reburied in their original location. The crew member placed tobacco near this location. This individual was satisfied with the resolution and felt comfortable with our reporting the information in the final archaeology report.

Fieldwork continued at the site, and our crew located human remains. These remains were immediately reburied by the same crew members. These same individuals then placed tobacco near the area where the remains were found and a dish with food for the spirit of that individual. They spoke to the spirit of the individual, asking the spirit to understand that they meant no harm and that they would move away from the area. The crew members discussed the situation with the field director and requested that the shovel tests be moved back at least 200 feet from this area, as they felt that it was a very sacred one that must not be disturbed. We complied, continuing our survey, and were able to delineate the site's limits without further disturbance to the sacred areas. We uncovered the remains of an important prehistoric ricing site and obtained the information needed to assess the site; the crew felt comfortable working in the area because proper respect had been paid to the sacred areas.

Truck Highway 169 Project

In the summer of 1995 we completed an archaeological survey for the Minnesota Department of Transportation along a portion of TH 169, just south of Mille Lacs Lake. We maintained daily contact with Mille Lacs Reservation staff, informing them of our progress. Prior to excavating test units, an intact catlinite pipe was found eroding from the cutbank above an old roadbed. When the pipe was discovered, we immediately contacted Mille Lacs Reservation staff, who met us at the site. The crew members left the pipe in situ for the Mille Lacs staff to observe. The Mille Lacs staff wanted the pipe reburied immediately because they felt that it indicated the presence of an Ojibwe burial site. They reburied the pipe outside the proposed right-of-way, west of the area where it was found. Our crew was instructed to place our test units away from the area where the pipe was originally located. We respected these concerns and completed our excavations away from this area. As a result of our fieldwork, we were able to determine that this site was eligible for listing on the National Register of Historic Places. We were able to complete the archaeological fieldwork, yet respect the concerns and traditional beliefs of the Mille Lacs Reservation representatives.

NAGPRA

In the fall of 1993, we received more than 200 museum inventories of sacred objects, unassociated funerary objects, and objects of cultural patrimony that may have been associated with the Leech Lake Anishinabe people. In order to begin the NAGPRA process, the Leech Lake Tribal Council created an elder council, called the Leech Lake Advisory Council on Cultural Resources. The council was to work with the Heritage Sites program director in deciding whether these objects were to be repatriated. After many prayers, meetings, and discussions, the elder council determined that the way to proceed was to combine oral and written histories regarding these objects. They asked the archaeology director to visit all the museums in Minnesota in order to determine if their collections contained items that could be attributed to the Leech Lake Anishinabe people. If so, these objects would be brought back to the reservation and dealt with in the proper, traditional manner. All of the meetings to date have involved much prayer and a great deal of discussion regarding the old ways, and the proper and respectful disposition of these objects. However, the council has chosen to rely on whatever museum records exist to determine which objects came from the Leech Lake Anishinabe people. They have combined both written and oral histories in their work with NAGPRA.

Pug Hole–Klein Lot Site

In the summer of 1995, we completed an archaeological survey on Leech Lake Reservation tribal lands prior to leasing a lakeshore lot. A previously recorded site was relocated, and the site limits were expanded to include the lot in question. Severe erosion was noted on the lake side of the lot. Later that summer, human remains were found to be eroding from the area. A representative of our elder council was contacted, and he came with us to the site to rebury the remains. He instructed us to remove only these remains that were actually visible. We were not to displace any soil to remove any human remains still located within the bank. The exposed remains were reburied on the lot further inland from the shoreline.

A meeting was held to discuss possible methods to halt the erosion. Because a site was on this lot, the Heritage Sites program director was consulted regarding erosion control methods. Would it be possible to plant trees on the lot, or should the bank be shored with large stones? I contacted a representative of our elder council for advice. The elder said that the shore should be left to erode, as it was a natural process that should not be fought. He said that the spirit of the person that was still buried there either wanted to move to the water in order to be near the water spirits or might be on the next step of his or her journey. The elder said that if we placed rocks on the eroded area, they would not stay put, because the spirits in that area would be much more powerful than any stones. He said that it would be dangerous for a heavy equipment operator to drive over this site, as he might be injured or killed because of his actions. The council member's decision was respected, and the site was left alone. Although it was difficult for me to allow the site to erode, I felt that we must heed the traditional knowledge of the elders. There was no alternative once we understood. It was a decision that respected the elders' traditional knowledge.

Discussion

These examples are specific to our reservation and tribal archaeology program. We understand that it may not be feasible for archaeologists to access traditional knowledge in many settings. However, we encourage communication between archaeological and tribal communities, if that communication is compatible with traditional beliefs. We believe that we have the same goals: site protection and a knowledge of past lifeways. Through frank communication on both sides, it should be possible to work toward these goals.

A Personal, Traditional Perspective

In my language my name is Bine-si-ikwe, Thunderbird Woman. I am an Anishinabe, Leech Lake Reservation enrollee, and a member of the Minnesota Chippewa Tribe. I was taught that the Anishinabe people are the Keepers of the Earth, and that as an Anishinabe person, it is our responsibility to protect the water and land, and all things related. I also believe that I have a responsibility to preserve my cultural ways.

Burial Sites vs. Other Archaeological Sites

I see archaeological sites as being of two types: burial sites and other archaeological sites. There is a strong distinction between these two types of sites and how they can be treated. Burial sites are the chosen places where the bodies of our ancestors are laid to rest, and they should not be disturbed. These sites must be respected. I consider my role to be one of protector of these sacred sites. From our perspective, there are risks and repercussions if we do not respect these teachings.

We are taught that when we die, we are intended to go back into the earth, and that Mother Earth will take care of us. Burials feed the underground spirits and small creatures through the natural decomposition of the body. This is part of the natural order—we all depend on each other to survive. We must not disturb this cycle.

Archaeological sites contain the history of our people, in different stages of their lives, according to the seasons of the year. I believe that useful information can be recovered from these types of sites that will be helpful and interesting to Native Americans. Future generations of Anishinabe people may not rice or hunt or gather, and they may be unaware that we lived off the land at one time. But archaeologists, working with our elders, can help us to understand our past connection with the land through our oral histories in conjunction with the scientific studies of our past diets, habitats, and lifeways. We can find out how the ancestors lived all those thousands of years before us—what they ate, where they lived, etc. This scientific knowledge supports our traditional knowledge of our past lifeways.

Role of Native Americans in Archaeology

My granddaughter recently told me that she wants to be an archaeologist when she grows up. I look at her and wonder, can she be a traditional Anishinabe woman and practice archaeology? I want to support her in her dreams of becoming an archaeologist. I would like to know that she could continue to retain her cultural boundaries. We believe that women are the caretakers of the earth, keepers of the water, and the lifegivers. The women will initiate the mending of the sacred hoop, which symbolizes the broken connection between the Anishinabe of today and those of generations past. Who better, then, to do archaeology on Leech Lake than an Anishinabe woman?

I strongly support the involvement of Native Americans in the field and future of archaeology. We truly understand the level of respect that is necessary in this field. This is not to say that non–Native Americans cannot be respectful or sensitive, but there has to be a strong bond and relationship between archaeologists and native people. There must be trust on both sides, or it will never work. Archaeologists must invite Native Americans to observe what they do and to communicate in a way that will be beneficial to both parties. It also follows that Native Americans must begin dialogue with archaeologists, in a manner that is respectful to our teachings.

We must have Native American input in the field of archaeology. We must learn to enter the non–Native American world and deal with these issues. Our Heritage Sites project director is a non–Native American who knows the language of the western society. That is why she is here. She also knows her boundaries and where her part ends, and she encourages the Anishinabe to do the rest for themselves. That is the key—archaeologists cannot be paternalistic and tell Native Americans whether burials can be excavated or which sites are worth saving. This has to be a cooperative effort, and Native American views must be respected. It is too painful for us to consider the alternative. We can work together with mutual respect. We must move beyond the fighting and set aside the anger of past injustices.

The choice is ours now that the 1992 National Historic Preservation Act amendments and NAGPRA are in place. If we don't make our own decisions, others will make decisions for us. We must take responsibility for our ancestors and learn about this field, because it is so important to us that these sites are preserved and that we have a say in the telling of our history. It may mean struggling through the educational system and applying the fieldwork and technical aspects in a way that feels comfortable for us. But we can do it. And we can work with archaeologists who possess this knowledge, as long as the level of trust is established.

The traditional knowledge that we possess is important and valid. We want the archaeological community to acknowledge this fact and work with us toward a stronger, more integrated and healthier discipline.

We want to thank the Leech Lake Tribal Council for allowing us to participate in the important symposium and discussion. It would not have been possible without their support and encouragement. We would also like to thank Dale Henning, David Kluth, and Delina Davis for their insightful comments and discussions regarding the final draft of this paper.

■ DOROTHY LIPPERT

Ten

In Front of the Mirror
Native Americans and Academic Archaeology

The role of Native Americans within the world of academic archaeology is currently undergoing a great deal of change and revitalization. In part due to legally directed consultation, more and more Indians are becoming involved in archaeology. A growing number of us have chosen to pursue the discipline of archaeology as a career, and in this paper I would like to consider some of the many factors that affect us as we work at this vocation.

The pressures involved in becoming an archaeologist are somewhat different for a Native American than they are for nonnatives. In addition to expectations from within the profession, other, more personal stresses can be involved. Some of these are directly related to the history of archaeology in America, while others relate to current political activities. University education about the Native American past may also serve as a barrier to one's desire to study our history in an academic context, as a distressing personal example shows. A key to presenting archaeology as a profession open to Native American input is communication. This is a very simple thing to say, but it is more complex in its execution.

Finally, I would argue that archaeology as a discipline must realistically consider not only the roles of Native Americans within the discipline, but also Indian perspectives on the past. We can bring many views on the ancient people to our work, the most important being an impression of the ancients as ancestors. As Indian archaeologists we feel the heavy burden of telling their stories, not just for reasons of furthering academic knowledge, but also out of respect for our elders and those who were here before us.

History

The history of interaction between academic archaeologists and native peoples fuels much of the resentment many Indian people feel toward the discipline. Anthropologists from the early years of the discipline sought to study and record as much information as possible about various tribes out of a fear that cultural ways were fast disappearing (Trigger 1989). For many tribes this was indeed the case, and, in fact, there have been instances in which knowledge preserved by anthropologists has become an important source of information for continuing cultural practices (Hubert 1989b). However, in many more cases native peoples found anthropologists to be intrusive and annoying. Much of the information shared with ethnographers was published, and tribes came to resent the fact that local and sometimes sacred knowledge was taken and used improperly. Many Indians were made to feel like interesting specimens rather than people.

Archaeology might have seemed to escape this problem because of a focus on past or extinct cultural groups. However, this formulation of the discipline reflected a divergent concept of the ancient history of the North American continent from that implied by anthropology. Publications in both the popular and scholarly press reflected a bias against existing tribes, seeing Indian peoples as remnants of a once noble past. With the days of glory long gone, contemporary Indian life could hold no keys to understanding the mysteries of the past.

The seeds for the repatriation dispute were planted in this era. The idea had been formed that the ancient past could only be unlocked using scientific reasoning, which belonged to the archaeologists. Native perspectives on what became known as "prehistory" were defined as myth and folklore, neither of which was as powerful as science. Such an understanding of the past cut out the only peoples who are actually related to the ancient North Americans. The need to make this point clear factored into much of the determination Indian activists felt when trying to explain why it is necessary to see the modern tribes as historically, genetically, and emotionally linked to ancient peoples.

Again, with the collecting of skeletal material, Native Americans were made to feel like specimens. This imagery underlies much of the dialogue about repatriation today (Lippert 1992). In part because native peoples and native knowledge were not seen as vital to the discipline of archaeology, few Indians attempted to gain academic credentials and participate in the profession. In addition, other factors, notably economic and social, played into this situation. Then, as today, Native Americans fall below the poverty level in staggering numbers. For many Indians, higher education has never been a viable choice.

In the fall of 1990, Native Americans made up less than 1 percent of the total number of students enrolled in institutions of higher education (Reddy 1993)—a figure comparable to their representation within the general population. However, it is certain that a fraction of these students are not, in fact, related to the original inhabitants of this continent. At the University of Texas at Austin, ethnicity is self-determined, and judging from lists of Indian students obtained by the Native American Student Organization (NASO), it is apparent that the original ancestry of at least 5 percent of the individuals listed was in India!

Further up in the academic strata, the number of Native Americans becomes smaller. In 1988–1989, less than a quarter of 1 percent of students receiving doctorates were Native American (84 out of 35,692). This rate moves up to nearly a third of a percent when one considers the social sciences, but it is still somewhat less than admirable. In 1990, out of a total of 2,047 doctorates in the social sciences, American Indians received 6 (Reddy 1993).

Academia and Native Americans

Many Native Americans who choose to study anthropology do so out of a desire to explore their ethnic background. It is not always easy to make or maintain this choice within the academic arena. At the University of Texas, I once enrolled in a course (not in the Anthropology Department) that promised to consider the ways in which the image of Indianness has been constructed using texts written by and about Native Americans. However, I found that the professor was so steeped in his own perspectives of the Indian as "Noble Savage" that he was somewhat less than knowledgeable or sympathetic to modern Indian concerns about identity.

Unable to escape the class after the drop deadline, I endured weeks of irritation. He compared the intellect of the painters of southwestern rock art with that of elementary school children because he thought the drawings looked similar to children's artwork. At one point, he seemed to regret that all of the Indians in Texas had either been killed or moved out of the state. Hearing a statement like this could indeed lead a Native American student to seriously question her presence at the university! In fact, according to the 1990 census, Texas ranks eighth in the country for numbers of Native American residents (Reddy 1993). I include this class description not merely to blow off some steam, but to point out that academia is not neutral in its approach to the study of Native American history: sometimes things can get downright hostile.

In addition, the opposite condition has begun to occur. In the wake of the quincentennial, it has become fashionable once again to mythologize Native American culture. Our history is sometimes transformed into an impossibly serene, all knowing, cooperative, gender-sensitive enterprise that is then held as a shining example for the rest of the world to follow. White culture, corrupted by civilization, could supposedly learn much from our heritage. This benevolent, though misguided, viewpoint again places Native Americans in a category other than human. At times it seems easier to contend with clear-cut ignorance rather than well-intentioned romanticization.

Archaeology classes are generally much better, but they often fail to make the connection between living Native American groups and the "prehistoric" past. In most of my archaeology classes, little or no mention has been made of the modern Indian tribes who are related to the various aspects, chiefdoms, and phases being studied. One gets the idea that living Indian people are irrelevant to the study of North American prehistory, and maybe within the current formulation of prehistory, we are. But I believe that this merely illustrates the need for a reconsideration of what we have defined as archaeology. Are we uncovering the past for its own sake or for reasons of our own? We may be trying to be objective and scientific, but isn't there a sense of wanting to connect with the ancient peoples that drew all of us into this profession? It seems to me to be dangerous to define a past that does not possess a human soul.

Communication

Communication between archaeologists and Native American groups has increased over the years, especially after the passage of the Native American Graves Protection and Repatriation Act. However, this term—communication—may involve different actions and have different meanings. If discussions only take place within the boundaries of legally mandated sharing of information, a true dialogue may not result. Let us consider the various Indian communities and ways in which archaeologists can open less formal communication with them.

Information about archaeological research need not be distributed only in cases where excavations take place on Indian lands. Members of tribes who are culturally or spatially related may be fascinated by studies that seem commonplace in departments of anthropology. It is vital that archaeologists come to view sharing information with Indian groups as an integral part of conducting research.

The method of transmission of information is also important. Sending a copy of the published report may be useful, but many of those who are interested may find it difficult to interpret. While technical reports may be useful to members of tribes who are considering archaeology as a career, academic language may obscure information fascinating to the general Indian community.

One interesting report has been published by the U.S. Department of the Interior's Fish and Wildlife Service about burials found at the Stillwater National Wildlife Refuge (Raymond 1992). This report discusses the project and the information learned from the burials in nontechnical language. It even describes paleo-pathological research in a clear manner. Because of financial constraints, reports like this one may be rare, but similar efforts should be undertaken where possible.

Other approaches to consider are giving talks at community centers, or tribal meetings, or inviting people to visit labs or excavation sites. I once arranged the NASO to take a tour of the Texas Archeological Research Laboratory. In an apparent long-standing tradition, members of the Caddo Tribe of Oklahoma regularly attend an annual conference on Caddo archaeology. The level of communication that takes place at the conference may be questioned, however; at the last meeting, a Native American student commented to me that "It all looks very interesting, but I didn't understand a word of it."

When considering a connection to the Indian community, archaeologists often overlook intertribal organizations. Texas has many organizations that enable Indian people of all backgrounds to come together to discuss common concerns. These groups should not be dismissed in attempts to educate the native public about archaeology just because they are composed of people from many different tribes. The majority of the 65,000 Indians in Texas don't live on tribal lands (Reddy 1993).

I have been privileged to be a speaker at the American Indian Resource and Education Coalition's annual conference on Indian education in Texas. At the 1995 conference, I gave a short talk on skeletal research, discussing what is actually done and the sorts of information that can be learned. I had been quite nervous about making that speech. On other occasions I have been made to feel like a traitor for studying human remains. In fact, the listeners seemed quite interested and asked thoughtful questions. It became clear to me that many had not known what could be learned from skeletal analysis. To me, this incident represents a clear breakdown in communication because this group has been one of the more active in Texas to push for repatriation.

I do not mean to state that with a little more education members of groups such as this would change their minds about reburial, rather I think that they should be fully informed about the nature of archaeology and about what can be learned. As Lynne Goldstein states, "Since Native Americans often have little idea of what we do, they may invent our culture for us, based on the limited information they have on hand" (Goldstein 1992:61).

Native American Archaeologists

There have been many calls for an increase in the numbers of Native Americans in archaeology, and in fact our ranks have grown. However, the number of Indians who acquire a college education remains small, and the number of Indian graduate students remains even smaller. At the University of Texas at Austin, 182 students out of 48,000 are listed as American Indian or Alaska Native. Native Americans are not considered a minority group with regard to recruitment efforts (Office of Admissions, University of Texas at Austin, personal communication 1996). In Texas, Native Americans are not considered minorities when applying for state-regulated financial aid specifically available to minority students (Red Elk 1995). NASO has made efforts to recruit Native American graduate students, but it is nearly impossible to recruit undergraduates since we receive no support for this from the university.

Calls for an increase in the number of Native American archaeologists are easy to make, but can be much harder to answer. In stating a desire for more practicing native archaeologists, we must address what it is the discipline really expects of us. We are capable of bringing perspectives to our work that go against standard archaeological knowledge about the peoples of North America. Will these be accepted, or rejected as nonscientific?

For example, we know that at one time these lands were inhabited only by our ancestors. This country was Indian for at least 20 times as long as Europeans and their descendants have been here. This knowledge can provide modern Indian people with a feeling of kinship that transcends tribal boundaries. I have found that my own studies in archaeology reflect an emotional connection that is a result of being related somehow to the "prehistoric" peoples of North America.

I think the best way to explain this is to relate an experience I had as an undergraduate at Rice University. I was visiting the Houston Museum of Natural Science to study an exhibit of precolumbian Central American artifacts. I remember wandering happily through the exhibit, comfortable in the feeling of kinship with the ancient makers of the objects. When I examined a case of personal adornment items, I stared into a black obsidian mirror and was struck by a deeply satisfying thought: the owner of the mirror had probably seen a sight similar to the one I was seeing when he or she looked into the polished glass.

As Native Americans, when we study the past, we see our ancient selves, living and acting in a world not yet impacted by 504 years of colonial confusion. When we work at archaeology, we do so with a sometimes unspoken responsibility: we know why we need to preserve the memories of those who went before us. It might be argued that this can lead to unobjective results; how can one scientifically study prehistory if one is also reverent of the ancestors? This question points me toward another difficulty of belonging to both groups. Is it reverent to the ancient peoples to pursue one of my interests, the study of health conditions in a "prehistoric" community through examination of their skeletal remains?

Skeletal Research

I believe that one can attempt to maintain appropriate reverence toward the ancients while continuing to learn from their material remains. For many of our ancestors, skeletal analysis is one of the only ways that they are able to tell us their stories. The forthcoming information may not be as clear as it is from other sources; it seems that it is difficult to speak with a voice made of bone. Nevertheless, while so much has been lost, these individuals have found one last way to speak to us about their lives.

While working on my dissertation research, I have observed many different people and their approaches toward skeletal analysis. Many appear to work quite casually, and I know that I have irritated some by insisting on following rules about working conditions to the letter. In doing so, I find that I am attempting to foster an awareness of the heavy responsibility of working with human remains. Bio-archaeological research is a privilege. It must not be taken lightly.

I could not conduct skeletal research against the wishes of a related Indian community. If possible, I would make known to concerned individuals the types of studies that could be done and what could be learned, as well as my willingness to follow procedures that address religious needs. In the end, however, I would be forced by my own ethics and humanity to comply with their wishes. One of the basic common beliefs among native peoples is respect for elders and their wisdom.

Conclusion

As a Choctaw and an archaeologist, I am often forced to defend my own work and my choice of archaeology as a profession to members of various Indian groups. This is one of the more difficult aspects of being a Native American archaeologist. As a member of both groups, I can't help getting drawn into various conflicts. Although this leaves me quite cynical at times, I still feel that more Native Americans are needed for the future of archaeology. It has been hard sometimes to clearly articulate why this is necessary, but I think it has something to do with the image I saw in the obsidian mirror.

When we study the people of the past, we do so with a frame of reference that is constructed in the present. However unknowingly, we carry our own perspectives and experiences into our studies, and this affects to various degrees our conclusions about the past. The next people to come along in the precolumbian exhibit I mentioned above were an older, white couple. They also stared appreciatively into the mirror, but I knew there was little chance that their images were comparable to the owner's. Yet there must be similarities; we share common, human characteristics.

I believe that Native American archaeologists can study the past in ways that are both divergent and complementary to the more traditional canon. For us, the past is strong. The precolumbian past of this continent is a powerful, almost mythic time that illustrates the accomplishments of native peoples: it serves as a source of strength when confronted with the struggles of the present. This is the perspective that influences my own attitudes and activities in archaeology.

In continuing my studies of the past, I do so gratefully, with the tools developed by generations of archaeologists, most of whom are not Indian. It is necessary, however, to recognize that Native American archaeologists may see some areas of the past more closely. We look through an emotional lens that is knowingly constructed through our blood, the genetic characteristics of which echo in the bones of our ancestors.

I do not think that it is impossible to know the American past without being related to the peoples being studied. In fact, if we consider the history of North America when we define our profession, we may recognize a justice of a sort. While so much of our native history was lost through the actions of European peoples, it is perhaps fair that so many of their descendants strive so hard to restore it. White archaeologists might try to consider their work as a sort of penance rather than a right.

We must reconsider what our purposes are when we conduct archaeological research. We must recognize that our actions do affect native peoples on many levels. Acknowledging this fact need not compromise a scientific study of the past, it should merely force one more step toward active communication. Archaeology must also consider what is implied in calls for an increase in the numbers of Native American archaeologists. How much of a native perspective is to be incorporated? How easy is it for a Native American to choose archaeology considering the social and economic pressures that may be involved? Increasing the numbers of Indians practicing archaeology is certainly desirable, but it should be just as necessary to educate tribes and intertribal groups.

Finally, I do not maintain that the Native American perspective on the past be privileged to the exclusion of any other approaches, merely that it be recognized as an existing canon. There should be room in this discipline for a variety of viewpoints. After all, we are all human. We all share genetic characteristics and fundamental concerns, and when we look in the mirror we all see basically the same thing: our very human selves.

I am grateful to Roger Anyon and Kurt Dongoske for the invitation to participate in this forum. I believe that my own paper was much improved through listening to the opinions and experiences of the other participants. In preparing this paper, I have received useful critiques and commentary from numerous people, including Sam Wilson, Gail Bailey, Aina Dodge, and A. D. Lippert. I am grateful to them for their advice and support.

Eleven

How Traditional Navajos View Historic Preservation
A Question of Interpretation

What is cultural resource management? What is repatriation? What is reburial? And why do we need a burial policy? These are questions traditional Navajos ask of the cultural resource managers and preservationists working with the Navajo Nation Historic Preservation Department (HPD).[1] Sadly, these questions at times come from our Navajo staff members as well. The concepts of managing cultural resources, repatriating sacred items and human remains and associated and unassociated funerary items, and making policies to protect burials and historic and traditional properties are alien to traditional Navajos. Traditionally, cultural resources were protected through moral teachings.

The Navajo Nation has been named repeatedly as one of the front-runners of tribes who are "managing their own cultural resources." In fact, we will be among the first to assume state historic preservation office responsibilities under the 1992 amendments to the National Historic Preservation Act. But does HPD preserve the Navajo Nation's cultural resources as the traditionalists would? The answer is both no and yes. To traditional Navajo people, cultural resources are vital living elements that need to be protected. In this paper, I use "cultural resources" to mean all archaeological and historical properties, sacred areas, and other areas of cultural importance. Burial sites were also protected by avoidance. Avoidance of culturally significant areas was the only traditionally accepted means of protection. This is one reason it is difficult for traditional tribal members to come to terms with burial policies, repatriation policies, archaeologists, and anthropologists. Generations of traditional people have protected cultural resources and burials with these unwritten laws.

If the Navajo Nation has succeeded in making headway in the management and preservation of our cultural resources while complying with federal and tribal laws, why aren't our traditional people comfortable? Their discomfort comes from allowing and even requiring testing and excavation on any type of archaeological or historic property on Navajo lands. As a tribal member, I am proud of the accomplishments of both the Navajo Nation Achaeology Department and HPD, but I often wonder if we will ever manage or preserve our cultural resources according to tribal customs. Having worked for both of these departments, I have come to realize that the worlds of anthropology and archaeology can be accepted to some extent, but not wholly, by traditional people. Only by providing adequate information about our jobs with HPD, a complete interpretation of federal and tribal laws, as well as a complete description of the work archaeologists and ethnographers do on Navajo lands can we help our traditional people begin to understand and accept our professions. Until all our traditional people are educated in these areas, they will continue to think HPD is in violation of unwritten tribal laws when it issues permits for testing and excavations.

In 1988, the Navajo Nation gave HPD the authority to advise the tribal chairman (now the president), the Navajo Tribal Council, and other tribal agencies or departments regarding cultural resource issues. Because HPD took over existing Bureau of Indian Affairs cultural resource programs, the policies and procedures for managing the tribe's cultural resources and burials are much like the federal government's. Essentially, we are almost a clone of the three state historic preservation offices that currently review projects on the Navajo Nation. In the words of a fellow Navajo anthropologist, Richard Begay, HPD is a Section 106 shop (see Downer and Roberts 1996); however, we should not place the blame on anyone other than ourselves. Most of the nine programs within HPD receive funds from the federal government and thus are mandated to comply with federal regulations that often conflict with tribal traditions. HPD's Traditional Culture Program does not receive federal funding and can therefore strive toward incorporating traditional concerns in tribal policies and preservation efforts.

Since the establishment of HPD the Navajo Nation has developed a position called "Navajo cultural specialist," or NCS for short. Prior to that time, the bilingual Navajo archaeologists had been doing the work of the cultural specialists as well as archaeology. While with the Navajo Nation Archaeology Department (NNAD) I worked with many Navajos who voiced concerns over issues including collecting of ceremonial items that had been left for protection and/or offerings at both Navajo and prehistoric archaeological sites. This led to consulting with traditional tribal members who were familiar with the sites or the items and recording oral histories. In the early 1990s, HPD came up with a solution that would enable traditional Navajos who lacked previous archaeology or anthropology experience or formal training to work as professional cultural resource managers. The NCSs now are working alongside both archaeologists and anthropologists and providing complete documentation of cultural resources. Ideally, the Navajo cultural specialists should have a broad range of knowledge and experience in traditional ceremonial activities. But this does not mean that Navajo archaeologists cannot work in dual roles as archaeologists and cultural specialists.

As HPD employs more Navajo archaeologists, anthropologists, and cultural specialists, preservation procedures are changing rapidly. Tribal members like Begay and our Navajo cultural specialists have greatly influenced changes in current management and preservation practices on Navajo land. Nontribal members who have had the privilege of conducting research that benefited only themselves and/or their scientific communities often find themselves defending their work. In fact, I have been told by fellow tribal archaeologists, "You are in the wrong field." Research is not totally disregarded; research is needed to answer important questions. Ethnographic research among our traditional people is needed on numerous topics ranging from preservation methodologies to the sensitive areas of cultural affiliation with the prehistoric people.

The Navajo Nation is fortunate to have numerous tribal council members who are sensitive to cultural resource issues and who have passed tribal laws and policies to protect and manage cultural resources. I can only imagine that when the tribal council passed the Navajo Nation's Cultural Resources Protection Act (CRPA; Navajo Nation 1986), they assumed cultural resource and preservation professionals would follow the intent and spirit of the law. Instead, CRPA and *Bulletin 38* (Parker and King 1990) are often set aside, while the national and scientific emphases of federal laws are accepted. The tribal council realizes the need for HPD and tribal archaeologists. One way of showing support is by funding Navajo college students to attend the Northern Arizona University in Flagstaff and Fort Lewis College in Durango, Colorado, in hopes of having more Navajos trained in the different fields of anthropology and working on the Navajo Nation.

While working as a field archaeologist, one tends to lose all sight of tribal traditions. It is easy to get caught up in making a name for yourself in the profession and making compliance people happy. It is easy to forget that the site you are recording, testing, or excavating belongs to "others" whose presence remains. Recalling my years in archaeology often embarrasses me. I think of crew members yelling "Look at this cool pipe in my unit!" without considering the fact that often these pipes are smoked in ceremonial contexts, or "Let's get this f——r out of here," when a burial is discovered at 4:55 p.m., and you want to get home for some cold beer. Even though I've been a part of these types of incidents, I still find myself defending the world of archaeologists to traditional Navajo thinkers. What would traditionalists do if they knew these types of incidents occur in the field? For that matter, what would they think of the lengthy discussions of venereal diseases that afflicted the early inhabitants? Traditional Navajos and people like myself are equally curious about the people who lived here before us, but we also think of the consequences of going too far in answering research questions. The concerns expressed are not only for the traditional community but for all individuals who work in the fields of cultural resources.

As time passes, the Navajo general public is becoming aware that archaeological inventories are required for any undertaking. When an undertaking goes beyond the inventory phase, and testing and/or data recovery is the only option, HPD automatically begins working against tribal customs. This is when traditional people look to HPD to come up with balancing solutions that allow the cultural heritage of the Navajo Nation to remain alive. As more of my people pursue the challenging work of anthropology on Navajo lands, my hopes are that they come up with new accepted mitigative measures that will not always include a shovel and, if so, will allow the spirit of the site to live on. Ultimately, it is people like myself who are asked by traditional people why the Navajo Nation sanctions the disturbance of "properties of other people" through federal and tribal laws. Through the efforts of Navajo speakers, cultural resource management laws/policies and even anthropological theories are shared and interpreted with traditional people.

Traditional people find the discipline of anthropology very interesting and sometimes appalling. Traditional protocols for particular situations and recommendations are often shared with people in the field. The Navajo cultural specialists working for HPD have also offered information that can benefit field archaeologists. For years, field archaeologists, including myself, have recorded multicomponent Navajo ceremonial locations as one massive site. The sorting of the components is impossible for field recorders who do not know the types of features associated with a particular ceremony. Cultural specialists can identify separate components of a ceremonial site by the placement of features and have begun to train our archaeologists in this knowledge.

Navajo field recorders are often asked by local people to give briefings on projects as well as on the archaeological profession. Curiosity and concern arises fast when noncommunity members are observed on archeological and burial sites. Community members, traditional or not, know where most archeological and historic sites and burials are located. They consider themselves stewards of the land and the cultural resources the land holds. An outsider's presence is noticed immediately. When Navajo archaeologists or ethnographers are approached in the field, there is communication for a few moments between tribal people and archaeologists. What starts out as a scolding for "disturbing the properties of others" turns into informative discussion for both parties, archaeologists and traditional thinkers. Ironically, the communication and understanding comes between two Navajo individuals rather than between a nontribal member archaeologist and a traditional Navajo. I am not complaining; in fact I am glad this happens because this is when people like myself have an opportunity to learn about the wide range of Navajo traditions and how it plays out with our chosen profession.

Through these dialogues with my Navajo people who are affected by projects, I have come to realize that speaking Navajo is not only a great asset, it is also a tool that can be used to change the feelings traditional people have toward anthropology. Traditional people retain a massive amount of information on places of importance to themselves, their clans, their community, the tribe, and other tribes. Often, these places are archaeological sites or landscapes tied to the sites. Most important, opportunities like these provide valuable and controversial information that is now adding a new dimension to the field of archaeology. Through these exchanges with my traditional people, I have been taught the magnitude of respect my elders have for places left by "those who have gone before us." Whether the sites belonged to the Paleoindian cultures, the *Anaasazi*, or Navajos, the sites are regarded as living elements of the natural landscape and the property of the former inhabitants. The traditional people consider themselves stewards of the sites. In most cases, the sites are considered traditional cultural properties, and for centuries the areas holding the resources have been avoided and left undisturbed.

I believe cultural resource managers who intend to work for tribal programs or work among tribal traditionalists should be required to learn the pertinent language and cultural traditions. Sharing information on cultural resources with elders opens another dimension to our profession. For years I have recommended that all nontribal archaeologists and ethnographers working for the Navajo Nation be required to take Navajo language classes. My pleas have always fallen on deaf ears. Cultural classes should also be required. One of my biggest peeves is interpreting for nontribal member archaeologists and anthropologists who have worked for Navajo tribal programs for years. If traders who work at trading posts can learn to speak Navajo, surely archaeologists/anthropologists can too; after all, don't they pride themselves on studying cultures? I have worked too often with nontribal members who do not know how to present themselves to the Navajo public or who do not want to deal with Navajos. Traditional tribal members are very impressed with nontribal members who know how to introduce themselves to the Navajo public and appear to be attempting to learn traditional protocol in working with their culture.

Oddly, it wasn't until after I went to work for HPD that I realized tribal members could have a lot of influence on the management and protection of cultural resources and burials on Navajo lands. HPD will continue to gain the support of our traditional community as we work to integrate tribal customs into preservation. I believe HPD provides a buffer for traditionalists who prefer not to work directly with sensitive issues such as writing policies for the protection of burials and repatriation. Through the National Historic Preservation Act consultation process, HPD has involved traditional community members in working with federal agencies on projects that might impact their traditional practices. The Glen Canyon Environmental Studies project and continuing consultation with the Bureau of Land Management on the Dinetah area are examples of how traditionalists are encouraged and utilized to advise both HPD and federal agencies on management of cultural resources. Traditional people are very grateful for opportunities to make recommendations on an undertaking or to provide oral traditions of the project areas on and off Navajo lands.

HPD recently completed the Policy for the Protection of Jishchaa', a revision of the Navajo Nation's burial policy. The revision was written with a strong emphasis on Navajo cultural traditions. The original policy had been written by non-Navajos without the input of the traditional people. The committee members—six Navajos and five non-Navajo staff members—were hand-picked by HPD Director Alan Downer. I believe I was picked to serve on the committee because I am Navajo and was working as an archaeologist at the time. Being a part of and observing the committee work was trying. The anguish over interpretation of Navajo words and protocol for dealing with burials often led to heated discussions between Navajo and non-Navajo committee members. The very thought of discussing death and treating human remains made one of our cultural specialists ill every evening following the sessions. These episodes of watching nontribal members having to be overruled by the Navajo staff leads me to believe that nontribal members need to learn to be merely tools in forming regulations rather than influencing tribal members on how they should manage cultural resources and burials on their lands. Tribal members need to be given opportunities to integrate traditional protocols into all tribal policies, and, if needed, the nontribal members can assist in the integration.

Because of the emotional ties to the landscape and the unacceptability of disturbance to any cultural resources, Navajos like myself know our mission at HPD is far from over. Developing research designs that allow for minimal disturbance is one solution. But, what do you do if there are still unanswered questions about your past and at the same time there are traditional people who believe that it is wrong to "disturb other people's homes"? What do you do when you've experienced unexplained occurrences as a result of your work? Can a hard-core researcher ever begin to understand the feelings traditional people have about cultural resources? Should the people of the ancient cultures be brought back to life in archaeological reports? To many traditional people, it is best for us to let the people of the past stay in the past and continue as a part of the landscape they live in.

For now, we at HPD will continue to make the small changes. We can begin by repatriating artifacts to the place of origin. This is certainly a better option than having items stored in curation facilities far from their homes. This brings back memories of my work with NNAD in the late 1970s when we were trained and instructed to surface collect from historic and prehistoric sites. Often we collected offerings and funerary items against our beliefs. Traditionally, prehistoric sites have always been a part of Navajo ceremonies and history and have played a part in the ceremonial life of the people. Long before *Bulletin 38*, Navajo archaeologists tried to discourage nontribal archaeologists from collecting cultural items that were placed at sites to deteriorate naturally in their environment. For instance, Navajo "remaking dolls" are often left at prehistoric sites. Even years later, removing the dolls during data recovery will affect the healing process of the patient for whom the ceremony was performed. In a larger picture, it will have an adverse effect on the ceremonial life of the Navajo people, not to mention the effect to the prehistoric component.

Developing methods that do not always call for 100 percent collection and excavation (with a shovel) should be paramount; sampling should always be an option. Redundant data collection should be frowned on. If our traditional people knew how testing, excavation, and analysis are actually performed, they would be overwhelmed with concerns for the archaeological community.

Traditional tribal members also provide HPD with guidance on the tribe's repatriation efforts under the Native American Graves Protection and Repatriation Act (NAGPRA). Initially, the whole concept of repatriation had to be explained, and even now the enormity of the task is not well understood. Most of HPD's Hataalii Advisory Council were appalled that ceremonial items were displayed and/or stored in museums. Again, traditional advisers are learning the technicalities of NAGPRA and the process of repatriation in the Navajo language. Knowing the Navajo language is critical for working with traditional people, and preservation programs need to be able to interpret laws and policies accurately.

As Indian tribes decide whether they should assume state historic preservation office responsibilities under the 1992 amendments of the National Historic Preservation Act, decisions should be weighed carefully. Traditional protocols should be integrated into all aspects of managing and preserving cultural resources in tribal preservation offices. Establishing cultural management programs and preservation offices are great accomplishments, but true integration of tribal customs into the programs is challenging if not impossible because of the way that federal regulations are interpreted with an emphasis on hard-core research.

NOTES

1. For a complete discussion of the organization and structure of the Navajo Nation Historic Preservation Department see Begay, this volume.

LORETTA JACKSON ■
ROBERT H. ("HANK") STEVENS

Twelve

Hualapai Tradition, Religion, and the Role of Cultural Resource Management

Traditionally, 14 bands, each having a distinct dialect and territorial homeland, made up the Hualapai Tribe.[1] In spite of the late-nineteenth-century relocation of the tribe from its more diverse tribal ancestral homelands, the Hualapai system of social organization is still in effect, maintained through descent and kinship linkages. Continuity is provided by the Hualapai language, traditional knowledge, oral history, social roles, and through the learned behaviors regarding responsibilities for and uses of natural and cultural resources (Hualapai Tribe 1993).

Resource preservation, especially of cultural resources, is one way indigenous people respond to threats to their traditional lifeways. Increasing numbers of nations and tribes of American Indians (or Native Americans) commit themselves to exercising *cultural sovereignty*. The Hualapai Tribe exemplifies this approach:

> [The] Hualapai Tribe places a great value on the oral traditions of its elders, and these traditions are an important part of the cultural heritage of the Hualapai people. When

Hualapai culture is the subject of research, it is the Hualapai people who are the cultural experts. Consequently, the Hualapai Tribe prefers that research using oral traditions be conducted by Tribal members so that sensitive information can be controlled and the Tribe can be sure it is used for appropriate purposes [Jackson, in Anyon et al. 1996:16].

In 1992 and 1993, the Hualapai Tribe embarked on a culturally based and community-supported program of cultural research as an exercise of Hualapai cultural sovereignty, with the intention of protecting cultural resources and enhancing cultural preservation. A research program was proposed, developed, and conducted through a cooperative agreement reached by the tribe with the U.S. Department of the Interior. The following discussion of this research will provide a context for understanding some of the issues facing Hualapai and other tribes concerning questions that are often associated with cultural, historical, and archaeological research.

The *Ba'a* or *Pai* (the People) have ancestral and contemporary territorial claims to the Grand Canyon and the Colorado River. This geographical placement has its origins in the Hualapai creation account, long maintained in oral history by traditional practitioners. Archaeological evidence and Hualapai rock writing also attest to the veracity of Hualapai territorial claims. Early ancestors of the Hualapai, historically spelled Walapai, are known by various terms. The name *Yuman-Hokan* comes from the language group associated with the Great Basin and includes areas surrounding the Colorado and Little Colorado drainages. *Cohonina* is used in tribal cultural-historical and oral accounts. The name derives from the Hopi term, *Ko Ho Nin'*, in reference to "the People that Live to the West" of the Little Colorado River, specifically the Hualapai and Havasupai people. However, archaeologists tend to use this term to define a prehistoric culture area that is not necessarily associated with the *Pai*. The term *Cerbat/Upland Patayan* is used in anthropology, archaeology, geography, and paleontology. Traditionally, "Old People" are referred to as *Patayan* and an ancestor is *Batayan* in the Hualapai language. These names for the early people from whom today's Hualapai are descended require further study. Care should be taken to use the terms as they are understood by the Hualapai people.

The *Walapai Papers* (U.S. Senate 1936) recount that only four generations ago (during the lives of the parents and grandparents of many of today's Hualapai elderly) many Hualapai individuals (in some cases, entire Hualapai families and family groups) were murdered by "Americans" who stole Hualapai lands, waters, and natural resources. To restrain the Hualapai from defending themselves against these crimes, and to "protect" Hualapai people from further offenses, the U.S. Department of War established a Military Reservation for the Hualapai Indians in 1881. The U.S. Department of the Interior acknowledged: "The Hualapai are rightful possessors of the real property and waters of the lands occupied by them." The federal government established the Hualapai Indian Reservation as a trust territory in an executive order in 1883. An act of Congress in 1925 again declared that the Hualapai Tribe is the legal owner of the entire Hualapai Reservation (Hualapai Tribe 1993).

The Hualapai Tribe now owns, uses, and inhabits less than 25 percent of the extensive aboriginal Hualapai ancestral homelands (which have been conservatively estimated at 5.5 to 6 million acres). The 14 bands of Hualapai people have resided in these areas since time immemorial. Through emergence, survival, subsistence, and struggle, they have sought to maintain and protect their families and homeplaces. For these reasons, to Hualapai people, their aboriginal homelands are imbued with sacredness. The Hualapai Tribe views the protection of Hualapai ancestral and sacred sites as being of utmost importance.

In 1993 a river trip by Hualapai tribal elders was conducted through the Grand Canyon for the Glen Canyon Environmental Studies program (discussed in more detail below). Hualapai elderly traditional practitioners conveyed much knowledge to the research project. In Hualapai worldview and religious thought, all the elements in and around the canyon have powers of observation and awareness. These include geological formations, the waters, the air, the wildlife, and the plants. The landscape and environment are filled with significant symbolism.

Hualapai elders maintain that all archaeological sites are sacred places—to be treated with respect. It has always been essential to protect ancestral sacred sites and to maintain the integrity of these sites. Physical contact with Hualapai ancestral cultural materials requires prayers and offerings to offset or reduce the dangerous consequences of intruding into these places of strong spirits. Some places are traditionally regarded as "off limits" (Hualapai Tribe 1993; Hualapai Tribe Office of Cultural Resources 1996).

Ancestral and sacred sites in Hualapai traditional lifeways have tangible and intangible qualities that make management and protection appear in conflict. As one elder put it: "We don't point our fingers to the places that are important to us; we do not tell; we just point with our lips or use our head for the gesture that it is over there in those hills. But we do not get specific."

Scientific techniques and archaeological management strategies for preservation and protection of cultural resources are obscure and foreign concepts to many traditionalists and religious practitioners. Discussions among and treatment by archaeologists, anthropologists, and historians of supposedly inanimate material objects, artifacts, and architecture are usually alien and appear disrespectful in the thinking and worldviews of traditional practitioners.

The Hualapai Tribe's Office of Cultural Resources and Department of Natural Resources have worked together to develop an ecosystem management program. This program has created a balance between traditional cultural practices and scientific methods to manage our resources effectively. The success of this integrated program will affect future generations of Hualapai people by ensuring the long-term yield and sustainability of our resources.

In order to seek balance, as difficult as it may be, it is often necessary to identify the cause(s) of imbalance. As demonstrated by the preceding summary of the historic encounters between Hualapais and Americans, the relationship has at times been sorely troubled with injustice and suffering. In many cases, materials from early cultures were removed from their contexts as though they were prizes of conquest by governmental agencies, educational institutions, and museums, which funded and professionally rewarded archaeologists (who were perceived by the indigenous peoples as little more than looters). Although these are worst cases, this pattern of behavior did occur, and it persists to a degree among some archaeologists, anthropologists, and historians.

A more subtle yet nonetheless harmful practice that continues to offend traditional practitioners among indigenous peoples is that anthropologists and historians extract knowledge from tribal cultures, claim exclusive interpretive authority and intellectual property rights, and exploit this knowledge in and as a domain unique to academics. It has been a common practice for primary sources of traditional knowledge and practices to be objectified as "informants" (at times romantically characterized as "the last members of their tribes," with academic opinions rendered regarding the supposed extinction or disappearance of the tribal culture, group, knowledge, or practice in question). Of course, this practice seems like nothing less than cultural genocide to traditionalists in the tribes. Traditional cultural practitioners warn us about these and other threats to our cultural continuity.

Catastrophic declines in American Indian populations by the end of the nineteenth and the beginning of the twentieth centuries spurred many anthropologists and archaeologists into salvage and curational modes of conducting research about the "vanishing" American Indians. A great deal of anthropological research was produced, some of which yielded reliable and accurate records of American Indian cultures (e.g., Boas, Powell, Kroeber). However, as American Indian populations began a phase of recovery, many traditional cultures survived, persisted, and even thrived. When these socially diverse groups began to reassert political, territorial, and cultural sovereignty, anthropologists, archaeologists, and historians often split ranks in disputes among themselves—and often against the tribes—as to the validity of tribal claims. The pattern persists today.

Partly as a response to pressures from tribal, federal, and state laws and regulations, the problems and inequities inherent in these situations are being addressed by increasing numbers of archaeologists, anthropologists, and historians in discussions and consultations with American Indian and Alaskan Native tribes.

The example of Hualapai Tribe is helpful here. In 1991 a Hualapai Tribe cultural resources program was started. Our first experiences with archaeologists demonstrated that the professional practices of collection, interpretation, and curation were extremely ethnocentric. Anthropologists and historians rely on a paradigm that history began in North America with the introduction of European systems of writing; the human experiences of the thousands of years of cultures of indigenous peoples is off-handedly labeled "prehistoric." Implementation of archaeological procedures has been laden with the colonial residue of Euroamerican concepts regarding western scientific-technological expertise in juxtaposition with the "primitive" cultures of Hualapai and other indigenous peoples. As we see it, this goes hand-in-hand with commercial exploitation of lands and resources according to what the market can bear and with the fact that this exploitation is the primary impetus for natural and cultural resource identification, control, and management (Stevens 1992).

Too often, the federal government has failed or fallen short in exercising its trust responsibility. Federal and state officials were charged with the responsibility of defining and managing *our* traditional cultural resources. But American society as a whole, and many American historians, archaeologists, and anthropologists, specifically ignored the need for or minimized any interactions with the Hualapai and other tribes (there are and have been exceptions). Failure of trust responsibility led us to feel distrust.

There are numerous examples. The National Park Service's (NPS) criteria for evaluation in the National Register of Historic Places fail to adequately recognize the roles and histories of North America's indigenous peoples in terms other than those subsidiary to the historical experience of the United States of America.

Superficially imposed political boundary lines and jurisdictions have restricted Hualapai people's free exercise of religion. Our oral traditions and ceremonial activities are connected with the dimension of space, and certain locations have significance to our traditional cultural practitioners (Hualapai Tribe 1993). For example, American Indian pictographs are characterized by many anthropologists as "abstract art." Yet knowledgeable Hualapai elders can read many specific details in the accounts recorded in our ancestral rock writing. Labels that we do not use and with which we do not agree are applied to our beliefs and practices. Traditional Hualapai beliefs in the consciousness of elements in the natural environment and the presence of spirits in certain places are simply that; they are not adequately described as "animistic."

We came to know of the removal, collection, and sale of Hualapai and other American Indian cultural resources by professional archaeologists who were engaged in salvage operations conducted as part of economic development. We encountered archaeological practices and research findings that, according to our contextual understanding and our cultural values, were methodologically and interpretively less than adequate.

The treatment and interpretations of Hualapai ancestral materials and human remains were of critical importance to us (as they are to other tribes). A nationwide effort to address these concerns led to the passage and signing of the Native American Graves Protection and Repatriation Act in 1990. During this process, we became aware of organized, formal opposition by anthropologists and archaeologists to tribal concerns and beliefs regarding these matters (see Zimmerman, this volume). Of course, this does not lend itself to cooperative relations.

The National Environmental Policy Act has provided us with an opportunity to address our cultural concerns through environmental assessments and environmental impact statements for various federal undertakings. A measure of success along these lines is exemplified by research conducted by the Hualapai Tribe and its Office of Cultural Resources through a cooperative agreement with the U.S. Department of the Interior's Bureau of Reclamation (BOR) for the Glen Canyon Dam Environmental Impact Statement (EIS). Initially, the Bureau of Reclamation and Glen Canyon Environmental Studies formulated a research design that incorporated as many elements and linkages in the ecosystems as the scientists of many disciplines could perceive in the Grand Canyon of the Colorado River downstream from Glen Canyon Dam.

Regarding the human species, the initial research plan called for studies of recreation and aesthetics. The Hualapai Tribe's residence, occupancy, and use of the Grand Canyon system had not initially been considered as an important factor in the Grand Canyon's ecosystem—which is, in fact, the ancestral and contemporary Hualapai homeland! This horrendous oversight was rectified in part when Hualapai and the other seven tribes associated with the Grand Canyon became cooperative agencies for the purpose of the EIS. Once this status was achieved, each tribe negotiated a cooperative agreement and received sufficient funding that enabled active participation in the EIS. This ultimately led to a programmatic agreement among the tribes and the other cooperative agencies (BOR, NPS, AZSHPO, and the ACHP) for research, long-term monitoring, and management of cultural resources in the Grand Canyon.

In designing and conducting interdisciplinary research regarding the environmental, cultural, and historical features of the Colorado River corridor, the Hualapai Tribe expanded on its earlier studies (Watahomigie, Watahomigie, and Uqualla 1989) of culturally significant plant species (i.e., plants used for foods, medicines, and other purposes). Hualapai researchers had determined that "plant-gathering areas"—vicinities of Hualapai horticultural practices—were culturally important. Further significant ethnobotanical field research was accomplished through Hualapai participation in the Glen Canyon Environmental Studies program; additional ethnobotanical research in tributary canyons on the south side of the canyon was undertaken in the first phase of a project funded through a National Park Service grant (Hualapai Tribe Office of Cultural Resources 1995a). Many riparian zones in the ancestral homelands of the Hualapai are now in the juris-dictions of federal agencies and private ranchers. Although the Grand Canyon's abundant riparian vegetation is taken for granted by most non-Indians who visit the Canyon (most of whom are brought in by commercial "river runners"), Hualapai people are profoundly aware, even reverent, regarding the amount and availability of arrow weeds, willows, medicinal herbs, and food sources. For the Hualapai people, this is about their long-term survival as a cultural people (Hualapai Tribe Office of Cultural Resources 1995b). It is also about their management of these cultural resources. The Hualapai Tribe is engaged in a program of assessing the plant communities and developing effective methods for monitoring, with the goal of restoring the range of traditional cultural practices that will make long-term sustainable yields of these native plants possible.

The principles of collaborative research used by the Hualapai Tribe in design of the Glen Canyon Environmental Studies program can be summarized as follows:

Hualapai cultural scholars and traditional cultural practitioners and the Hualapai government are legally acknowledged to have an active, authoritative role in determinations regarding identification, description, monitoring, and management of Hualapai "sites" and cultural properties and resources. These determinations should take place within the contexts of the Hualapai cultural, political, social, religious, and economic systems, with advisement from the Hualapai Cultural Advisory Committee and the Hualapai Tribe Office of Cultural Resources and with reference to any and all impacts to these sites and systems. This process is not only mandated by legislation and regulation designed to protect Hualapai civil and property rights, it is also theoretically sound in terms of the conduct of scientific and humanities research. It is appropriate and necessary, therefore, that Hualapai cultural scholars be actively engaged in the peer review process regarding research designs, documentation, and results.

Tribal, federal, and state governments and their respective agencies need to interact collaboratively, in mutual consultation, and as cosignatories to any agreements affecting Hualapai cultural and natural resources. The Hualapai Tribe is a *sovereign nation.* Management policies and operations regarding cultural resources, natural resources, and/or public lands must not be in derogation of Hualapai territorial and cultural sovereignty. Government-to-government interactions are required by law. Failure by any party to adhere to these protocols will seriously jeopardize any collaborative research and negate any public benefit that might have accrued because of the efforts of the Hualapai Tribe and its traditional practitioners.

As a result of developing and conducting programs using multiple methods of research (e.g., archaeology, oral history, ethnographic interviews in the Hualapai language, site visits, life experience narratives, rock writing (petroglyph) research, ethnobotany, mapping and recording of place names), we find greater convergence and validity in the findings as well as in the methods (Stevens 1992, 1995). It is the burden of the tribe to provide reliable evidence for our ancestral and territorial affiliations, our cultural and natural resources, our traditional cultural practices and religious activities. We find that we can use methods of scientific and historical research to fulfill this task. By developing workable partnerships and collaborations with archaeologists and other scientific, social, cultural, and historical researchers whom we find over time to be trustworthy, the adversarial stance between the tribes and the anthropologists can be reduced, and more effective research can yield important findings beneficial for all involved.

NOTE

1. The 14 Hualapai bands are Cerbat Mountain (White Rock Water), Grass Springs, Clay Springs, Milkweed Springs, Peach Springs, Pine Springs (Stinking Water), Blue-Green Water (Cataract Canyon), Hackberry Springs, Walapai Mountain (Pine Tree), Big Sandy River, Mahone Mountain, Juniper Mountain, Burro Creek, and Red Rock. Of these, the Red Rock Band had completely intermingled with the other Hualapai bands by the period of European American contact, and it is no longer recognized as a distinct band. The Blue-Green Water Band is now known as the Havasupai Tribe, a sovereign, federally recognized tribe.

Thirteen

A Me-Wuk Perspective on Sierran Archaeology

The Sierran Me-Wuk people of Central California for many years have been vitally concerned with the rapidly accelerating loss of our cultural landscapes contained within our aboriginal territory. As we have watched and reflected with sorrow, our occupation, gathering, and cemetery areas, and our ceremonial and spiritual landscapes have been destroyed as a result of direct and indirect impacts from projects on both private and public lands. The direction the nonnative society has taken has been to erase all evidence of our presence from the land.

This purposeful cultural eradication demanded our immediate attention. The Sierran Me-Wuk people chose to address cultural resource management immediately and to take major steps in a more positive direction than had been done in the past when we believed we could do nothing. We began to address these issues by forming a coalition of Sierran Me-Wuk people so we could directly impact the future of archaeology in our aboriginal territory. In this essay I share the ways we implemented activities that had significant results for the preservation of our cultural and traditional heritage for future generations. One of the rewards of our work has been the recognition of and the development of a working relationship between the Central Sierra Me-Wuk Cultural and Historic Preservation Committee (hereafter Central Sierra Me-Wuk Committee) and various federal, state, and local agencies. But the most significant reward has been the elevation of acknowledgment and respect of the Sierran Me-Wuk by the nonnative professionals, public agencies, and the private sector.

The Tuolumne Band of Me-Wuk Indians, a federally recognized tribe located on several rancherias in the Central Sierras of California, sanctioned a committee that would provide a forum for the Sierran Me-Wuk community to address cultural resource issues. The tribe sanctioned the Central Sierra Me-Wuk Committee to review, discuss, and implement activities surrounding the identification, interpretation, and management of historic sites within our Sierran Me-Wuk territory.

I was delegated committee spokesperson by the tribe. Holding to tradition, a person from the tribe is chosen to speak on behalf of the people. A spokesperson is a carrier of words to ensure that the people are heard and acknowledged. I speak on behalf of our tribe for our cultural resource issues.

Soon after its inception, the committee invited other Sierran Me-Wuk communities to participate in our cultural resource program. The Central Sierra Me-Wuk Committee thus incorporated federally recognized tribes and nonfederally recognized tribes, allowing all groups to participate equally under the umbrella coverage by a federally recognized group. The bands and/or councils presently involved are two federally recognized tribes, Tuolumne Band of Me-Wuk Indians (Tuolumne County) and Jackson Rancheria/Band of Miwok Indians (Amador County), and three nonfederally recognized Me-Wuk Bands and/or councils, American Indian Council of Mariposa County (Mariposa County), Calaveras Band of MiWuk Indians (Calaveras County), and Sierra Native American Council (Amador County).

Our active involvement in Sierran archaeology began in February 1991. Since then, the Central Sierra Me-Wuk Committee has actively sought to participate in archaeological and cultural resource management studies. During this short time, we have been innovative in the development of agreement documents that set forth procedures for the disposition of cultural items encountered during ground-disturbing activities, thereby assuring preservation and/or proper mitigation measures for resources located on the cultural landscapes of what is now legally considered federal, state, and private lands. We have worked closely with various project proponents, including federal, state, and local agencies, to assure our native community the right to be involved in the compliance process. We have been successful in negotiating these agreement documents prior to any earth-disturbing activities.

The committee's responsibilities and activities developed as we became more involved in various projects. We began by notifying federal, state, and local agencies of the committee and its functions and requested that we be acknowledged and included in the notification process regarding proposed projects. Also at this time, I realized the significance of scientific documentation and the knowledge required to review the voluminous documents generated for each project. As I began to review documents, I realized that the committee representatives lacked the education, professional training, and associated resources to participate in a professional and timely manner in the compliance process.

Being truly blessed by our Grandfathers, on our first project we were introduced to and began to work with Michael Moratto and Dorothea Theodoratus, scholarly authorities on our traditional territory and well respected by the Sierran Me-Wuk people. They have given generously of their expertise and time to educate and train the committee members in all aspects of historic preservation law and the associated processes. From their inspiration and encouragement, I realized the imminent need to educate and train our committee in the compliance process. It became apparent that professionally trained Native American monitors would ensure that our cultural and traditional heritage would be properly identified, documented, and preserved, and that all phases of project investigations would adhere to federal and state laws. With guidance from Moratto and Theodoratus, I developed a curriculum for a training class for the Sierran Me-Wuk people and other California natives to serve in the capacity of Native American monitors. With the assistance of these and other recognized anthropologists and our local community college, we provided a college-certified 12-hour class on monitoring. In addition to the anthropologists, two state agency officials instructed us in the legal aspects, Dwight Dutschke, associate governmental program analyst of the California State Office of Historic Preservation, and Larry Myers, executive secretary of the California State Native American Heritage Commission. This was an excellent opportunity for the native people to learn about the significant roles and duties the Office of Historic Preservation and the Native American Heritage Commission fulfills for California native people.

The course curriculum provided intensive and comprehensive training on historic preservation laws (both federal and state) and an introduction to various aspects of archaeology and ethnography. Monitor trainees learned basic anthropology research skills including interview techniques, how to read and understand site forms, use of maps and compasses, artifact identification, and most important of all, accurate record keeping. We provided information on procedures to follow in case human remains are encountered during field investigations; we reviewed the proposed draft of the California State Primary Record and Archaeological Site Record Forms; and we addressed the role of the "California State Recognized Most Likely Descendant List," established and maintained by the Native American Heritage Commission.

Our classes have been very well received by the committee representatives and other California natives and have proven to be very useful for the participants. As a result, the committee representatives and other California natives have been able to participate in and have established credible standing in cultural resource management. We successfully certified 40 Native American monitors, ranging in age from 16 to 62.

The most significant hurdle for the committee was to bridge the gap between the native community and the archaeology community. For many years, professional archaeologists did not consult with the local native community because they thought our input would be of no value. Early scholars had already provided "acceptable scientific theory" regarding native values. The native people of today were considered too "civilized" (too acculturated), and it was believed they had not carried forth their traditional cultural heritage. This obviously has not been the case. Some professional archaeologists are not even cognizant of what tribe occupies our area, let alone know how to approach or communicate with tribal members. And if communication was attempted, it was usually via a letter or telephone call requesting information.

On the other hand, the native community has had deep suspicions about these intruders. Why do they come and dig up our ancestors? Why do they destroy our ancestors' areas? Why do they destroy our gathering areas? They cannot be trusted! Why are they always writing or telephoning us for information when we do not know who they are? They only want to make money off of us! We never get anything in return, not even reports! Take, take, take, is all they do! I believe this suspicious attitude on the part of the native people and the reticence to communicate on the part of the nonnative community was the greatest hurdle I had to overcome.

But as time passes, and with some effort, changes in attitude may also occur. After the native community professional training, we better understood the "why" of archaeology and the significance of ethnography. Archaeologists now realize that the significant value of a resource may not be totally within their specified project boundary and that impacts on a cultural landscape may be far reaching. These professionals must learn to look at and listen to the surrounding area as well as the circumscribed area. The site's "integrity" can only be ascertained when all aspects are considered (see the second contribution by Fuller in this volume). As a result of these efforts, the professional archaeologists who perform investigations in the Sierran Me-Wuk territory now seek native community involvement. They are now cognizant of how essential information from the native community is in any determination of the significance of cultural landscapes. Further, this communication has resulted in the development of better working relationships. This cross-cultural experience has directly influenced professional archaeologists' perspectives by introducing the elements of understanding, respect, dignity, and sensitivity toward our traditional cultural heritage. These are the essential elements of anthropology.

The committee became aware early on of the significant value of agreement documents. We began by implementing policies developed by consensus so our future would take a more positive turn. These agreements would be our assurance and a tool for compliance with historic preservation laws and would ensure our right to participate. They, in turn, would ensure that our ancestral remains would be treated with the integrity and respect due them and would ensure the proper disposition of human remains, associated and unassociated funerary objects, and other cultural items discovered in our territory. We realized these agreement documents should address all project activities, such as biological, archaeological, and geomorphological investigations, as well as all planning and construction activities on a project that might result in the inadvertent discovery of human remains, associated and unassociated funerary objects, and other cultural items. Agreement documents outline provisions for establishing an area for reburial, providing for a Native American monitor, and requiring annual review of the agreement if the project is ongoing. Copies of the executed agreement documents are sent to all the project contractors and subconsultants, to the county sheriff/coroner, and to the California State Native American Heritage Commission. An unexpected benefit of these signed agreements is the procedure for quick resolution of unanticipated problems during the construction phase. At this point, all parties to the agreement have developed a feeling of trust and respect, which allows them to move quickly to resolve problems, avoiding substantial project delays.

As our knowledge of historic preservation compliance has increased, we have become more aware of the essential role of the Native American Graves Protection and Repatriation Act of 1990. Under this act, the section on intentional excavations has had an immediate effect on archaeological investigations. The act also mandates consultation with the native community. And, as prescribed by the act, the consultation process results in the establishment of detailed agreement documents between the native community and the federal land-managing agency. Committee representatives and other California natives asked me to organize and develop a training class to educate them on compliance and explore the far-reaching implications of this law. This successful training class resulted in a request by tribes in Southern California for this specialized training. Our most recent class was conducted at the University of California, Los Angeles, in January 1996.

In conclusion, I would like to discuss private land ownership in our area. Recognizing our serious efforts, the majority of owners now seek our local native community's involvement of their proposed land projects. Acknowledgment of the native community's ancestral lands demonstrates their respect for our cultural and traditional heritage. We frequently receive requests to walk land now owned privately and to make recommendations for cultural landscapes preservation. This is another positive result of the committee's active involvement in preservation. In many cases, anonymous phone calls alert us to possible desecrations on private and public lands. The caller may be employed on a project and may have been given specific instructions not to report any cultural resource finding or risk being fired, may be the adjoining landowner, or may wish not to disclose an identity for fear of community reprisal. Nevertheless, we are grateful that some members of the nonnative society acknowledge and respect our ancestral lands and are not afraid to demonstrate their concern publicly.

In closing, we, the Sierran Me-Wuk people, have taken major steps in developing and planning the future of Sierran archaeology and cultural resource management. One positive result is the preservation of our traditional cultural heritage for future generations. The doors of communication must continue to be opened so that a working relationship is established and maintained. We, the Me-Wuk people, must be taken seriously. We believe the acknowledgment of our rich and proud heritage will continue to benefit the state of California and the United States of America, and specifically those people living and working in the Sierra Me-Wuk territory. I caution you, do not let the direct act of annihilation of the past continue. The Sierra Me-Wuk people have demonstrated a unity in achieving our cultural resource goals. Let us, the professional archaeological community and the Native American community, continue to work together and learn from one another.

As a spokesperson for the Central Sierra Me-Wuk Cultural and Historic Preservation Committee, I still wonder to what degree would professional archaeologists work with the native people had federal and state laws not required their involvement?

Relevance of Archaeology to Tribes

Fourteen

Straight Talk and Trust

I am a writer and Caddo historian, but I suspect I was invited to participate in the SAA forum and contribute to this volume because 21 years ago my research created a need for me to understand how archaeologists reach their conclusions. It was then that I first stuck a metric tape in my pocket, picked up a trowel, and scraped my fingers screening dirt during an Arkansas Archeological Survey/Society Training Program and University of Arkansas Field School at a Caddo site. There I studied fundamentals in a classroom, learned basic excavation techniques on site, and earned provisional certification under strict tutelage.

That same summer, in Shreveport, Louisiana, I became acquainted with the late Clarence H. Webb, often referred to as the father of Caddoan archaeology. It was also then that I began a long-term friendship with Hiram G. "Pete" Gregory at Northwestern Louisiana State University in Natchitoches. He impressed me with his strong belief that the science of archaeology cannot and should not be isolated from connection with living descendants of a defined culture. This was not a widely accepted theory in the early 1970s.

Since that summer of my archaeological initiation, I've participated in other field schools, inspected many sites, and learned to read the esoteric language archaeologists use when writing reports. Along the way I've enjoyed meeting and working with a hundred or more professional and avocational archaeologists in the Caddoan area of Arkansas, Louisiana, Texas, and Oklahoma. I respect the work of most, rely on the expertise of some, and trust the advice of a few. Just as elders in my Caddo Tribe have taught me Caddo history, archaeologists have taught me Caddo prehistory.

In January 1993 my tribal chairman asked me to serve as an unpaid cultural liaison for contacts outside the Caddo Tribe. A few months later, I became the tribe's unpaid Native American Graves Protection and Repatriation Act (NAGPRA) representative. When a 1995 National Park Service grant made it possible for us to staff a NAGPRA office, I withdrew from active participation. I currently chair the Caddo Heritage Committee.

My experiences in fulfilling these duties, together with participation in a half dozen NAGPRA training workshops and various conferences where tribal representatives shared experiences, lead me to conclude that tribal views of archaeology can generally be grouped according to whether or not a tribe remains within its aboriginal territory. In either case, the relationship between tribes and archaeologists appears scarred by distrust.

The people of those tribes still occupying the land of their ancestors have an unbroken link with their past. The youngest generation sometimes lives on the site of an ancient village. Their parents and grandparents are familiar with sacred grounds and can locate the graves of ancestors. They know when outsiders with an interest in their past come to investigate, survey the surface of their ground, or dig below it. For too long, these people had little control over such activities on their reservation and no control over ancestral territory now owned by nontribal corporations, ranchers, or other individuals. With or without tribal agreement, excavations were conducted and items were carried away, along with pieces of the people's pride. There should be no wonder that archaeologists find it hard to win the trust of these people.

For the people of tribes who were coerced into leaving their original homelands, either by treaty or threat of violence, the experience is different. Generations have been born in a foreign land, and the youngest have scant knowledge of the homeland occupied by their ancestors. Few, if any, of their parents or grandparents have had the opportunity to visit the old homeland, but all know where their people came from, and the feeling of attachment to that place is strong. Removed from the lands of their ancestors, the people did not know when strangers came to investigate old home sites and sacred places. Until recently, only a few were aware that bones of the ancient ones and objects buried beside them had been dug from the earth, examined, analyzed, discarded, sold for profit, or stored on a museum shelf. Tribal members are incensed and saddened by the shocking discovery that *anyone* would violate a grave. They find little consolation in being told that archaeological evidence documents their cultural history and their people's long occupation in the old homeland. They have preserved important aspects of their ancient culture, they know where they came from, and they can discern no real benefit coming to them from archaeological science. Is it any wonder that so many distrust the motives of archaeologists?

Implementation of the consultation mandated by NAGPRA has promoted an exchange of information leading to better understanding between tribes and the community of archaeologists. At least we are coming to know one another and talking about mutual benefits. At most we are able to veil past hurts and establish trust.

NAGPRA, however, applies only to lands that are controlled or owned by the United States and to tribal lands. No authority is given to tribes when sites are discovered or burials are disturbed on ancestral lands that are now privately owned. State unmarked burial laws, the National Historic Preservation Act (NHPA), and the Archeological Resources Protection Act (ARPA) also have limited application. Lobbyists for certain agencies, institutions, industries, and politically influential artifact collectors weakened the language of unmarked burial laws before they were enacted. The effect of the NHPA and ARPA depends on how willingly the rules, regulations, and intent of the acts are enforced by decision makers for the Army Corps of Engineers, National Park Service, Fish and Wildlife Service, archaeological contract firms, the Environmental Protection Agency, state historic preservation offices, museums, corporations, private landowners, local law enforcement, and various other state and federal agencies, institutions, or individuals. In some instances, lack of familiarity with legislation or personal bias blinds a person from seeing the *intent* behind the laws. In other cases, a deliberately narrow interpretation of regulations is used to exempt an agency or individual from protecting or preserving a site.

When this happens, tribal effort to influence the preservation of a site or to protect a disturbed burial is discredited; tribal sovereignty is disparaged; religious and spiritual practices are disregarded; requests for responsible action are denied; and both preservation law and archaeology lose relevance for Native Americans. The greatest affront in my experience is the policy of a colonel in a Corps of Engineers district office, who, following advice of Corps' attorneys rather than that of the agency's archaeologists, the state historic preservation officer, and the Advisory Council on Historic Preservation, chose to use the narrowest interpretation of regulations and ignore the intent of NHPA. By doing so, he abrogated responsibility for aiding in the protection of human remains eroding from a riverbank.

I do not imply that the majority of decision makers involved with archaeology are unwilling to support both the word and the intent of legislation. Aside from that dismal experience with a Corps of Engineers district's policy, one speech by a biological anthropologist whose primary concern seemed to be that limitations on skeletal analysis would destroy his career, and the knowledge that human remains and artifacts have been taken from the earth by a landowner who exhibits them in his private profit-making museum on the same property, I've been encouraged by an increasing sensitivity toward the concerns of Native Americans.

Mutual respect is improving. Proposals for partnerships are emerging. Tribes that have established their own preservation offices have invited non-Indian archaeologists to join their boards or advisory councils. Other tribes have formed committees willing to reassess the relative value of archaeology as a source for knowledge concerning tribal history, health issues, and territory.

I know of one proposal that is an especially hopeful sign that archaeology will increase in relevance for Native Americans. It is a suggestion that professional archaeologists should consider a practicable plan beyond the implementation of NAGPRA. The plan offered for consideration is that professional archaeologists assist tribes in identifying grant sources and preparing grant proposals; offer expertise and consultation relative to federal and state laws that affect archaeological and cultural properties of direct interest to tribes; and direct archaeological activity toward establishing definitions of aboriginal territory. All tribes, and in particular smaller tribes with few resources of their own, might perceive benefit if such steps are taken.

For now, there are steps that each individual involved with archaeology can take to promote trust and demonstrate that your work has relevancy for Native Americans.

You can make sure that the tribe is not the last to learn that you have made a discovery or that a planned activity may result in the excavation of human remains or cultural items (despite regulations to the contrary, failure to notify the tribe or a long delay in notification often happens).

You can reserve scientific language for reports issued to your colleagues and regularly communicate your archaeological findings to tribes in plain language that nonprofessionals can understand. (Your discipline may require references such as "sites xxx and xxx are found in a biotic transition zone," but such a description has about as much meaning for tribal representatives as Inuit language has for you.)

You can avoid professional acronyms, or at least define them, when communicating site information to tribes. You can be mindful of the fact that your colleagues recognize the significance of strata colorations by number, but, without interpretation, the data may mean no more to tribal representatives than a child's paint-by-number chart. Your colleagues also identify foci, phases, classifications assigned to sherds and lithics, but an untrained tribal representative probably does not.

The most important thing you can do is to question yourself. Ask "Does excavation add anything we don't already know about the cultural history of people or is collection of scientific data just an excuse?" Ask yourself "Will analysis of human remains actually contribute to the well-being of living descendants, substantiate their territorial claim, identify genetic traits that aid diagnoses and current treatment of disease, or will my analysis primarily be of benefit to the advancement of *my* professional standing or the satisfaction of *my* scientific curiosity?" Ask yourself "Is the protection of sites from vandalism or destruction part of my job, and am I willing to argue strongly with anyone who thinks it is not?" And, though you may be tired of hearing it, ask yourself "If this were the grave of one of my ancestors, would I want better reasons for excavation?"

Remaining shadows of doubt that cloud Native America's perception of the relevance of archaeology can be dispelled when each person whose position influences the direction of American archaeology can justify his or her work with honest answers to questions like these. Accept responsibility for the protection of cultural resources, acknowledge tribal sovereignty, respect traditional religious and spiritual beliefs—these tenets are the touchstones of trust.

Fifteen

The Role of Archaeology in the Seminole Tribe of Florida

The role archaeology now plays in the Seminole Tribe of Florida would have been unthinkable 50 years ago. The practice of archaeology was something that white scholars did and that Seminoles did not do. It was understood that once a native person was laid to rest in a wooden box on an isolated hammock somewhere in the Everglades, the place became a site of reverence and spirits. No Seminole thought of returning to disturb or to alter the burial in any way. To do so would have risked the wrath of evil spirits or a state of spiritual disharmony, which would jeopardize the health and state of mind of Seminoles. Rituals were performed by medicine men for the protection and well-being of the Seminoles in general during the death and burial of deceased tribal members.

We knew that Euroamericans would do things that the Seminoles would not think of doing. The whites were "scientific" and did not believe in "superstition." They were capable of excavating a burial mound, digging up the human remains, and studying them. They did not fear any spirits. They kept their spiritual and physical selves separate, so they could do all this and not feel the trepidation and trembling that the Seminoles felt when confronted with the prospect of excavating burial mounds. To this day, none of the tribe's college graduates is an archaeologist.

With these thoughts as background, I want to discuss the role of archaeology in the Seminole Tribe of Florida. Other tribes and groups share the heritage and culture of the Seminole Tribe of Florida. The two other federally recognized tribes are the Miccosukee Tribe of Indians of Florida and the Seminole Nation of Oklahoma. Independent groups such as the Independent Traditional Seminole Tribe of Florida choose not to belong to any of the federally recognized tribes (Goss 1995). My discussion will concern only the Seminole Tribe of Florida and our relationship with archaeology and archaeologists within recent times.

As the Seminole Tribe has progressed into a modern tribe complete with economic development and self-sufficiency, we realize that there are cultural resources that must be studied in order to be protected. Certain knowledge has to be learned. We must know what is on the reservations, their number, their location, and their characteristics. I am talking about burial mounds, middens, historical Seminole war forts, trading posts, and any other historical sites and associated data.

In 1992 the Seminole Tribe applied for and obtained a National Park Service grant for a project called the Seminole Heritage Survey. The plan was to contract with the Archaeological and Historical Conservancy (AHC) of Miami, Florida, to compile information on the known Seminole historical and archaeological sites throughout Florida. It was "the first systematic attempt to provide such an inventory since no such list had been available to the Seminole Tribe of Florida, who are keenly interested in adding to the tribal knowledge and public awareness of their heritage" (Carr and Steele 1993:2). The idea for this project came from earlier work with the Seminole Tribe's Big Cypress Reservation (Figure 2), the largest of the five Seminole reservations in Florida (Goss 1995:Map 4). That work was done with a small grant from the Florida Division of Historic Resources. It resulted in the assessment of 31 prehistoric and historical sites within the reservation boundaries. The report states: "It was obvious from the results of that survey that many of these sites had not been known to tribal members, and that this information was not only important to supplementing tribal history but to effectively managing reservation lands in regards to proposed land improvements and development" (Carr and Steele 1993:2). Nevertheless, more refinements and fieldwork are needed to get a more accurate picture of the Seminole sites of Florida.

Other work by the Archaeological and Historical Conservancy for the tribe has been done with the Housing and Citrus Farming programs. AHC has surveyed the Brighton Reservation to locate cultural resources so that home sites will avoid cultural resources, especially burial mounds. Significant findings have been made. Fieldwork in proposed citrus farming zones on both the Big Cypress and Brighton

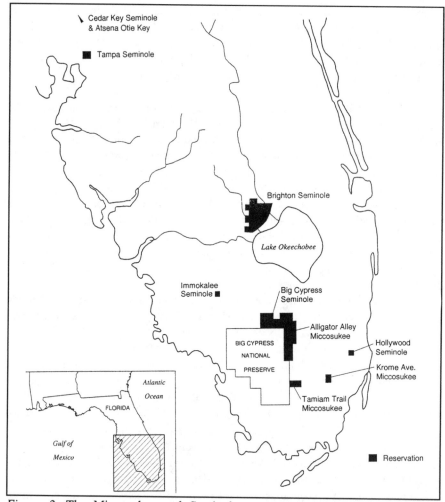

Figure 2. The Miccosukee and Seminole reservations of Florida (after Goss 1995:Figure 4). As of May 1996, a sixth Seminole Reservation (Cedar Key) has been added, near the historic site of Atsena Otie Key on the gulf coast above Tampa.

reservations has ensured that cultural resources would not be destroyed by agriculture. The tribe has had to make difficult decisions balancing the need for the protection of cultural resources and the need for business development. Archaeology has been extremely helpful and informative in business and land use planning on the reservations.

No discussion about archaeology and the Seminole Tribe would be complete without mention of the Native American Graves Protection and Repatriation Act (NAGPRA) and related activities. Because of this law and attendant requirements, the Seminole Tribe has received numerous surveys and inventories about Seminole-related artifacts, human remains, and possible items of cultural patrimony. While the tribe has not repatriated any human remains as of yet, it is only a matter of time before the Seminole human remains will be repatriated, wherever they may be in the rest of the country. We will be dependent on archaeologists who will define and identify these human remains, grave goods, and items of cultural patrimony. Of course, we will add our knowledge to this in order to make decisions regarding which items will be requested from institutions and which items will not be requested.

Because of NAGPRA and the tribe's renewed interest in both historical and precolumbian cultural resources, the public is calling the tribe more and more about commercial and private destruction of burial mounds and middens. At times, the tribe can work with the state to preserve cultural resources. Other times, it seems that destruction is inevitable. The tribe depends on the work of archaeologists in most cultural preservation work, especially material culture.

One such example is Atsena Otie Key in Cedar Key, Florida. Atsena Otie Key was the headquarters of the U.S. Army when the Second Seminole War ended in 1842. It was also a place where Seminoles who were captured or surrendered were forced to board ships heading toward the Indian Territory. A Seminole cemetery is reportedly located at this location where those who died en route were buried, although the exact location is not known. The Seminole Tribe would like to have an excavation done to locate the cemetery so that a proper memorial can be created, and some protection can be offered to the site. No additional study is envisioned other than for this purpose.

Another event that involved burials and led to creation of new reservation lands occurred in 1982. A construction company building a parking lot in downtown Tampa unearthed a cemetery. Archaeologists determined that the remains were Seminole, possibly those who were captured or surrendered and died while waiting to be deported to the Indian Territory. The chairman of the tribe, the Honorable James E. Billie, asked that the remains be reinterred in an area 10 km away. There, a Seminole Cultural Center was built over the entombment of the Seminole remains. The 8.5-acre parcel of land was brought into trust by the federal government, paving the way for the tribe to build a bingo palace and to sell cigarettes on a profitable basis. While some of the public expressed surprise about the quick development of this enterprise and the nature of the development, the majority of the tribe was in favor of the economic windfall arising from the discovery of ancestral bones. Billie remarked that it seemed providential that the bones of the tribe's ancestors reached out throughout the years to lend a financial hand to their long-suffering descendants.

In summary, I can say that the Seminole Tribe has not worked with archaeologists very long. But several conclusions can be reached about the role of archaeology toward the Seminole Tribe of Florida.

1. Archaeology is neither good or bad. The discipline is a tool that can be used to further knowledge and to support business and land use planning.
2. Most of the work of archaeology is mundane and routine. It is when archaeologists excavate graves and burial mounds that the Seminole Tribe or any Native American tribe usually becomes involved in disagreements and controversies.
3. The philosophical outlook of the Seminole Tribe may be different from those of archaeologists toward excavation of graves, burial mounds, and items of cultural patrimony. Therein lies the root of most problems between archaeologists and tribes. These problems will have to be solved in order to affect the long-term relationship between the two camps in a positive way.

In a democratic society, not everyone believes the same way, every time, on every issue. The Seminole Tribe has members whose opinions on the role of archaeologists may differ. A very traditional, fundamentalist viewpoint may state that graves and burial mounds should never be disturbed, obviating the need for a discipline such as archaeology. Very few may subscribe to the view that anything goes, and archaeologists may do whatever they want. For the most part, I agree with the traditional, fundamentalist view that graves and burial mounds should not be disturbed. If they are disturbed, they should be immediately reinterred in the same location or close to the original location. But I feel that any exceptions to this position must be spelled out.

At times, graves and burial mounds may have to be disturbed for the sake of knowledge. Study of remains may uncover information about the health of the individuals that could benefit present and future generations of Seminole tribal members. But limits as to the length and time of these studies should be agreed on by the tribe and archaeologists. Tribal concerns should be given paramount importance in the decisions.

As a modern progressive tribe, the Seminole Tribe of Florida needs archaeologists for selected projects that meet worthwhile goals. The archaeologists, in turn, must respect the cultural wishes and practices of the tribe. Therein lies the future role of archaeologists in the Seminole Tribe of Florida.

Sixteen

The Role of Archaeology on Indian Lands
The Navajo Nation

The demand for systematic archaeological work on Navajo lands was precipitated in the mid-1970s by the Navajo Indian Irrigation Project near Farmington, New Mexico. The Navajo Nation established the Cultural Resources Management Program (CRMP) to conduct that work, thus initiating modern archaeology on Navajo lands. With the passage of the Navajo Nation Cultural Resources Protection Act (Navajo Nation 1986), CRMP became the Navajo Nation Archaeology Department.

Also under the act, the Historic Preservation Department (HPD) was established to ensure compliance with federal and tribal cultural resources legislation (Begay 1991). The Navajo Nation is mandated to comply with federal laws, including laws that protect cultural resources. Today, HPD, through its office on cultural resource compliance, ensures that all cultural resource managers working on Navajo lands comply with the Archeological Resources Protection Act, the National Historic Preservation Act, and the Native American Graves Protection and Repatriation Act. In addition, archaeologists and ethnographers working on the Navajo reservation are responsible for complying with tribal laws and policies.

The Navajo Nation must respond to the needs of its citizens. All ground-disturbing activities, even obtaining one-acre homesite leases, require federal involvement. This is a tremendous task considering the size of the Navajo Nation. The Navajo Indian reservation encompasses about 25,000 square miles in Arizona, New Mexico, and Utah. The total enrollment of the Navajo Nation is about 220,000, of which 170,000 or so live on the reservation in towns and isolated settlements in an area about the size of West Virginia. Navajoland has an estimated one million archaeological sites, and each must be considered if they are to be impacted by federal undertaking. Basically, any ground-disturbing action on the Navajo reservation requires a cultural resources inventory. To meet the demands of federal and tribal legislation, the Navajo Nation employs more than one hundred archaeologists, archaeological aides, and technicians.

How are these archaeologists relevant to Navajo people? Navajo people believe they have a sacred duty to protect archaeological sites, human remains, burial items, and cultural items found on sites. Navajo traditional history incorporates all aspects of Navajoland, and many traditional people believe that non-Navajo versions of history do not contain as much information about history as their own. In short, there is a tremendous amount of Navajo traditional information regarding the preservation and management of cultural resources. We know how to take care of cultural resources—we have been doing this for centuries, long before cultural resource protection legislation existed.

HPD has made tremendous progress since its inception in incorporating traditional Navajo cultural values and teachings in its overall mission (see Martin, this volume). The department is charged with overseeing the management and protection of Navajo cultural resources, while being responsive to traditional needs. It has established a Traditional Culture Program and a Hataalii Advisory Council to give it guidance on traditional concerns. The council is made up of 16 traditional chanters: "medicine men and women" from all parts of Navajoland who specialize in various ceremonies. HPD's traditional components have been instrumental in the revision of tribal policies.

For example, in the revised burial protection policy, *Anaasazi*, not Anasazi, is defined as "the Diné term for all ancient peoples who inhabited Diné customary lands, including all peoples whom archaeologists call 'prehistoric.'" The definition has caused some commotion among archaeologists on Navajo lands, including archaeologists and cultural resource managers who work for the Navajo Nation.

Archaeologists have had a detrimental impact on Navajo culture. They have taken a perfectly good Navajo word and institutionalized it to refer only to "puebloan" peoples, assigning temporal affiliations based on material culture complexity. Many archaeologists have even offered their own interpretation of the word *Anaasazi*. By their words and actions, nonnative archaeologists seem to be trying to define the past for the Navajo people without any regard to Navajo cultural traditions. As Navajo cultural resource professionals, we are faced with cleaning up the ensuing mess. We must take the word *Anaasazi* back and apply it as it is traditionally used. Perhaps this calls for an overall revision of the archaeological nomenclature.

The role of the archaeologist on Navajo lands is completely intertwined with Section 106 of the National Historic Preservation Act. Very little personal archaeological research is allowed on Navajo lands, especially if that research involves excavation, removal, or destruction/disturbance of the resource. Most archaeologists who work for the Navajo Nation, as well as for private contractors, are involved in surveying, writing reports, and submitting them to HPD for compliance review. Although the department would like to see more Navajo involvement in archaeological projects, the only legal mechanism is the enforcement of the Navajo Preference in Employment Act. This does not necessarily guarantee Navajo input into projects conducted on Navajo lands. A few projects like the proposed paving of the Navajo Mountain road require more intensive work, such as excavations. Often, what archaeologists do and how the Navajo public reacts to their work can lead to confrontation and raises many issues.

For instance, the Anaasazi are part of Navajoland, part of Navajo history, and part of the Navajo people today. It doesn't matter if an archaeological site is Basketmaker II or III, or Pueblo I, II, III, or IV, or if it is Archaic or Paleoindian; for Navajo it is all Anaasazi. No "prehistory" exists in Navajo traditions. Our history begins at the creation of life and at the creation of this world. As a people, we sing the creation of the earth, the placement of mountains, the waters, and the people. Navajo people can tell you their version (and with remarkable specificity of detail) about what happened at Kin Teel (Pueblo Bonito in Chaco Canyon), Tse niihooghan (Cliff Place at Mesa Verde), Kin nii na'ighaii (White House in Canyon de Chelley), Betatakin and Keetseel in Navajo National Monument, and even the Grand Canyon.

Navajo people came from a number of ethnic groups who became clans within our nation. Each of these clans brought with them a rich history and cultural tradition that contributed to the overall Navajo culture. The story of the diverse gathering of peoples from different areas explains who we are as a people and where we came from. To this day we honor that history by preserving and strengthening our traditions.

Yet, very few nonnative archaeologists accept our knowledge and understanding of what they call "prehistory." In their view, we cannot possibly know anything about archaeological sites and the people who inhabited them because we have the hogan, our traditional round home, and live in dispersed residences. What would we know about community living, pottery, masonry, corn, dancing, pictographs and petroglyphs, turquoise, or even cotton? The archaeological interpretation of our past ignores and refuses to accept the traditional interaction between past cultures and Navajo people.

In 1992 the Navajo Nation received funding from the Bureau of Reclamation to document Navajo cultural resources and history in the Grand Canyon as part of the environmental impact statement for the operation of Glen Canyon Dam near Page, Arizona. Before this project, the general public, the National Park Service, and even some Navajo people did not believe that the Navajo people and their ceremonies had any connection to the Grand Canyon. Through the Navajo Nation's participation in the project, we were able to document the oral history of the canyon, identify specific sites (trails, plant and mineral gathering areas, etc.) of importance to the Navajo people, and to make management recommendations to the bureau and the park service on all resources important to Navajo people (Roberts, Begay, and Kelley 1995). This project is only one example of intimate Navajo knowledge of their homeland. Cultural resource managers who work in the Grand Canyon must now recognize Navajo history in the canyon.

Given Navajo traditional cultural knowledge of the past, why does the Navajo Nation still require archaeological contractors and its own Archaeology Department to classify sites by cultural affiliation, period, and formal type according to the Pecos Classification, when this activity has no meaning for the Navajo people and, to be honest, little or no meaning to modern archaeology either? To put it simply, it is because nonnative archaeologists wrote the cultural resource laws, regulations, policies, field recording standards, report writing standards, and even the personnel descriptions for the positions they occupy.

Increasingly, we see Navajo archaeologists in the work force. Many of them are faced with choosing between the archaeological discipline and tribal tradition. Must they choose between the two? I don't think so. I've worked as an archaeologist on Navajo lands, and although I do complain about archaeologists and archaeology, I know they are an essential part of development on the reservation. Like many Indian nations, the Navajo Nation is dependent on federal monies and agencies to construct roads, houses, and power and water lines. Federal involvement means compliance with federal cultural resource laws, and that, my friends, makes archaeologists essential on Indian lands.

Furthermore, the Navajo Nation must sometimes consult with other Indian tribes (see Swidler and Cohen, this volume) when it comes to the management of our resources on our lands—resources that we as a people have a long cultural tradition of managing. This consultation and the resultant management decisions may not always honor Navajo traditions. Some Indian tribes who claim affinity to past cultures do not acknowledge Navajo traditions, and this is problematic for all parties involved. Native and nonnative archaeologists are often caught in the middle of these controversies. Of course, archaeologists on each side support their employers, whose views may also contradict conventional archaeological theory (see Dongoske and Anyon, this volume). Many questions arise and beg to be answered, and some just can't be, but that's okay.

Often, conducting archaeology on Navajo lands leads to questioning our own traditions and our judgments about preservation. For instance, traditional people want archaeological sites protected, but when it is within a right-of-way for a highway it may not always be possible to "let sleeping *Anaasazi* lie." We must sometimes make decisions between tradition and modern conveniences. It would be much better to make decisions based on our traditions. If traditionalists concede to excavations, are they foregoing their values so they can have an all-weather paved road serving their community? Is it okay to leave the dead in place, cap the site, pave the road over it, and drive over the dead on a daily basis? I believe traditionalists who agree to data recovery realize the alternatives and consent to disinterment and reburial. Every day we must make decisions to preserve our land and traditions, and it is not always easy.

Clearly, archaeology has a vital role to play on the Navajo Nation. Archaeological techniques such as surveying and excavating are indispensable in federal undertakings—and these undertakings benefit Navajo people. They help the public receive the services most of the people in the United States already enjoy: running water, electricity, paved roads, and other amenities. Archaeology as a purely academic discipline, and archaeologists who have "pure" research on their agenda, have an unwelcome role in the lives of Navajo people. Navajos know who we are as a people, where we came from, who and how past cultures figure into our past, and we do not need nonnative archaeologists giving us misguided information based on "research."

What can be done to change the way archaeologists do business on Navajo lands and, for that matter on all Indian lands? An easy question to ask, but not easy to answer.

First, recognize the people's version of their own history. Indian interpretation of the past is just as valid as yours, and you can only benefit by listening to us.

Second, make archaeology as a discipline useful to Indian people. Counting sherds and lithics and presenting the results in complex graphs are useful only to archaeologists (and sometimes not even then). Make your work available and understandable to the community with whom you are dealing.

Third, be adventurous and interact with the people—see how they live, eat their foods, and go about their daily lives. You may find out how those "unidentifiable ceremonial objects" are used.

Tribes need to do their part as well. The Navajo people, as well as other Indian peoples, need to get involved in archaeology. Tribes need to encourage young people to get into the field of archaeology. The more native archaeologists there are, the more quickly we can make positive changes. Indian peoples must take control of the archaeology that is being done on their lands.

Most important, archaeologists must consider the larger issues of cultural preservation and the consequences their discipline has on Indian cultural identity.

The discipline of anthropology has defined the Navajo as "Athabascan." Our children are taught in schools that we as a people came across the Bering Strait, and that we only settled our homelands in the 1500s. We do not want our children to be taught history as you believe it—it will destroy the very fabric of Navajo people. We must interpret the past from our perspective. The Navajo and non-Navajo views of the past need not be so different, but nonnative archaeologists must drop some of their preconceptions and listen to what we have to say to bridge the existing gulf. We will not let non-Navajos write our history or chart our future.

JEFFREY VAN PELT ■
MICHAEL S. BURNEY
TOM BAILOR

Seventeen

Protecting Cultural Resources on the Umatilla Indian Reservation

The Confederated Tribes of the Umatilla Indian Reservation (CTUIR) in north-eastern Oregon consists of three tribes: the Umatilla, Cayuse, and Walla Walla. Pursuant to the Treaty of 1855, the three tribes were forced to cede approximately 6.4 million acres to the U.S. government. Specific rights, however, were retained, including the right to continue with our way of life as we have always known it.

The CTUIR's Cultural Resource Protection Program began about nine years ago with a plan to develop and manage a wholly tribal program specifically driven by our Indian worldview, a cultural perspective quite different from the non-Indian view of Mother Earth and the natural and cultural resources she provides and cares for.

For the past decade the program has been sustained by soliciting cultural resource contracts from a variety of private, state, and federal entities. As a result, the program has been successful in providing training, education, and employment in cultural resource management for many tribal members. Much of this success is the result of the support from within the tribe's governing body through the Cultural Resource Commission, elders, and leaders. Our program encourages these tribal members to participate actively and to provide time and information when they can. In turn, much of the guidance provided by the program is the result of many hours of speaking with our teachers and elders about sensitive issues addressed through anthropology, archaeology, oral history, and archival research.

The program's cultural resource archives housed in Mission, Oregon, contain approximately 4,000 site forms, hundreds of maps, dozens of oral history tapes, and numerous photographs. Much of the archaeological and historical site forms are computerized for easy reference, assisting tribal staff in preparing file and literature searches, overviews, reports, responses, and other documents. This resource allows the program to serve the tribe's governing body and private, state, and federal entities so they can make informed decisions about how these natural and cultural resources should be utilized and managed.

During the past two years the program has been assisted by various contracts and partnerships (e.g., Earth Conservation Corps/Salmon Corps) that have provided approximately 25,000 hours of education, training, and employment for tribal members in cultural resource management, including important expertise in the consultation process. This process is based on the tribe's active participation in the decision making of what happens to those resources—resources vitally important to our people today and to future generations.

We, as native peoples, absolutely must be involved in the management of those resources that have provided us with food and medicines for thousands of years. With the advent of dam construction on the Columbia River, the Snake River, and other smaller tributaries, native peoples of the Pacific Northwest have observed the virtual extinction of their sacred salmon, eels, and other natural resources so abundant before the arrival of non-Indians. In short, these resources, even in the face of countless studies and ridiculous management practices (such as barging salmon upstream), are being annihilated.

Our program emphasizes tribal members working directly with tribal elders in the field, thereby providing day-to-day historical information on past and present land use to younger tribal members. This traditional method of teaching provides our youth with the knowledge unique to our elders. By adhering to this oral tradition of teaching and learning, our program supports the native system in which we live. However, by following our traditional way of passing on information from one generation to another, difficulties can arise. As a tribal program, we strive for a balance in our attempts to walk between two widely divergent worlds—the Native American and the nonnative—because we must. That balance, through the oral teachings of our elders, has given us the direction to succeed in creating a program that makes our Indian youth proud of who they are and of their native heritage. This is not because we are teaching them our history and culture through the study of archaeology. The discipline of archaeology as developed by the nonnative culture is not a useful method of teaching about tribal culture. Likewise, archaeology is not particularly useful in making decisions about how Indian people may choose to manage natural and cultural resources. Rather, archaeology is a highly *destructive* method of "preservation." However, when preservation cannot be achieved, standard archaeological methods are still necessary.

The Native American Graves Protection and Repatriation Act (NAGPRA) passed in 1990 has the potential of helping bring back tradition and a way of life within many North American tribes. With this and other legislation, along with the memorandum signed by President Clinton on April 29, 1994, regarding government-to-government consultations between federal agencies and federally recognized Indian tribes and the Executive Order signed on May 24, 1996, regarding the protection and preservation of American Indian religious practices, Indian people may once again be able to fulfill their inherent responsibility as indigenous caretakers of the land they have managed for thousands of years.

Cultural resource management is nothing new in Indian Country. American Indians have always managed their natural and cultural resources with respect, by remembering where we originated from—Mother Earth. By remembering those who came before us, native people of today inherited the responsibility to protect our traditional way of life for generations to come. Our tribal program has fought many battles during the past nine years. Many of these battles have been simply to gain recognition as indigenous people who have the right to manage the very resources connecting us with the past. At the same time, we have also been forced to witness aboriginal resources being destroyed by dams, timber harvesting, mining, irrigation, and development.

As tribes go through the NAGPRA process and see, for the first time, the lists of thousands of ancestral human remains, associated burial items, and sacred objects, our native people are seeing what the "science" of archaeology has done to our family members and ancestral way of life. To say this is shocking is an understatement! As the 1996 New Orleans meeting of the Society for American Archaeology has demonstrated, the discipline of archaeology is changing—but what have American Indians lost since the beginning of American archaeology? To Indian people, archaeological sites are a physical key allowing us to take our spirits back to a time when we had the right to be one with the very spirits residing in the natural world: that is, our ancestors and teachers.

The separation of the spiritual from the mundane and the Manifest Destiny policy of the U.S. government have had an impact on Indian people that needs to be looked at very seriously. What do we owe our future generations? Non-Indians have a very hard time dealing with the past and learning from it. This lack of sensitivity and respect is difficult to comprehend. Everything in American Indian culture and way of life is directly connected to the past. If nontribally trained archaeologists want to engage in cultural resource management studies in Indian Country, they must work in concert with the tribe or tribes that have a vested interest in the aboriginal lands considered for study. We must realize we can learn from one another as equal partners to combine our knowledge and invest in learning from the past.

Through our Treaty of 1855, the Umatilla, Cayuse, and Walla Walla tribes were recognized by the U.S. government as a sovereign nation. We are an independent nation with our own political structure, economics, laws, religion, and way of life. By recognizing the tribes as sovereigns, the U.S. government acknowledged our inherent responsibility to manage our own resources. Sovereignty is not a right, but rather a responsibility, and trying to fulfill that responsibility has been very difficult. The U.S. Supreme Court developed principles called "canons of construction" to guide them in interpreting what rights the tribes really meant to cede when "negotiating" a treaty. Therefore, you have to try and understand what was in the hearts and minds of the native people at the time they were forced to accept the terms of their particular treaty or treaties.

The fiduciary trust responsibilities of the U.S. government, and the many federal agencies within that government, are just now really being recognized. These trust responsibilities are necessary and vital to preserve what few treaty rights tribes were able to retain while being weakened by disease, starvation, alcohol, war, and forced assimilation (e.g., boarding schools, reservations, allotment acts). Unquestionably, tribes reserved the right to manage their cultural resources.

Over the past two years the Cultural Resource Protection Program of the CTUIR has invested approximately 34,000 hours of effort in contract archaeology, working with private, state, and federal groups to provide on-the-ground protection of cultural resources and tribal input on the various ground-disturbing projects that would have an impact on our culture, a culture in which our Indian people share throughout their lives. Archaeology, history, and oral history are the kinds of education our tribal members are experiencing as part of our program's evolution. Each project and partnership allows the program to educate tribal members and our non-Indian colleagues in identifying and managing tribal resources from a native perspective.

In addition, the program and CTUIR has assisted eight out of nine Oregon tribes in working with the state legislature to create stronger laws on the comanagement of resources so valuable to native peoples of the Pacific Northwest. For example, NAGPRA provisions were applied to state and private lands, and penalties were increased for convicted grave robbers from $500 to $10,000 per disturbed grave. By seeing the tribes come together, the Oregon state legislature has assisted in sending a strong message to people throughout the Northwest. By working through the state legislature and applying federal legislation, tribes can support the comanagement strategy developed by our program over the past decade.

In closing, as our elders always tell us, remember those who have been here before, work with those who are here now, and prepare for those who are coming. We must stand tall like the bear who walks on both feet and also on all fours. Walk in balance in both worlds. See through the eyes of the eagle to better achieve a comprehensive view of all that is going on around us. Use our wits like the coyote so we can once again manage our resources so very, very valuable to all our people.

■ JOHN C. RAVESLOOT

Eighteen

Changing Native American Perceptions of Archaeology and Archaeologists

In my view, the title of my paper reflects one of the most important issues currently facing our profession. The nature of American archaeology is rapidly changing, and many of the changes that have occurred since the mid-1980s are the result of Native Americans exercising their legal rights to be equal and active participants in the historic preservation process. Indian communities across the nation are establishing their own cultural resource management programs, historic preservation offices, and cultural centers (e.g., Klesert and Downer 1990; Anyon and Ferguson 1995). Native American programs are conducting cultural resource inventories, making assessments of National Register eligibility, excavating sites, writing reports, and curating artifacts and records in their own repositories and museums.

In the past several years, some tribes, like the Gila River Indian Community, have been recognized as self-governance tribes by the Department of the Interior. The Tribal Self-Governance Act of 1994 (P.L. 103-413) authorizes Indian tribes to negotiate annual funding agreements to plan, conduct, consolidate, and administer programs, services, functions, and activities currently administered by the Department of the Interior. Self-governance serves as an effective mechanism to implement President Clinton's historic 1994 directive to federal departments and agencies mandating that the rights of sovereign tribal governments be fully respected.

On October 13, 1995, the Gila River Indian Community (GRIC) and the U.S. Bureau of Reclamation negotiated the first annual funding agreement to plan, design, construct, operate, and maintain a water delivery and distribution system to irrigate 146,330 acres of tribal and allotted lands on the Gila River Indian Reservation. This agreement provides GRIC's Cultural Resource Management Program with the resources to conduct the archaeological inventories and subsequent mitigation studies anticipated as a result of the construction of the water delivery and distribution system. A following amendment to this agreement was signed on February 27, 1996, to develop a partnership between GRIC and the bureau to design, construct, and operate a cultural repository for Central Arizona Project (CAP) artifacts and records.

The Gila River Indian Community lies 35 miles south of metropolitan Phoenix in south-central Arizona. The reservation covers about 600 square miles of land that is home today to 13,000 Pima (known as Akimel O'odham, or "River People") and Maricopa (known as Pee Posh, or "People") Indians. Prehistoric Hohokam settlements, including Snaketown (Haury 1976), the type site for the Hohokam Cultural Tradition, and early historical Pima and Maricopa settlements exist in large numbers along the entire length of the Gila River, which bisects the reservation. The Hohokam were the prehistoric desert farmers believed to have been the ancestors of the modern-day Pima Indians.

The most significant impact of self-governance on cultural resource management is that tribes are being provided with the financial resources to conduct cultural resource functions, make determinations of eligibility and effect, and curate artifacts and records that previously were the sole responsibility of federal agencies. Self-governance will undoubtedly have additional repercussions of an unknown magnitude on how federal agencies such as the Bureau of Indian Affairs and Bureau of Reclamation deal with and consult on cultural resource issues, given that the Tribal Self-Governance Act is relatively new and the question of "inherent federal functions" as they relate to the National Historic Preservation Act and the Native American Graves Protection and Repatriation Act (NAGPRA) has not yet been resolved. This self-governance act is clearly a significant development since the vast majority of archaeology conducted in North America is funded by the public, and much of this work occurs on Indian reservations. Ten years from now the subject of "who owns the past" will not be a major topic of discussion among archaeologists and Native Americans. Archaeologists can either accept the fact that American archaeology is changing and establish dialogue with Native Americans to develop common ground and objectives, or bury their heads in their federal regulations and/or academic ivory towers. If avoidance behavior is the path selected, we can be assured that new federal statutes will be introduced to force archaeologists to change business as usual.

As an archaeologist working for an Indian community, I strongly believe that the future of American archaeology is with Indian communities functioning as active, not passive, participants in the interpretation, management, and preservation of their rich cultural heritage. While I know many archaeologists who would argue that no one owns the past, the reality is that our profession has spent more than 100 years studying someone else's cultural past. As archaeologists, we must recognize and acknowledge the fact that, despite all of the significant contributions that our profession has made to an understanding of North American prehistory, we have not done a very good job of communicating with and involving the descendants of the past societies we are studying. How often do we discuss the results of our research with Native American communities and present it to them in terms understandable to nonarchaeologists? Typically, at most we distribute copies of our reports, written for the funding agency and the archaeological community, which for the most part sit unopened on tribal officials' desks. How often do we include oral histories in our interpretations of the archaeological record? What efforts do we make to educate Native American communities about what we do and explain, at least from our point of view, why it is beneficial to them? We know that federal agencies are required by law to consult with tribal leaders and/or their designated representatives about projects that require Section 106 review, including consideration of traditional cultural properties and NAGPRA consultations, but what substantive efforts do we make in the actual communities?

Despite all of the efforts that the Gila River Indian Community's Cultural Resource Management Program has made in the past several years to inform community members about these and other important issues, the vast majority of the community's members do not have a clue about what we are saying or, for that matter, what archaeologists do, with the exception of the commonly held perception: "Archaeologists. Oh! Aren't they the people who dig up the graves of our ancestors and carry off their remains to museums?" This perception must change if we have any hope of including Native Americans as equal participants in the study of the past.

Acknowledging that changes in this perception must occur, how do we as archaeologists go about ensuring that a serious effort is made to improve dialogue with Indian communities? Sessions at annual meetings are clearly a good start, because they demonstrate our professional society's commitment to this important issue. However, improving dialogue and relationships between Native Americans and archaeologists on a local and national level will take considerably more time and effort on the part of many dedicated individuals and organizations, such as the Society for American Archaeology and the Keepers of the Treasures. These efforts must reach a much wider audience than they have thus far. So, where do we start? More specifically, how do we as archaeologists go about changing Native American perceptions of our profession?

Before I offer some suggestions from my own personal experiences as a tribal archaeologist, let me make it clear that I believe it is our responsibility as a profession to radically alter the way we deal with issues of concern to Native Americans, rather than to place the burden on them to conform to our way of thinking. Archaeologists must take a basic anthropological approach to acquire a better understanding of Native Americans and their worldview.

In my opinion, the kinds of changes that must occur in our profession will not materialize unless anthropology departments, which are responsible for training future generations of archaeologists, make substantive changes in the content of their course curriculum for undergraduate and graduate students and reconsider their goals and objectives. Most archaeology students graduating from anthropology departments are ill prepared to deal with the types of issues we are talking about today. I know I was! Anthropology departments are still training students to be primarily researchers and educators, when most graduates will ultimately fill positions in the private sector with archaeological contract firms or with federal and state agencies. One might ask, "How many of these recent graduates have had any formal exposure to Native Americans and their viewpoints? How many graduates have taken a course in archaeological ethics? How many anthropology departments require their students to take a class in public archaeology?" My personal experiences and those of archaeologists I have recently hired to work at Gila River would suggest the answer to all these questions is "Very few!"

My first exposure to working with Native Americans was as a student attending Southern Illinois University's Black Mesa archaeological field school in northern Arizona, where Navajos had been hired to work as laborers. I was an anthropology major specializing in archaeology, soon to graduate, and most of the Native American employees knew a whole lot more about archaeological fieldwork than I did. To them it was just a seasonal job, but to me it was something that I hoped to make my career. Looking back, I am sure that it didn't even seem odd to me that no Native American students were attending the field school. It should have. Regrettably, more than two decades later, the participation of Native American students in archaeological field schools has not changed significantly. There are some exceptions, but not nearly enough to make a substantial difference.

Following the field school experience, more than a decade passed before I had my next significant interaction with Native Americans in a professional role, but this time it was in the context of repatriation (Ravesloot 1989, 1990). Like many archaeologists at the time, I didn't fully comprehend the ramifications of the issue. In my mind, Native Americans were using repatriation as a political tool to get back at white society, in this case the archaeologists, and to further other political agendas. Although in some cases this may have been true, for the majority of Native Americans, my perception of the situation could not have been further from reality. As I have learned, particularly from my experiences at Gila River, it is never a question of whether human remains and associated funerary objects should be reburied, but more importantly, if any disturbance to the ancestors' final resting places should be allowed in the first place (Ravesloot 1995). So, when I was recently asked by tribal members of my staff to prepare a cultural resource program policy that would forbid photographing of human remains and associated funerary objects during excavations and as part of the documentation process, I had no problem abiding by their wishes. There is no question in my mind that their concerns about disturbing the dead are genuine. On the other hand, many in the archaeological and physical anthropological community would accuse me of being negligent in my responsibility as an archaeologist by not fully documenting the archaeological record.

My experience at the 1995 Pecos Conference held at the Gila National Forest, New Mexico, indicated to me that some archaeologists have not yet developed a sufficient respect and sensitivity to Native American views of the dead, since jokes about burials were made during the first morning of formal paper presentations. A large number of the audience found the jokes amusing. I found this lack of sensitivity to be amazing and embarrassing; to make matters worse, tribal employees from Gila River's Cultural Resource Management Program were in the audience. Not surprisingly, not one of our tribal staff members attended any more of the sessions following those episodes. For many of them, it was their first exposure to archaeology and archaeologists outside the boundaries of the reservation. What a great introduction to archaeology! A lot of perceptions were changed that day.

Anthropology departments could and should play a critical role in changing perceptions and improving relationships between Native Americans and archaeologists. Awareness of cultural traditions and values is clearly a must, although as suggested earlier, students should also be required to complete course work in Native American worldviews, ethics, and public archaeology as part of their undergraduate and graduate training. Archaeologists must first be trained as anthropologists!

Anthropology departments also need to place a much greater emphasis on recruiting Native American students. How do we go about doing this? One way is for both the departments and Native American cultural resource programs to develop training programs and partnerships. The training program that has been developed between the Navajo Nation Archaeology Department and the departments of anthropology at Northern Arizona University and Fort Lewis College is a good example of the direction we should take. Programs must also provide opportunities for non-Indian archaeology students so they can interact more frequently with Native Americans and be exposed to alternative viewpoints.

The recruitment of Native American students to our profession must begin much earlier than college, as has been recently emphasized for non-Indian students. Two years ago we began a program at the Gila River Indian Community, which fills some of this need. The Red Earth Summer Archaeology Program for high school students was developed in cooperation with the Gila River Indian Community's Employment and Training Office. The primary goal of this program, which lasts for eight weeks, is to introduce high school students to archaeology. Activities included introductory lectures on anthropology and archaeology, presentations by tribal elders, field trips to local museums and national monuments, an introduction to archaeological field and laboratory methods, visits to the Indian program offices at the University of Arizona and Arizona State University, participation in the latter's summer archaeological field school, and a one-week stay at the Arizona State Museum at the University of Arizona to learn about the goals and everyday operation of an anthropological museum.

While it is our hope that one or more of the high school students who have participated in the Red Earth Summer Archaeology Program will elect to pursue a career in archaeology, that result is not absolutely necessary for the program to be a success. More important is the fact that the program has provided Native American students with an opportunity to participate in the study of their past and that it has introduced some to higher education who most likely would not have had the experience. In the process of introducing Native American students to archaeology, I also believe we have managed to change some perceptions about archaeology and archaeologists. Because of the Red Earth Summer Archaeology Program, the Gila River Indian Community's Cultural Resource Management Program is slowly developing a broad base of support throughout the community.

Tribal support of archaeology at Gila River is coming about because of our program's emphasis on the community's young people and involvement of tribal elders, rather than solely from our scientific contributions to understanding the past. Archaeologists can change Native America's perceptions of and interest in archaeology, but we cannot expect traditional approaches to work.

A Look at Consultation

Nineteen

Aspects of Consultation for the Central Sierran Me-Wuk

In the Central Sierra of California, the Sierran Me-Wuk people were hosts to numerous early scholars who understood the pressing need for and significant value of documenting a culture that, it was believed, would soon disappear. The Sierran Me-Wuk consider these to be the earliest efforts to establish "professional consultation." These scholars developed a consultation process for documenting what they believed to be the most significant information. For example, they wrote about material culture (Barrett and Gifford 1933), language and territories (Merriam 1907; Barrett 1908; Kroeber 1908), kinship and moieties (Gifford 1916, 1926, 1944; Kroeber 1917), mythology (Kroeber 1907; Gifford 1917; Barrett 1919) and ceremonies (Gifford 1955; Merriam 1957).

Now, we wonder how adequate and valid this information is. The Me-Wuk at that time may not have been cognizant of the specific research dimensions nor of the full meaning of the English language. Sometimes, the scholars' biased attitude is reflected in their published and unpublished works, and this may have resulted from several factors. Language and behavioral nuances could contribute to cross-cultural misinterpretations. For example, how well were English words translated into Me-Wuk thought processes and vice versa? Was understanding sufficient for good communication? For the anthropologists, time was of the essence. Did they spend adequate time to really understand the culture's complexity as they moved through a tribal territory, literally one day here and one day there? Funding was generally insufficient for any prolonged studies and/or detailed observations. Often, researchers had only enough money to consult for about a day in each native community and to purchase whatever was available on that day. For the native people, some subjects were forbidden, and some topics were considered impolite. These scholars did what they thought was good documentation in a limited amount of time. The Sierran Me-Wuk consider the early part of the century the "First Gold Rush for Native California Collections" in central California by institutions and individuals.

Since this gold rush era, the anthropological consultation process has become nearly extinct. In the same manner the nonnative community acknowledges our presence—as a vanished culture and society. For example, not long ago, a nonnative contacted me regarding an article entitled "Patterns in the Landscape" for a series, *Quest for the Unknown,* published by Readers' Digest. A quote from this article will make the point: "In North America the Miwok Indians (now extinct) made perfectly straight tracks that ran for dozens of miles through the California sierras, from one mountain peak to another." How provocative! To the Sierran Me-Wuk this reflects an inability to identify the living Me-Wuk culture and the blatant failure to locate easily identifiable academic publications regarding our traditional and cultural heritage. Clearly, the authors neither consulted with the Sierran Me-Wuk community nor undertook adequate journalistic research. We wonder what led their professional writers to make such a misleading determination.

Ironically, the Sierran Me-Wuk bands hold traditional festivals and celebrations throughout the month of September every year to pay tribute to Mother Earth for her bountiful givings to the people. These festivities constitute one of the many traditions that have been carried forth from our past. Other natives and nonnatives have attended our celebrations and festivals—often coming from great distances. Perhaps the Sierran Me-Wuk should contact Readers' Digest and invite them to our next series of celebrations and festivals so they can publish an article entitled "The Miraculous Reappearance of the Sierran Me-Wuk Indians in North America"— including photographs!

For many years, professional archaeologists who conducted cultural resource investigations in our area seldom spoke with the local native community. They preferred to rely on "acceptable scientific methods." That is, they preferred to reiterate those data collected incompletely and hastily by the early scholars. They followed their predecessors' tradition of not allowing the native people access to the data to assure them that the scholars had accurately reflected their input even though it was the native people who provided the data in the first place.

Today, what constitutes an acceptable standard for consultation has changed dramatically from that of the past because it is required by law, and native communities have begun to exercise their rights throughout the mandated process. Thus, agency officials and professional archaeologists *must* consult these communities on proposed projects. It is interesting that agencies and/or organizations have been providing classes for those professionals on just how to "do" this Native American consultation. Classes address subjects like: What is an Indian? Where do you find them? How do you talk to them? What "rights" does the native community have, and by what laws? What does federal recognition have to do with being an Indian? What is consultation?

From the native perspective, consultation first and foremost involves the recognition and respect of the indigenous people and their territory of yesteryear and now. Given this premise, consultation then constitutes the exchange of information regarding a proposed project so that both the native community and the archaeologist can address direct and indirect impacts to cultural landscapes that may have far-reaching effects. This is accomplished through discussion, one human to another. For the archaeologist, consultation requires listening to explanation, and to be successful it necessitates the ability to understand and document significant values regarding that native community's cultural and traditional heritage. For the community, it is imperative to participate from the beginning in order to establish "standing" and to follow the process of compliance until the completion of the project.

Another determining factor affecting the outcome is the attitude demonstrated by the consulting parties from the beginning. Many academics perceive our culture as existing only in the past and do not realize that it has been carried forward into the present. They often do not appear to be cognizant that all living cultures are dynamic. Professional archaeologists often believe they are the "recognized experts"; they have bought and paid for their scholarly education, and what they have been taught is academically correct. We often hear, "Oh no, now we have to talk to the Indians!" "What do they know?" "We know more about their culture than they do!" This is where the consultation process may begin to break down.

Each community, especially the native one, has a unique process for communication. Agencies have specific procedures and rules for communication, depending on the chain of command or infrastructure; the native community refers to these rules as protocol.

First, the doors of communication must be established. This should be demonstrated by the agency acknowledging and respecting tribal protocol and by the native community acknowledging and respecting that of the agency. Second, trust must be established and, henceforth, must reflect continuity. When good faith efforts are made to communicate (development of trust), the consulting parties should be able to enter into agreements addressing site preservation and/or proper mitigation measures and procedures for the disposition of human remains and cultural items (reflecting continuity). Third, the dignity of and respect for the cultural and traditional heritage must be acknowledged, even though the academic may not fully comprehend the significance. This is usually where the list of "acceptable scientific methods" may have to be expanded. "Science" may not be the problem. In fact, the fault may lie with the scientist who is inflexible, ignorant of the existence of acceptable options, or denies the existence of a living culture.

Professional archaeologists consider themselves trained scientists and their profession as based on a body of data and theoretical propositions. I would like to demonstrate problems inherent in "acceptable scientific theory" with an example. Archaeologists' perceptive difficulties may be as simple as the inability to recognize what constitutes a cultural landscape (Theodoratus 1993). Professional archaeologists will document a site that includes a stream, an oak tree, and bedrock mortars, with an associated midden area. Through the eyes of a scientist the site is identified by the presence of physical and cultural evidence that can be scientifically evaluated; thus these areas will usually be documented as separate loci. They draw a little circle around the mortars, and another little circle around the midden, and the stream and tree are omitted from the scene.

The native people see this cultural landscape from a very different perspective. For them, the stream and the tree link the areas, revealing the activity performed there. Acceptable scientific theory totally neglects the human aspect because there is no tangible evidence to show that people gathered acorns, used the water in the stream for processing, and used the midden area for cooking and eating. Mortar sites are usually not considered significant because they have no "integrity." Few archaeologists recognize that the trees and the water alone can provide integrity. The depth of the midden deposits is often the sole characteristic used to determine significance. Further, the traditional archaeologist's approach does not make any provision for spiritual and religious aspects that may make the site a complete area and endow it, from the native view, with both integrity and significance.

Consultation may be most advantageous when addressed at the earliest opportunity. The earliest opportunity may be before the project's sponsor spends thousands of dollars for development plans that have to be altered because of cultural resources. When projects are delayed because of the discovery of these resources, the sponsor usually will blame the present-day native people for their ancestors living everywhere and/or the archaeologists for their inability to recognize significant sites when they see them. If consultation had been initiated at the earliest opportunity, interruption may possibly have been avoided. Professional archaeologists need to realize that the native people know their traditional territory, and it is important to them. Our grandfathers, grandmothers, and other elders taught us when we were young children which areas were used and the way they were regarded by our people. I remember riding in a car with my grandparents, or out walking with my grandfather, or gathering with my grandmothers. These are the times they would teach me about our cultural landscapes, telling me about gathering and hunting areas, cemeteries, and ceremonial areas. Native people today continue to teach our children about our heritage in this traditional manner—passing information orally from one generation to another.

I would like to share with you two projects in our area that fall under the jurisdiction of the California Environmental Quality Act (CEQA)—one progressing extremely well and another plagued with a multitude of problems.

The Central Sierra Me-Wuk Committee was brought in at the earliest opportunity on a proposed golf and county club project. The project sponsor had architects do a preliminary design for the golf course and then performed a first review of the area for historic sites. At the point when the sponsor became aware of the cultural components, communication had already been established with the local native community. We walked the land together and shared our perspective on the area. The sponsor began looking at the locality the way we viewed it and realized that the remnants of an old village were on the property. We began discussing what could be done with the sites and what type of impacts, direct or indirect, might occur, and how to address mitigation, whether by data recovery or preservation as open space. We readily agreed that all prehistoric areas would be kept in open space with 10-m buffers. Once these areas were established the project was redesigned, and we all became participants in a win-win situation. The sponsor was eager for our participation in developing and presenting to the public our inter-pretation of our heritage, not only at the visitors center, but also on the golf course. This golf course and country club not only would be a place of recreation. It would also educate the public about the significance of this historic area that reflects use by not only native people, but also homesteaders, Chinese workers, and gold miners. Successful consultation has provided us with the first golf course in the state of California that will share knowledge of native culture, specifically the Sierran Me-Wuk heritage.

Approximately six months ago, Barden Stevenot, the managing general partner of Greenhorn Creek Associates, the firm that developed the golf course and country club, asked if we would be a part of the official groundbreaking ceremony. We readily agreed. At the ceremony, we spoke of the good working relationship we had, the respect for our heritage he had shown by going that extra step, and our prayer of thanks to our grandfathers for our new shared success. We ended the presentation with prayers and songs to bless Mother Earth for this bountiful giving. The audience was emotionally moved, and for the first time in many years the non-native community shared their respect for our cultural and traditional heritage.

This project has now been underway for approximately three years, and today we are still involved in consultation on its development. We have agreed on a five-year monitoring plan once the project is compete to ensure compliance with the historic property treatment plan, demonstrating a continued commitment to good faith effort in consultation and to mutual trust and respect. Good faith effort in consultation has led to well-written documents, which are a key tool to protecting not only the native people's interests, but also the project sponsor's interest. The name of this golf and country club is Greenhorn Creek, located in Angels Camp, California, and we encourage all novice and avid golfing archaeologists to come, see, and play.

More recently we became officially involved in another golf and country club project, only after the project's sponsor was notified that consultation with the local native community was required by the U.S. Army Corps of Engineers' permitting procedures for developing the wetlands and also by Section 106 of the National Historic Preservation Act. The sponsor had already complied with CEQA requirements for cultural resources but now discovered that it was necessary to meet federal requirements. Unfortunately, this was going to cost money and downtime. Because we were brought into the process late, problems soon developed. Archaeologists were performing investigations while the construction crew was within a few meters of sites that did not have established boundaries. We red-tagged the project, requested the California Native American Heritage Commission to mediate, and called the Army Corps of Engineers to inform it of the project's noncompliance with the stipulations of the permit. Eventually, we worked through the maze of problems, but the experience created a lot of negative feelings among the participants—the sponsor, the professional archaeologist, and the native community. I believe what really astonished the sponsor and the archaeologist was our knowledge of laws and how to use them. We believe what went wrong with this project was the result of the attitude that the sponsor and the archaeologist demonstrated toward the native community. Certainly no trust or respect was established among the consulting parties. We repeatedly needed to have discussions with the archaeologist regarding his investigations. "Why are you doing it this way when the scope of work reflects something else?" "Where are the buffers as requested?" And six months later, "Where are the draft reports for review?" This golf and country club has since had numerous other problems, such as insufficient water and difficulty with highway access. We can only wish them well.

In closing, I hope the archaeological community will begin to understand the importance of establishing a good working relationship with the native community at the earliest opportunity when working within a group's traditional territory. We are not omitting or negating nonnative scholarship; instead we are anxious to learn the nonnative techniques and perspectives in obtaining and documenting our history. We are very proud of our heritage, and the archeological community can only benefit from the involvement of native people. But archaeologists must be open and willing to learn about our culture. Consultation, at its best, is a two-way street.

Cultural resources are nonrenewable. Therefore, let us all take active responsibility in preserving the proud and rich Native American heritage that will continually benefit not only the state of California, but the United States of America as well. We are interested in this as a mutual objective. Are you?

My gratitude and appreciation is extended to Sandra Bietz, tribal chair, Tuolumne Band of Me-Wuk Indians; Larry Myers, executive secretary, Native American Heritage Commission; Michael Moratto; and Dorothea Theodoratus for their sincere dedication, continued support, and comments on my writings.

■ KURT E. DONGOSKE
ROGER ANYON

Federal Archaeology
Tribes, Diatribes, and Tribulations

As archaeologists working for the Hopi and Zuni tribes in Arizona and New Mexico, we are faced with situations uniquely different than those experienced by most professional archaeologists and cultural resource managers. We are expected not only to understand the tribal positions regarding archaeology and cultural resource management, but also to act as advocates for these tribal positions, even if they are at odds with those of cultural resource managers, professional archaeologists, academicians, or in some rare instances our own professional positions. At the same time, we are responsible for explaining the positions of archaeologists to our tribal employers in ways that allow them to understand the roles and professional and legal responsibilities of archaeologists and cultural resource managers. Generally, this is not easy. We are often misunderstood by both our tribal employers and our professional colleagues.

Our intent in this paper is to provide a personal perspective on the particular situations we face by focusing on our different roles. As tribal employees and tribal advocates, we represent the tribes and thus present their positions to our professional colleagues through meetings, letters, reports, and review and comment on the research designs and reports of archaeologists. Conversely, as professional arch-aeologists and nontribal members working within a distinctly nonwestern cultural context, we advocate the values of archaeology to the tribes primarily through face-to-face discussions. Before addressing the issue of advocacy, however, we provide some general background to establish the context for our discussion.

Background on the Different Perspectives

Native American tribes are increasingly involved in the practice of archaeology and cultural resource management in the United States, primarily as a result of recent federal legislation that provides tribes a legal role in federal projects. Many tribes, such as the Hopi and Zuni, have established their own cultural and historic pres-ervation programs dedicated to the appropriate management of culturally affiliated archaeological sites and other traditionally important cultural resources located on and off reservation lands (Anyon and Ferguson 1995). It is becoming common for tribes to hire professional archaeologists to act as their technical experts. Never before in the history of American archaeology have Native Americans been so dynamically involved or in such a unique position to influence the future of American archaeology and cultural resource management.

Vast philosophical differences separate the western scientific view from the tribal view of the world, and these differences are especially acute when dealing with tribal ancestral cultural resources. To archaeologists, an archaeological site rep-resents a body of data (Willey and Phillips 1958:18; Joukowsky 1980:35). From an archaeological perspective a site, and the materials contained within, are considered dead, static, and inanimate objects that have a primary importance for yielding quantifiable data vital to the scientific understanding of past human lifeways and adaptation. In addition, the prevailing archaeological perspective is that these sites have been abandoned by their former inhabitants. Consequently, archaeological research, in both academic and contract settings, is designed to treat archaeological sites in an objective and unemotional manner.

In general, the Hopi and Zuni view ancestral archaeological sites as being imbued with life; they are inhabited by the spirits of their ancestors who once occupied the site. Moreover, these archaeological sites are not conceptually dif-ferentiated from the present, but are viewed as important living spiritual places that maintain an intrinsic and vital role in the continuance of the Hopi and Zuni cultures and lifeways (Dongoske et al. 1993; Anyon and Ferguson 1995). Thus, these sites are viewed as never having been abandoned. Archaeological sites validate Hopi and

Zuni traditional histories, and as such, they are considered to have been left there for a specific purpose, that is, to serve as markers on the landscape (Dongoske, Ferguson, and Jenkins 1993:27; Ferguson et al. 1993:27). For the Hopi and Zuni, archaeological sites are imbued with religious and spiritual cultural values that are very alien and intangible to a western-trained scientist. Ceremonies and rituals continue to provide a connection to these ancestral sites and a reason why the Hopi and Zuni are still here (Dongoske, Ferguson, and Jenkins 1993; Hart and Othole 1993).

Human burials offer a similar stark contrast. The Hopi and Zuni consider the people interred in the grave to be on a journey and to retain property rights to the grave goods with which they were buried (Ferguson et al. 1993:33). They should never be disturbed while on their journey (Pueblo of Zuni 1992). Archaeologists, on the other hand, consider burials and grave goods as part of the "abandoned" archaeological record and, therefore, available for scientific study.

For example, in 1992 Hopi clan elders and priests visited a large archaeological excavation project being conducted by Arizona State University in the Tonto Basin of central Arizona. During this visit the Hopi examined artifacts in the laboratory, and one Hopi priest identified the large and long pestle-shaped ground-stone artifacts as the same type of objects being used in Hopi ceremonial settings today. These artifacts had most likely been categorized as plant-processing tools by the archaeologists, but to the Hopi these are sacred objects embodied with a specific spiritual energy and only employed in specific religious ceremonies. These sacred objects are to be handled only by those who have been spiritually instructed and prepared. The handling of these sacred objects by others, including archaeologists, can have negative physical and spiritual consequences for those individuals.

Moreover, the context in which these artifacts are found is also extremely important to the Hopi, because it can tell them whether or not the artifacts had been ritually retired and under what circumstances. If the Hopi were to determine that these sacred artifacts had been ritually retired, then from their perspective the excavation of these artifacts would have violated that ceremonial retirement. Additionally, if the artifacts had been ritually retired under negative circumstances, their excavation could result in the release of the negative spiritual force contained within these objects back into the physical world. For Hopi, certain artifacts recovered from an archaeological excavation continue to have significant power in the present, as they did in the past—power that may be either positive or negative. Zuni beliefs are very similar to the Hopi view of ritually retired objects.

The following examples, although not directly applicable to archaeological contexts, exemplify the Hopi and Zuni certainty that there are negative consequences for unprepared individuals who handle sacred objects. In 1978 two pot-hunters from Safford, Arizona, stumbled on a cave and came across four ceremonial objects, known as *Taalawtumsi*, at Second Mesa on the Hopi Indian Reservation (Brinkley-Rogers and Robertson 1993:A-16). These ceremonial objects are an integral part of a Hopi initiation ceremony that is conducted every four years. Between the initiation events these objects are ritually "laid to sleep" on a bed of feathers in this cave. The pothunters stole the four ceremonial objects and eventually sold them to a collector.

In the Hopi religion and culture there is a penalty for the misuse of sacred objects and that penalty is death—a prolonged, painful death. One of the two pothunters who stole the sacred objects was nearly killed when he was struck by a car while riding his motorcycle. The injuries he received from this accident left him with a useless arm and leg. The other pothunter began experiencing kidney, liver, and gallbladder failure approximately three months after the theft (Brinkley-Rogers and Robertson 1993:A-17).

While finding a buyer for the ceremonial objects, the pothunters used the services of three Indian art dealers. Each of these individuals extensively handled the objects in the process of finding a buyer. Of these, one began having serious encounters with law enforcement officials, which eventually led to his imprisonment, and he later died in a traffic accident in 1992. The second dealer suffered a serious heart attack, and the third died in New Mexico in 1983, at the age of 40, when he drove off the road (Brinkley-Rogers and Robertson 1993:A-17).

In the fall of 1992 an individual illegally sold certain Zuni ceremonial items, sacred masks, and other objects to another individual who traded in Native American artifacts. These items were removed from the Zuni Reservation, a clear violation of the Native American Graves Protection and Repatriation Act, and also a clear violation of Zuni cultural values. The trial, conviction, and sentencing of these individuals did not occur until fall 1995. Zuni belief is that transgressions of this kind will result in serious misfortune to the offending individual within a four-year period after the transgression. By the time of the trial one of the defendants was so ill with cancer that he was unable to attend the court proceedings in Albuquerque, and before the four-year period had elapsed this individual succumbed to his cancer.

A skeptic could consider these injuries and deaths to be a matter of happenstance; however, to the Hopi and Zuni there are no coincidences. From Hopi and Zuni perspectives these individuals' misfortunes are a direct result of their inappropriate handling of these sacred objects, which was compounded by their iniquitous and illegal intent.

Our Role as Advocates

As employees of the Hopi and Zuni tribes, one of our roles is to present these emotional and spiritual tribal positions concerning cultural resources to archaeologists and agency representatives. When conveying tribal concerns regarding the impact of federal projects on properties of traditional importance, we act as advocates for the tribes. In effect, we present the tribal position while acting as culture brokers, trying to bridge the differences among federal agencies, archaeologists, and the tribe.

As archaeologists, we respect and adhere to our obligations to abide by professional standards and ethics. In so doing, we are compelled to educate tribal representatives about archaeology, why it is performed, and what can be learned from archaeology. An example of our work in this regard was the effort funded by the Salt River Project to explain, to the Hopi, Zuni, and Acoma advisory teams, how burials are excavated by archaeologists and what can be learned from human osteological and funerary studies.

The three teams, composed of religious and clan leaders in their respective communities, spent two days listening to archaeologists and physical anthropologists explain the details of analysis and the benefits in knowledge that can be gained from burial excavation and human osteological studies (Ferguson et al. 1993: 32–33). After considering this information, the teams decided that the burials should be avoided and not excavated. However, if the burials could not be avoided, then they should be excavated by an archaeologist, but with restrictions; there would be no studies on the bones other than basic metrics, sexing, and aging. After acting as advocates for archaeological and human osteological studies when working with the advisory teams, we then had to turn around and act as tribal advocates with the federal and state agency archaeologists to ensure that the tribal position on the treatment of the human remains and funerary objects was accommodated—not an easy task since the agencies were demanding more studies than the tribes desired.

Essentially we find ourselves giving a sales pitch for the worth and advantage of archaeological research to the tribe, a pitch Native Americans sometimes find bizarre. Then, after the tribe has decided its position on the matter, we advocate that position to the agencies, a position with which the agency representatives and archaeologists usually have major problems because it generally requests limits on their ability to perform scientific studies. It is equally true, however, that we may find the tribal pitch sometimes outlandish, and it places us, as advocates, in a position with which we may or may not agree. Yet, this is the nature of the beast.

The issues surrounding traditional cultural properties, otherwise known as TCPs, are another example of our role as tribal advocates, which also places us in a difficult position as culture brokers. Here we present two situations that exemplify this issue: first, the point of archaeological sites as TCPs and, second, the matter of funding TCP identification and evaluation.

As we noted above, the tribal perspective on archaeological sites is often radically different from that of the archaeologist and effectively the federal agency and state historic preservation office (SHPO). For example, there are significant differences between the way the Hopi and Zuni tribes and the way the agencies view the National Register eligibility determination of archaeological sites as TCPs (e.g., Dongoske et al. 1995; Sebastian 1995a, 1995b). The Hopi and Zuni tribes believe that many of the prehistoric archaeological sites in a large portion of Arizona and New Mexico are TCPs. As advocates for the tribes, we agree with the agencies that these prehistoric sites are indeed eligible for the National Register under criterion d (36 CFR 60.4) and have the potential to inform us about prehistory. On the other hand, we find ourselves in complete disagreement with the agencies when it comes to a determination of eligibility of these sites under criteria a, b, and c.

The tribal position is simple. These sites are often eligible under more than one criterion—sometimes all four. The Hopi and Zuni consider them eligible under criterion a because they are associated with events that have made a significant contribution to the broad patterns of Hopi and Zuni history (e.g., clan migrations). It should be noted here that the nature of oral history (and history in general) necessarily focuses on those portions of history and culture that are of significance; if it were not of great significance, it would not have been recounted through multiple generations.

Under criterion b, these archaeological sites can be considered eligible because they are associated with the lives of persons significant in the Hopi and Zuni past (e.g., Hopi and Zuni ancestors). Additionally, many archaeological sites can be associated with the lives and deeds of such cultural figures as the War Twins, Salt Woman, and the Katsinas.

These archaeological sites can also be eligible for the National Register under criterion c because they are representative of a significant and distinguishable entity (e.g., clan migrations) (Ferguson et al. 1993:30; Hart and Ferguson 1993).

Eligibility under the first three criteria (a–c) apparently creates problems for the state and federal agencies and SHPOs in both bureaucratic and research terms. This means that the business-as-usual approach of using mitigation of effect through archaeological data recovery may not be an option for either the agency or the archaeologist, because tribal perspectives and values must be taken into account in making determinations of effect and the subsequent appropriate mitigative actions. Clearly some agencies realize this, and in at least one instance an agency and a SHPO has flatly dismissed the Zuni position without even consulting the tribe. This happened even though the agency specifically requested that the Zuni perform a TCP identification and evaluation of eligibility for the National Register within the project area.

The Zuni noted that all the archaeological sites were ancestral Zuni and were regarded by Zuni as TCPs. These particular archaeological sites were recommended as eligible for the National Register under criterion a by the Zuni Cultural Resources Advisory Team, a group of traditional religious leaders (Othole 1993). The agency had previously recommended that these sites be determined eligible

under criterion d, a finding that Zuni did not oppose. After receiving Zuni recommendations, the agency consulted with the SHPO regarding the eligibility of the
sites, recommending to the SHPO that the sites be found eligible under criterion d,
but not under criterion a. No consultation with Zuni occurred during this period of
bureaucratic activity between the agency and the SHPO. The SHPO concurred with
the agency, effectively invalidating the Zuni position and, through a simple
bureaucratic maneuver, eliminated meaningful Zuni participation in the historic
preservation process. Since the sites were officially eligible only under criterion d,
archaeological data recovery was recommended and implemented.

Our advocacy for the tribal position has generated a great deal of antagonism
from some quarters, even to the point of our being accused of taking the high moral
ground while historic properties are destroyed around us. Not so. We are doing
nothing more than advocating the equitable consideration of the tribal position,
which maintains that many archaeological sites are associated with important
persons (e.g., ancestors and cultural figures) and events (e.g., migrations) in tribal
history and thus also merit a determination of eligibility under other criteria. Moreover, we feel that if the national historic preservation program in the United States
is truly representative of and responsive to our multicultural society, it *must* be
capable of respecting and integrating other value systems in determining significance
for a historic property and rely not solely on values generated from a western
scientific perspective.

In the 1970s, after many years of struggle, funding for archaeologists to conduct
archaeological surveys under Section 106 of the National Historic Preservation Act
became routine. Although TCPs have been eligible for the National Register for as
long as archaeological sites have, it is only recently that agencies have begun
considering TCPs in anything approaching a routine way. Even so, there are huge
disparities in agency perspectives. Some agencies have funded TCP identification
and evaluation at a comparable level of effort to that expended on archaeological
site identification and evaluation. Tribal members and tribal employees are compensated for their time and expenses in performing the identification, generating the
appropriate technical reports and making recommendations about evaluations of
TCP eligibility for the National Register. In general, this level of effort is acceptable
to the Hopi and Zuni.

Some agencies, however, either simply ignore the TCP issue or request that the
tribes conduct their own TCP identifications and evaluations without federal agency
assistance (Othole and Anyon 1993; Ferguson et al. 1995:13). These two approaches
unnecessarily burden the tribes. Agencies that ignore the issue usually receive a
clearly worded letter about the necessity for full compliance with Section 106.
Those that suggest tribes work without assistance are challenged on their dis-
criminatory practice of paying archaeologists but not tribes. Some of these agencies
argue that if any TCPs were in the project area, then surely the tribe must already

know about them and be able to identify them without fieldwork. Determining the precise location of TCPs, however, often requires fieldwork in order to situate esoteric knowledge in a contemporary geographical framework.

These issues put us, as tribal employees, at immediate odds with both the contract and the agency archaeologists. As advocates for the tribes, we demand adequate funds for them, noting that there is no reason to fund archaeologists if tribes are not being funded. When the agencies cry poverty, we suggest that the Section 106 compliance funds be split between the archaeologists and tribes, something that does not go over well with our colleagues. In addition, we point out that it makes as little sense to insist that tribes should already know all their significant traditional and/or ancestral cultural resources within a project area as it does to insist that archaeologists should know the locations of all the archaeological sites they would recommend as significant. This also does not sit well with our colleagues, but given that archaeological sites and TCPs are both historic properties, why should TCPs be treated any differently than archaeological sites? We see a double standard being used by some federal and state agencies when considering the values that make a historic property significant. That is, if a historic property is considered significant from a western scientific perspective, then there is adequate funding and effort by the agency. However, if a property is significant to a tribe, the agency rarely provides adequate funding for tribal identification and evaluation. The reality is that many agencies apply an ethnocentric approach to the management of historic properties that favors western values over Native American values.

Conclusions

The primary point we wish to emphasize in this paper is the inherent complexity and seemingly contradictory roles we play as archaeologists employed by tribes. In our role as archaeologists, we advocate the value and benefits of archaeology to the tribes for whom we work, and we hope that some of our advice is assimilated into the position that the tribe takes on any particular project. Sometimes we are more successful than others. In fact, our success often depends on just how much direct and unambiguous utility the archaeology may have for the tribe—for example, if the results of archaeology can assist the tribe in making a clear case for cultural affiliation under the Native American Graves Protection and Repatriation Act when otherwise the situation would appear somewhat clouded or under dispute. Establishing claims to use areas for traditional purposes might also be a situation where archaeology can directly benefit the tribe.

In other cases, we may not be so successful. It is in these situations that we, as tribal employees, then advocate the tribal position to the agencies and archaeologists. We do not see a contradiction in our arguing for archaeology to the tribe and then, when the tribe opposes certain aspects of the archaeology on a certain project, arguing against doing those archaeological aspects to the agency. This is because the tribes are very clear about why they may oppose some archaeology, and it is invariably because they would rather preserve the sites in situ, without disturbance, than have them excavated. When it is clear that a project will have adverse impacts to archeological sites, the tribes generally give their full support to professional archaeological excavations within the impact area.

Finally, although many tribes such as the Hopi and Zuni may have similar, if not identical, positions on many archaeological and cultural resource management issues, tribal views are not always compatible. In cases of divergent tribal views, we sometimes find ourselves in the strange situation of advocating different positions. These positions are not congruous with each other or with those of the archaeologists to whom we are presenting these positions. The bottom line is that on any project, as tribal employees, we can never be quite sure what position we will be expected to take as tribal advocates in the realm of cultural resource management.

This paper was written when Roger Anyon was director of the Zuni Heritage and Historic Preservation Office. He has since moved to Tucson, Arizona. The tense of this paper thus reflects Anyon's situation at the time of writing.

NINA SWIDLER ■
JANET COHEN

Twenty-One

Issues in Intertribal Consultation

In 1989 a contract between the Navajo Nation and the Bureau of Indian Affairs (BIA) authorized the Navajo Nation Historic Preservation Department (HPD) to assume administrative control of selected cultural resource management and historic preservation functions on Navajo lands. This contract was negotiated under the Indian Self-determination and Education Assistance Act (P.L. 93-638, as amended), and is commonly referred to as a "638 contract."

The terms of the contract shifted the oversight responsibility for compliance with federal cultural and historic preservation laws from the BIA to HPD. A 1994 programmatic agreement for the management of cultural resources located within road improvement projects on Navajo lands further amended the traditional relationship between the tribe and the federal government. As a result of these shifts, HPD instead of BIA is responsible for consulting with neighboring tribes concerning the effect federal undertakings may have on historic properties according to Section 106 of the National Historic Preservation Act (NHPA). The purpose of this consultation is to enable tribes, in the role of interested parties, to identify places of traditional, cultural, religious, or sacred importance. These places, commonly called traditional cultural properties (or TCPs; Parker and King 1990), range from prayer offering places, herb or mineral gathering areas, and landscape features, to what are typically identified and recorded as "archaeological" sites. Although such places are in areas used historically by many tribes, many are now within the sovereign boundaries of the Navajo Nation (Navajo Nation 1991).

To deal with this new responsibility, HPD developed procedural guidelines for consulting with other tribes. These efforts coincide with similar nationwide attempts to involve tribes in the Section 106 process, to ensure that tribal cultural preservation interests are considered before federal development projects are undertaken (USDI 1993). Using road improvement projects as an example, this chapter examines issues involved in intertribal consultation.

Mandates for Consultation

The implementing regulations of Section 106 require that agency officials invite interested tribes to become consulting parties and to concur in any agreement affecting historic properties prior to initiating federally funded projects *on Indian lands.* "When an undertaking may affect properties of historic value to an Indian tribe *on non-Indian lands,* the consulting parties shall afford [tribes] the opportunity to participate as interested persons" (36 CFR Part 800.1(c)(2)(iii), emphasis added). The 1992 amendments to the NHPA codify this directive in the law and instruct federal agencies to consult tribes whenever and wherever a tribe attaches significance to places on federal land or within federally funded or licensed projects.

> Properties of traditional religious and cultural importance to an Indian tribe or Native Hawaiian organization may be determined to be eligible for inclusion on the National Register [of Historic Places]. In carrying out its responsibilities under section 106, a Federal agency shall consult with any Indian tribe or Native Hawaiian organization that attaches religious and cultural significance [to these properties] [16 U.S.C. 470(a) §§ 101(d)(6)(A–B)].

Thus, federal law is now exceedingly clear that tribal concerns must be considered when identifying significant places and properties. The most effective way, perhaps the only way, to identify tribal concerns is to work directly with knowledgeable tribal individuals and/or groups.

Similarly, the Navajo Nation's policies encourage consultation with neighboring tribes before ground-disturbing activities. The Navajo Nation Policy to Protect Traditional Cultural Properties says that the tribe is "committed to protecting traditional cultural properties of other Native American groups on lands under its jurisdiction [provided] that other tribes on whose lands Navajo traditional cultural properties are located will make a reciprocal commitment" (Navajo Nation 1991:10). The Navajo Nation has systematically begun to address its responsibilities by developing consulting relationships with neighboring tribes on a program- or project-specific basis.

In March 1994, after nearly two years of negotiation, the Navajo Nation ratified a programmatic agreement with the BIA; the Arizona, New Mexico, and Utah state historic preservation offices (SHPOs); and the Advisory Council on Historic Preservation to achieve two interrelated objectives (NNHPD–RPP 1994a). The first was to consolidate the preservation, protection, and management authority of cultural resources located on Navajo land with HPD. Under the agreement, and for the first time in its history, the Navajo Nation has the prerogative to make decisions about cultural resources located within the boundaries of one class of projects—road improvements—with minimal involvement from federal or state officials. The other objective, expediting road improvement projects, is possible because the agreement streamlines the standard Section 106 compliance review process. Thus, project sponsors can begin work within a shorter time frame than was previously possible.

A controversial stipulation in the agreement affords non-Navajo tribes the opportunity to identify cultural resources, review eligibility and effect determinations, and comment on proposed treatment or mitigation measures for road projects on sovereign Navajo land. This stipulation was included in the agreement at the insistence of the SHPOs and the Advisory Council, and it held the Navajo Nation to a higher standard for consultation than many federal agencies. Consider for a moment that (1) some federal agencies still do not live up to the letter or spirit of NHPA and, to this day, fail to consult programmatically with tribes; and (2) the requirement for federal agencies to consult is not consistently enforced by regulatory agents. That this directive is in the agreement underscores the lack of trust the regulatory agencies had that the Navajo Nation would fulfill its newly assumed federal responsibilities to consult in "good faith." However, the lack of good faith consultation for federally sponsored projects on Navajo land is the very reason the Navajo Nation pushed for the 638 contract years before. Further, the SHPOs and Advisory Council directed HPD to contact surrounding tribes who historically used lands within the current boundaries of the Navajo Nation *before* the agreement was ratified, to *ensure* that the Navajo Nation engaged in good faith consultation efforts. Given the history of good faith consultation efforts by federal agencies and enforcement by regulators, the irony of this directive was not lost on the Navajo Nation.

The purpose of this initial consultation effort was to let neighboring tribes know that the agreement was being considered and to find out if these tribes had interest in any or all, current or future, road improvement projects on Navajo land that may affect historic properties. If the answer was yes, these tribes were to be invited to participate as interested parties pursuant to the agreement's stipulation. Our first efforts to contact other tribes likely mirror the experiences of federal agencies and other land managers. HPD sent 34 tribes and two tribal organizations a copy of the draft agreement by certified mail. Tribes were asked if they had concerns about any or all road construction activities on the Navajo Nation. If they were concerned, what was the nature of their concern? Was it in a specific geographical area? Was it for a specific type of place, site, or resource? After a couple of weeks, follow-up telephone calls were placed to each tribe. It was both difficult and time consuming to contact the appropriate tribal representative or department to find out if they (1) received the initial letter; (2) understood what we were contacting them about; and (3) wanted to declare themselves an interested party. To document our efforts, we kept logs of all correspondence, including telephone conversations and faxes. After almost a year of negotiation, only 6 tribes provided written declarations of their interest: the pueblos of Acoma, Laguna, Zia, and Zuni; the Hopi Tribe; and the San Juan Southern Paiute Tribe. Other tribes verbally expressed interest, but never followed through with a written declaration as required.

The directive to consult with other tribes was, and perhaps remains, the most contentious provision of the agreement for the Navajo people. The federal mandate for consultation was little understood or accepted, and, initially, HPD employees and Navajo Nation officials objected to the very idea of consultation with other tribes. Objections were raised that consultation would violate Navajo sovereignty. Some worried that Navajo concerns would be subjugated to those of other tribes. Long-term, unresolved land disputes with neighboring tribes fueled and intensified these feelings. Some employees regarded this mandate as a conflict of interest, especially when they were required to conduct the consultation as part of their jobs. Concern was also expressed that consultation could result in project delays. Further, many perceived the requests for compensation received from other tribes for their consultation efforts as unwarranted and inflated. Despite these apprehensions, the Navajo Nation is now in the awkward position of funding identification efforts, protecting, and managing places on Navajo lands that are important to other tribes.

The Consultation Process

The Navajo Nation recognizes two distinct aspects to the consultation process, although the difference between them is often fuzzy. One aspect is the actual identification effort; the other is the opportunity to consult with land managers and licensing agencies about issues of general concern. Identification efforts specifically enable interested tribes to identify places of concern within a project area. Comments about procedural issues, such as eligibility and effect determinations made pursuant to Section 106, are considered expressions of general concern. The Navajo Nation concluded that it is both fair and reasonable to provide financial compensation to interested tribes for their identification efforts, but not for their efforts to express comments of a more general nature.

While *National Register Bulletin 38* (Parker and King 1990) provided a general level of guidance on "how to consult" with tribes for the identification and evaluation of traditional cultural places, no precise consultative procedures actually exist (cf. King 1993). Similarly, although the Navajo Nation has a policy that suggests a willingness to consult with other tribes, standard procedures for consultation were never explicitly developed. As noted above, this was because the responsibility for compliance with consultation directives rested with the lead agency or project sponsor, and, until recently, the tribe had little reason to get involved in intertribal consultations or develop consultation protocols. Due to the internal tribal pressure for self-determination and the resulting assumption of federal responsibilities, this situation changed. While the policy to consult with other tribes has been in place since the late 1980s, the procedures to carry out consultation are still evolving: it has taken time and the maturation of HPD to develop an awareness of the myriad levels of legal and ethical responsibilities. Today, on Navajo Nation road projects, the process to identify places important to Navajo people and communities is led by Navajo cultural specialists aided by ethnographers. Our consultation efforts with neighboring tribes have similarly recognized the need to involve knowledgeable members of these other tribes, aided by their cultural resource management staff.

To achieve a measure of consistency among projects and project managers, it was imperative to develop internal procedures describing "how to consult" with tribes. The first step was taken in January 1994 through the issuance of program-specific consultation procedures that explained how to establish government-to-government relations on a project-specific basis with each interested tribe (NNHPD–RPP 1994b). The procedures provided the framework that facilitated identification of cultural resources by interested tribes. They contained examples of introduction letters, set a time frame to initiate consultation, and listed the types of information provided to tribes. Also addressed were issues of confidentiality of information and a standard approach for the treatment of human remains and associated cultural items that could not be avoided through project redesign.

In the earliest consultations, tribes would typically visit the project area, examine the "prehistoric" archaeological sites, and look for other places of concern. After the field visit we assumed a formal response from tribes would be forthcoming, expressing tribal interests. But since the procedures didn't require this, responses varied and were usually quite informal: occasionally, concerns were relayed to us right in the field; other times, tribal staff followed up with a short letter or phone call; sometimes, we heard nothing. After several months and many consultation episodes, HPD realized that the procedures were fine for establishing a consulting relationship, but that the framework was inadequate for managing actual identification efforts. For example, the procedures didn't require tribes to submit a justification for consulting on a particular project; declaration of interest was enough.

Nor were they required to present a description of the work they intended to do, furnish budgets for compensation of tribal experts, or provide written documentation summarizing the results of their efforts.

Problematically, consulting tribes didn't distinguish between activities related to identification and those related to expressing concerns about other general project issues; they requested compensation for both types of activities. As discussed earlier, the Navajo Nation was only willing to compensate tribes for their identification efforts. At this point, however, HPD lacked specific definitions to consistently distinguish between identification-related activities and those addressing general concerns. Similarly, with little prior experience in this arena, HPD had no basis for evaluating and negotiating the salaries requested for tribal experts. Additionally, tribes wanted to consult on more projects and at a greater level of intensity than expected. These problems combined to create frustration and confusion, as well as an unexpected, increased workload for those charged with carrying out consultation for the Navajo Nation.

Under these circumstances, consultation on individual projects proceeded informally, and each project was managed idiosyncratically. Tribes occasionally took advantage of our informal procedures. In the worst-case scenario, a consulting tribe brought 15 people on the project visit, including children and relatives of a tribal official. Later, the tribe demanded that each of these individuals be compensated for their time! On the other hand, many instances of informal field consultation went very smoothly. The Navajo Nation was just never quite sure what kind of documentation would be received, or if any documentation would be received in return for expended funds.

To clarify and formalize the consultation process, HPD subsequently issued additional guidelines mandating that the tribes submit a formal proposal to justify their interest in each project, with a proposed scope-of-work and budget attached (NNHPD–RPP 1994c). The proposals had to explain the tasks to be accomplished, identify participating individuals, and provide a fieldwork schedule. The guidelines also outlined reporting requirements and required tribes to submit a written report with descriptions of resources and management recommendations, along with site forms and maps, within a certain period after concluding identification efforts. To remedy earlier problems with payment requests, we clarified the difference between allowable and unallowable costs as related to identification efforts and expression of general concerns. If tribes wanted to be compensated for their identification efforts, itemized budgets had to be provided for our review and approval. Before paying tribes for completed work, we required an accounting of all expenditures relevant to the submitted budget. We also formalized procedures for notifying Navajo Nation tribal and community officials of pending project visits. The guidelines were sent to interested tribes for review before a meeting, where the guidelines were reviewed in detail.

Results and Observations

Although not our intent, the Navajo Nation has received far fewer requests from tribes to engage in identification efforts since the release of our more stringent guidelines. While the invitation to identify places of concern within project areas remains open, the guidelines made it clear to interested tribes that they had reciprocal responsibilities in the consultation process.

If the consultations conducted over the past few years are any indication, however, mutually beneficial results have been attained. On some projects, HPD recommended avoidance or protection of cultural places and historic properties based upon concerns expressed by tribes. As a result, BIA engineers modified project design plans to adapt to these concerns. BIA was happy because it didn't have to expend scarce funds to excavate archaeological sites. The Navajo Nation and consulting tribes were equally pleased because culturally sensitive places were left undisturbed or disturbance was minimized. A somewhat surprising result is the expressions of gratitude from both local residents and interested tribes at being asked for their input. After years of quiet resignation, people have been given an opportunity to take an active role in the management of their resources.

For the most part, the problems encountered have not been with the consultation process HPD developed pursuant to NHPA and corresponding tribal statutes. Problems developed because of differences in interpretation of the ownership clause in the Native American Graves Protection and Repatriation Act (NAGPRA; 25 U.S.C. 3002[3]) and the ramification that claims of ownership and control of human remains and cultural items have in the political arena. Insufficient time and a lack of funding proved to be another problem for tribes, including the Navajo Nation. Although many tribes want to be consulted about cultural resources, they do not have sufficient funds to hire and train staff and to compensate knowledgeable tribal members in order to accomplish a comprehensive identification project. Furthermore, tribes are still figuring out ways to handle requests for culturally sensitive information.

Even with an influx of funding for consultation, tribes must already have a programmatic infrastructure in place to engage successfully in consultations. Even with the necessary infrastructure, tribes are inundated with requests for consultation from all quarters, both with and without funding, usually within unmanageable time frames (for example, 30 days). Add to this the release of the hundreds of NAGPRA inventories that require review and response by tribal staffs. Additionally, most tribes have development projects on their own lands that demand priority attention. A lesson we learned is that silence from interested tribes does not necessarily mean lack of concern or interest. It may just be a matter of juggling to address multiple priorities. And tribes have their own ways of decision making; often this process is not as straightforward as that to which western-educated scientists or managers are accustomed. Reaching a decision may take much longer than the normally allotted 30 days.

A lingering problem, and one that nontribal organizations have difficulty accepting, is that tribes don't necessarily know the exact location of all their historic properties (any more than any citizen knows the location of all historic properties of national significance). For example, the Navajo Nation often receives vaguely worded replies from tribes in response to our initial requests for information. Their first request is usually for a copy of an archaeological report, followed by a request to visit the project area. Providing reports may not be possible at the beginning of a project; it may have to wait until a comprehensive inventory and report are completed. Thus, tribes may request additional time to respond based on receipt of additional information. This request for additional time, however, may be incompatible with management needs. Taking all this and more into account, is it any wonder why tribes let many requests for tribal participation go unanswered, or provide an inadequate and incomplete response, or respond later than the stipulated time frame?

In our case, out of the six declared interested tribes, only three consult on a somewhat regular basis. The San Juan Southern Paiute have defined a geographical area in which they have interests; this limits the number of contacts the Navajo Nation has with them. The Hopi and Zuni tribes typically attempt to consult on every project. For all their intentions, however, many requests for input still go unanswered. Although the other three tribes, Acoma, Laguna, and Zia, have stated a concern for many cultural resources on Navajo land, they simply don't have the time or staff to respond to the multiple requests for consultation HPD and others send to them. These tribes have repeated that their main concern is for the respectful treatment of human remains and cultural items, and to avoid adverse impacts to cultural resources if possible. Each has supplied HPD with a definition of respectful treatment but declined to participate in any type of identification activity, or reburial action or ceremony. In return, HPD has forwarded its standard treatment policy for human remains and associated cultural items that cannot be avoided by project redesign: reburial as soon as possible in the same orientation as found, as close to the origin site as possible. Thus far, this appears an acceptable compromise for all interested tribes, including the Navajo communities.

Another potential complication for the Navajo Nation is the likely entrance of other neighboring tribes into the consultative process (those who previously expressed only a verbal interest in projects on Navajo lands). Over the years, and especially since the passage of NAGPRA, tribes have become better funded and are currently developing the necessary infrastructure to cope with the many requests for consultation. They recognize the need and opportunity to become more actively involved in the management of cultural resources and places of concern. As these tribes formally declare themselves interested parties, the Navajo Nation's job will become that much more complex.

Conclusions

To consolidate tribal control of cultural resources, tribes can be proactive. They can develop replacement regulations under NHPA to modify and supersede all or a portion of existing federal cultural preservation regulations. Currently, 14 tribes, including the Navajo Nation, are pursuing this option. Another option is the more focused approach of a programmatic agreement analogous to the one discussed here. Tribes pursuing either option need to realize that they will be not only regulating pursuant to their own tribal regulations, but also administering the assumed federal responsibilities (Downer and Roberts 1996). The situation described for the HPD is a microcosm of what can happen when a tribe totally substitutes for those regulatory agents. Nevertheless, on a positive note, tribal initiatives such as these may "ensure that the full range of resources of concern to the tribe is protected, and that the tribal preservation program meets the real needs of the tribe, is sensitive to the tribal culture and is organized in a fashion that suits the nature and organization of the tribal government" (Downer 1990:90).

Other means of achieving a reasonable level of control in an era of competing multicultural objectives could come about through face-to-face negotiations between and among tribes, without involving federal and state officials. Many problems that tribes experience have their roots in imposed federal land and resource policies, despite treaties to the contrary. Very visible and disruptive results of these policies are water, mineral, and land claim disputes within an individual tribe, between and among tribes, among tribes and the federal or state government, and between tribes and private landowners. Resource disputes, as well as cultural differences between Navajo and neighboring tribes, directly contribute to the lack of accord among southwestern tribes regarding the cultural affinity of historical populations to present-day tribes. Although perhaps naive or overly optimistic, we suspect that if the political ramifications of reaching a consensus regarding cultural affiliation were resolved, then tribes could probably reach agreement for the care of these "resources" and respectful treatment of human remains. In our experience, tribes agree that the best management strategy is to leave cultural resources undisturbed. In cases where avoidance isn't possible, tribes seem in relative accord regarding general treatment measures, particularly when human remains are involved. This is not to imply that culturally appropriate treatment measures among tribes don't vary; they do. Whether tribes can reach accord on these differences is unclear given today's political climate.

Like many other sovereign tribes, the Navajo Nation's ultimate goal is self-governance. Currently, whether or not it is culturally relevant, the Navajo Nation must observe federal preservation law (Holt 1990) as outlined in our 638 contract. Unfortunately, compliance with the law may be contrary to the goals of tribal sovereignty (Downer 1990) and may, in fact, conflict with the tribal perspective.

The Navajo Nation's Cultural Resources Protection Act (CMY 19–88, 1988) says that "the Navajo Nation, in cooperation with the states, federal government, other Indian Tribes, and private organizations and individuals, [will] administer Navajo Nation owned, administered or controlled cultural resources in a spirit of stewardship and for the inspiration of present and future generations." Clearly, the Navajo Nation has expressed an ethical and legal commitment to the appropriate care of cultural resources on Navajo lands. However, until some of the larger, political issues are addressed, the consultation process, and the decisions made as a result of consultation, will continue to be contentious. Difficulties in establishing productive consultative relationships will remain clouded by issues of sovereignty, ownership, and control, as well as by the cultural, historic, religious, and spiritual ties people have to the land. Meanwhile, the Navajo Nation will continue to consult both to comply with the law and to foster cooperation between tribes.

The opinions expressed here are those of the authors and do not necessarily reflect the views of the Navajo Nation. Previous versions of the paper were presented at the 1995 meeting of the Society of American Archaeology in Minneapolis, Minnesota, and at the 1995 meeting of the Society for Applied Anthropology in Albuquerque, New Mexico. This presentation has been revised and edited for inclusion in this volume. The ideas presented here developed over time. Our thinking was enhanced through ongoing discussions with coworkers, as well as through conversations with and published works by Kurt Dongoske, Roger Anyon, T. J. Ferguson, and Alan Downer. This chapter also benefited from the insightful comments offered by Michael Yeatts and Tom King. We gratefully acknowledge the Navajo Nation Historic Preservation Department for allowing us the opportunity to write and present this paper.

ROBERT L. BROOKS ■

Twenty-Two

Compliance, Preservation, and Native American Rights
Resource Management as a Cooperative Venture

Many papers presented in this volume deal with various issues of Native American rights as they pertain to treatment of human remains, the study of ancestral settlements as archaeological sites, and protection of traditional properties. In general, preservation has been accomplished through the formulation and implementation of laws, regulations, and policies on federal and Indian lands. Although a series of problems have been discussed for these settings, there is a relatively straightforward legal relationship between federal laws and regulations and the responsibilities of land managers on federal or tribal lands. The implementation of such laws becomes much more complicated when dealing with state or private landownership. In this paper, I examine the relationship between state and federal agencies, archaeologists, and federally recognized Native American societies as they pertain to preservation issues in Oklahoma.

Oklahoma Archaeological Survey

The Oklahoma Archeological Survey was established in 1968. It has the dual role of a state agency as well as a research unit of the University of Oklahoma. The Archeological Survey's enabling legislation mandates that it conduct basic research on Oklahoma's prehistoric and early historical record, work with the citizens of Oklahoma to preserve important archaeological sites, and report on the results of its efforts. Because of the highly visible nature of Native Americans in the state, the Archeological Survey has worked to establish a cooperative relationship with the native peoples of Oklahoma, especially the indigenous tribes (the Caddo and Wichita). Examples include working with the Caddo Tribe of Oklahoma on their tribal history and with the Muskogee Nation on reburial of historic Creek remains. The survey has also worked to bring various programs on tribal heritage to native people in Oklahoma. While these efforts crosscut our mission of research, management, and education, the focus of this paper is preservation and management. Over roughly the past 20 years the Archeological Survey has been involved with enforcing the various state and federal laws as part of the state's historic preservation program. It is from this dual role as a state agency and as an enforcer of federal laws and regulations that problems at the state level are most clearly recognized.

Oklahoma's Native American Populations

Oklahoma has one of the most numerous and diverse Native American populations in the United States. Based on the most recent census, there are approximately 221,000 people of documented Indian ancestry living in the state. This is 8 percent of the population of Oklahoma and also only reflects those who are legally defined as Indian. It does not include the many individuals who fail to identify themselves as Native American. It is not unreasonable, therefore, to estimate the overall population of Native Americans in the state as being in excess of 10 percent of the total state population.

The Indian people of Oklahoma represent a variety of regional populations. There are the Five Civilized Tribes (the Choctaw, Cherokee, Chickasaw, Creek, and Seminole) from the Southeast; the Iroquois from the Northeast; the Shawnee, Pottawatomie, Sac and Fox, Miami, and Delaware from the Midwest; Plains groups such as the Pawnee, Comanche, Cheyenne/Arapaho, and Osage; and people indigenous to Oklahoma such as the Caddo, Wichita, and Apache. Oklahoma has members of 37 different federally recognized tribes within its boundaries—the most diverse population of Native Americans anywhere in the United States. A number of these tribes also hold either reserved or allotted lands within the state (Figure 3). Because it has such a large and diverse Indian population, the Native American presence is well expressed in the state. However, because of the overlap between indigenous

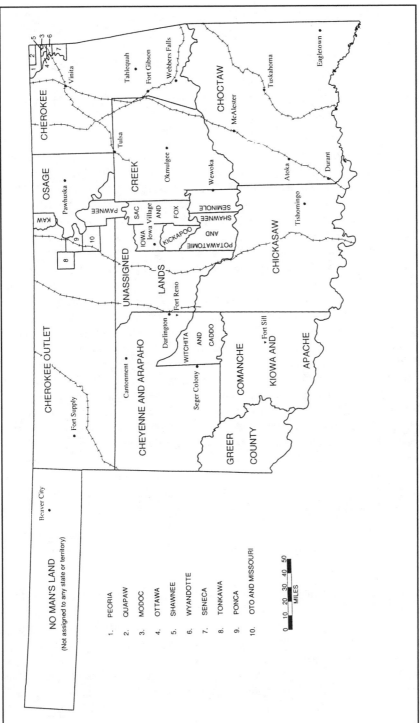

Figure 3. Indian Territory, 1866–1889 (after Morris, Goins, and McReynolds 1976).

and removed groups as well as differences in historical origins, there exists an incredible mix of political systems, cultural values, and traditional practices.

Land/Resource Management

Presently, within the boundaries of our state, some 22 state and federal agencies are involved with regulatory compliance under the National Historic Preservation Act (NHPA). They can be divided into agencies with land management responsibilities, those with regulatory roles, and those that provide financial or technical assistance. Oklahoma has a modest amount of land under federal ownership or management, which involves six federal agencies. There are also six state agencies with land-managing or regulatory responsibilities under federal laws and others with state-level land management roles. Within this mosaic of agencies resides a complex combination of resource management responsibilities. For agencies that are land managers, their responsibilities are clearly identified. However, managerial responsibilities for regulatory and technical and financial agencies are less well grounded. This is because they are frequently working on state and/or private lands where other legal, economic, and political considerations are operating.

During an average year, some 6,000 projects originating from these federal agencies will be evaluated under various provisions of the National Historic Preservation Act. In situations involving human remains, federal and state agencies may deal with tribes through the Native American Graves Protection and Repatriation Act (NAGPRA). Within the context of these laws and the diversity of Native American interests, the Oklahoma Archeological Survey has worked with federal and state agencies and Native Americans on a variety of issues. These include the protecting Native American cemeteries and unmarked graves, identifying traditional properties, training of Native Americans as cultural resource technicians, and including the role of Native Americans in the review process.

Protecting Native American Cemeteries and Unmarked Graves

Like many states, Oklahoma has a history of site vandalism (pothunting), which has resulted in the destruction of many prehistoric sites. We have also had to contend with looting of historic and unmarked Native American cemeteries where looters are seeking valuables placed in the grave. In 1986 and 1987, tribal officials of the Caddo and Pawnee tribes and the Muskogee and Choctaw nations expressed their concern to us over destruction of their peoples' graves and cemeteries. In the fall of 1987, working with state Senator Enoch Kelly Haney (a Seminole), a bill was drafted to make unauthorized digging of graves or cemeteries a felony. The bill also provided similar penalties for buying or selling burial furniture and provided for reburial of inadvertently exposed human remains where tribal identity could be established. Despite opposition, the Burial Disturbance Act was signed into law in June 1988.

Since the law's enactment, there has been some decline in pothunting at prehistoric sites and a dramatic decline in the digging of historic Indian graves. Other portions of the law have been used to return remains of Cheyenne/Arapaho and Wichita individuals to the tribes as well as to preserve Cheyenne/Arapaho and Creek freedman cemeteries. The law has also been used to pursue prosecution of individuals responsible for destruction of a prehistoric site related to the Caddo Tribe. Until the passage of NAGPRA, Oklahoma's burial disturbance law served as the most severe penalty for vandalism or disturbance of human remains. It remains our only effective tool for dealing with these problems on state or private land. However, the state law is not without its own set of problems. The greatest one is that the law does not prohibit authorized removal of an unmarked grave but rather provides for reburial at another location (this is consistent with the current Oklahoma law pertaining to movement of cemeteries).

In the recent case of an unmarked grave of ancestral Wichita remains in the right-of-way of a city waterline, the Archeological Survey was obligated to remove the burial pending reburial by the Wichita at another location. The project was rerouted only when additional burials were located. Thus, we ultimately had a situation that was unsatisfactory to the tribe as well as the city, even though our goal had been to protect/preserve the remains. In discussing this with the Wichita, we found that tribal members did not understand that the Oklahoma burial law operating on state or private land does not provide the same provisions as does NAGPRA on federal or Indian land. The difference between NAGPRA on federal land and state laws on state or private land will continue to be a problem until NAGPRA can be effectively used outside of Indian or federal land jurisdiction.

Identifying Places of Traditional Value

The draft guidelines for the treatment of traditional cultural properties that were published for comment in 1988 recognized that certain categories of Native American places did not receive adequate protection or consideration under existing Section 106 guidelines. Beginning in 1990, the Oklahoma Archeological Survey started a program of working with tribes to identify places of social, ceremonial, and sacred value. These might include locations of Native American Church ceremonies, ghost dance locations, dance grounds and ball grounds, and origin places. The intent was to establish an inventory for places of traditional value that could be used to avoid these locations where typical land alteration practices were planned.

However, there was also a concern with not violating tribal ethics pertaining to rights to this type of "special knowledge." We developed a system where specific locational information was not provided to the Archeological Survey. We only requested a general location (usually within about a 10–20 square-mile area). This general area was subsequently defined as sensitive for Native American issues related to traditional values. Where we had such information, we informed applicants to contact the appropriate tribe.

One problem in dealing with traditional properties was that there are no clear guidelines for establishing what constitutes a "significant" place of traditional value, nor was there a set of procedural guidelines for contacting tribes about such properties and their protection. The Archeological Survey also encountered a number of problems with the documentation of places of traditional value as well as a means of bringing this information to the tribe. First, conducting an inventory of traditional properties was much like doing ethnography—it is very time consuming. We were typically limited to talking with only a few informants. Second, even with Native Americans conducting the interviews, tribal people had difficulties understanding the reason for our "survey." There were also cases where informants did not divulge information that would compromise their position in regard to traditional practices within the tribe. At this point, we have undefined levels of information for the Comanche, Kiowa, Cheyenne, Chickasaw, and Creeks. In 1994, because of funding limitations, we had to abandon the traditional properties survey. Fortunately, the 1992 amendments to the National Historic Preservation Act require this effort on an individual project basis.

Cultural Resource Workshops for Tribes

Another means of enhancing Native American understanding of cultural resource management has been through workshops. The goal of these training sessions has been to create a group of tribal people who can function as "cultural resource technicians." In 1994, the Archeological Survey participated in a program administered by the U.S. Forest Service to train Bureau of Indian Affairs personnel as well as Native Americans on the historical background, archaeological culture history, and procedures for conducting cultural resource management programs on tribal lands. The Archeological Survey was involved in presenting the culture history as well as a summary of applicable federal and state laws. Tribes participating in this program included the Cherokees, Chickasaw, Creek, and Osage. In summer 1995, the Wichita Tribe, with assistance from the National Park Service, conducted a training program that included information on the tribe's culture history as well as enforcement of state and federal laws. In a NAGPRA workshop, the Caddo Tribe received similar kinds of information. Informally, programs have been presented to members of numerous tribes including the Cheyenne/Arapaho and the Absentee Shawnee.

These programs have resulted in an increased awareness of preservation laws on the part of some tribal members.

Consultation Under Section 106

Since the passage of the 1992 amendments to the National Historic Preservation Act, some regulatory and assistance agencies have ignored or shown only token acceptance of provisions calling for consultation with Native Americans on Section 106 undertakings. To deal with this situation, the Archeological Survey has instituted a policy where our formal response includes an opinion that additional consultation with tribes is needed to complete the Section 106 process. The Archeological Survey has also compiled a list of the appropriate tribes to contact based on the area of Oklahoma affected by the project. This list is sent out to applicants and agencies. While this system does not ensure compliance, it reinforces the mandate to consult with tribes on various federally funded or regulated actions. Furthermore, with the provision of lists of appropriate tribes to contact, there is no valid reason for an applicant or agency to claim they lacked sufficient information for Native American consultation.

Problems in Cooperative Efforts

Despite efforts by the Archeological Survey and many federal and state agencies to preserve archaeological sites in Oklahoma, there are obvious problems in bridging the relationship with tribes. In reviewing our efforts over the past five years, I have attempted to observe some of the concerns from an objective and, I hope, anthropological perspective. These problems are focused around three areas: (1) a basic communication failure regarding the mission of archaeology; (2) a failure of tribal people to understand the limitations of the law; and (3) failures of archaeologists, museums, and agency officials to consult with tribes in an effective fashion. In this last area, I would add that some of the failings are a function of overreacting to situations through efforts at political correctness.

1. Despite our education efforts, the increased communication with tribes, and our battles to preserve archaeological sites, many tribal people remain distrustful of archaeologists and the government. Archaeologists still are perceived as having the goal of digging up their ancestors' bones. From an archaeological perspective, we labor to preserve Native American heritage through our excavations and analyses with the goal of a better understanding of the lifeways of past Native American societies. However, to Indian people, this is too much like the government relocation, confinement on a reservation, and modification of traditional economies that took place in the late nineteenth and early twentieth centuries. It is understandable

that tribal people, especially those that hold closely to traditional values, are suspicious.

2. Even with our efforts to conduct workshops on historic preservation, tribal self-governing preservation programs, and communication/consultation on outcomes of projects, tribal people and tribal governments do not fully understand historic preservation laws. For example, within the context of Section 106, we have multiple mitigative strategies for National Register properties ranging from preservation in place to labor-intensive data recovery. Tribes have difficulty in comprehending these different paths. In most cases, they will say, "Just leave it alone!" We also have not made clear the distinction between laws operating on federal and/or Indian land as opposed to those operating on state or private property and why laws such as NAGPRA cannot be as widely applied in the latter settings. Native Americans also struggle with the relationship between NAGPRA and NHPA. Of course, I might add, some of us working with the articulation of these two laws have this problem as well. My impression is that tribes have a much better grasp of NAGPRA than of the NHPA. This is probably due to better education and the establishment of tribal NAGPRA liaisons. However, I also suspect that the basic premise of return of their ancestors' remains to the tribes is a more palatable concept than excavation of additional ancestral sites of their people.

3. A wide range of problems exists as a result of our current means of communicating with tribes on matters of historic preservation. One major issue is the conceptual distinction between what consultation means to many in the archaeological/museum community and state and federal agencies as opposed to its meaning to tribes. If we substitute the word "contact" for "consult," it would perhaps be more accurate. Tribes are notified of actions or intentions on projects; they are not necessarily consulted. As one tribal person said to me recently, "What consultation means is that you are going to tell us what you are going to do."

From my experience, this, in many cases, is exactly what takes place. A couple of reasons explain this. The problem stems partially from most state and federal laws, including the National Historic Preservation Act, having no means of dealing with the extensive time required for in-depth consultation. Typically, a Section 106 review has a 30-day time limit. It is rare for tribes to come to a consensus in such a short length of time. By the time the tribe has discussed the project, a course of action has already been determined without their input.

There are also procedural problems in contacting tribes. As noted, many of Oklahoma's resident native people were relocated or removed from distant states. While we can ensure in Oklahoma (for example) that the Choctaw are contacted about projects in the state potentially affecting their historic post-1820s settlements, we have no means of ensuring that the states of Mississippi and Alabama are contacting the tribe here in Oklahoma concerning their undertakings.

There are additional problems in establishing the appropriate consultation in Oklahoma where different tribes have to be contacted regarding sites from the prehistoric and historic periods. The Wichita would be an appropriate contact for late prehistoric sites in western Oklahoma, whereas the Cheyenne/Arapaho might be appropriate for ca. 1870s Native American sites. However, sometimes it is not handled in this fashion. Agencies may simply look for who held the land under treaty, ignoring the implications of prehistoric origins. There is also the long-recognized problem of the proper individual(s) to contact. Even with the establishment of NAGPRA liaisons and historic preservation coordinators, many tribes have basic divisions between traditionalists and those in political (appointed) offices. This problem is further accentuated by some tribes having political appointees who are more proactive in dealing with historic preservation issues than their traditional leaders are. In other tribes, this situation is reversed, with traditionalists being more advocative. Thus, there is no consistent pattern for either party that can be used when consulting on preservation issues. Consequently, we all find ourselves working through each issue on a case-by-case basis and unfortunately never building on past resolutions.

Political Correctness

As in most areas of political sensitivity, historic preservation has developed politically correct ways of doing business. The problem lies with many of these, in fact, not being the correct means of handling issues. It might be more realistic to consider this to be "Political Incorrectness." In at least three different scenarios, consultation with tribes through politically correct behavior has exacerbated the problem rather than remedying it.

The first scenario concerns responding to those who speak the loudest. It is not uncommon to encounter very vocal individuals who are upset or angry about archaeological or preservation concerns. Archaeologists, museum officials, and state and federal agencies have frequently dealt with these individuals without first examining whether they are speaking for the tribe in an official capacity. This often results in agreements or arrangements that have no official tribal representation and ultimately lead to discord. A similar situation is where more than one tribe is involved. It is my impression that we frequently first attempt to satisfy those most proactive in their position and secondarily consult with tribes that are less vocal in their concerns. In many cases, the less vocal tribe is offended by this loss of prestige. In the end, archaeologists and agency officials send a message that the most effective means of bringing about consultation with your group or tribe is by being the most vocal. From my perspective, this is counterproductive to effective communication.

Another scenario is where agencies insist on formulating their own policies and consultation procedures in isolation. There are instances in which one agency consulted with one tribe, and other agencies talked with other tribes or groups about the same site and tract of land. To an observer, the great deal of procedural inconsistency and lack of communication is obvious. Agencies also have experts in the archaeological and anthropological fields (as well as Native Americans) who can assist them in determining the appropriate group for consultation, yet, in some cases, archaeologists pursue consultation without receiving input from those more knowledgeable about the state's culture history and tribal relationships.

My final scenario concerns appeasement. Too often when dealing with tribes, I hear archaeologists or agency officials recite exactly what the tribe wants to hear— in some cases, making commitments that obviously cannot be delivered. When expectations are not met, the agency and archaeology in general lose credibility. Regardless of other issues, we must be honest in our dealings. Of course, this also applies to the tribal side as well. Neither group should make promises that cannot be kept or propose agreements that are impossible to bring to closure. Even if the initial set of circumstances is confrontational, it is better than defaulting to an unworkable solution.

Concluding Comments

In this paper I have presented a number of general examples of how Oklahoma has attempted to bridge communication gaps and bring about greater involvement of tribal people in preservation matters. In viewing these efforts, I have also identified a number of areas where problems exist. From my perspective, there can be no quick or simple solutions to establishing a strong link between Native Americans and the archaeological/preservation community. It will require meeting on a common ground and identifying where we need to focus efforts to resolve differences in perception, actions, and formal procedures. More importantly, we must all look to the potential of the future and learn from the failing of the past.

Twenty-Three

The Seeds of Common Ground
Experimentations in Indian Consultation

Over the past decade and within certain regions of the United States, archaeological field research has become much affected by the wishes of contemporary Indian tribes and communities. Federal legislation has placed requirements for consultation with tribes when sites on Indian lands, Indian trust lands, or impacts to significant cultural properties on federal lands may occur. Yet many archaeologists and other professionals remain remarkably aloof from this impact to their research domains and postpone or fail to carry out this requirement.

Today, archaeological research involving excavation on federal lands necessitates tribal consultation as either a contract or a permit condition. Existing federal legislation, however, does not give clear guidance concerning an appropriate consultative process. This has become a sensitive issue among Indian tribes that wish to define for themselves what consultation should mean. Agency archaeologists, archaeological contractors, and consultants need to be aware not only of the requirements for Indian consultation, but also of the differences among Indian tribes, and different levels in the consultation process itself. Many who initiate discussions with tribes become frustrated when tribes insist that they have not been consulted. This presentation emphasizes the importance of a government-to-government relationship between tribes and agencies, and a face-to-face relationship between tribal staff and professional archaeological staff. Examples of different kinds of successful Indian consultation provided here illustrate that professional integrity and basic communication lie at the heart of Indian consultation.

Tribal Consultation: Changing Tribal Views of Archaeologists

Native American views of archaeologists range from benign to detrimental, with few seeing benefits from the studies conducted by archaeologists. Archaeologists, coming at first from colleges, universities, and museums, and more recently from government agencies, rarely had contacts with Native Americans as an integral part of their plans and studies. An exception is the special relationship of Washington State University archaeologists in working on the Ozette Archaeological Project at Cape Alava, Washington, with the Makah Tribe at Neah Bay, and the establishment of the Makah Tribal Heritage Center in the 1970s. Also during that decade, the U.S. Army Corps of Engineers and the University of Idaho worked with the Nez Perce and Yakama tribes to establish a burial relocation program in the lower Snake River canyon. Apart from these exceptions, things only began to change with the legislative requirement for tribal consultation.

The significance of tribal consultation lies not so much in its definition as in what has not been captured in any definition thus far. Inherent in the tribal consultation process are the elements of sovereignty, the government's trust relationship, government-to-government communication, respect for cultural and linguistic diversity, and sensitivity to traditional cultural and religious practices. Tribes have also been treated differently according to their federal recognition status. In many ways, tribal consultation has become a matter of trust. Tribes and federal agencies alike continue to struggle with a working definition for consultation. Ultimately, it is not the definition that is important, only that tribes and governmental organizations are beginning to communicate and work together toward common goals.

Within the context of tribal consultation, archaeologists are often viewed with distrust and concern because of their common association with digging in the ground and with digging up graves. These are disrespectful activities in the eyes of many Native American cultures, so archaeologists are often met with reserve and concern, if not open hostility. In sharp contrast, most archaeologists are scientifically oriented, university-trained individuals who want to share their knowledge and show Native Americans the benefits of scientific insights and perspectives. This clash of cultural values continues to be a problem for American archaeology in general, but increased frequency of contact between archaeological professionals and growing participation of Native American tribes in archaeological activities through the tribal consultation process have provided the basis for common ground.

The Rise of Native American Consultation in the Northwest

Today, 54 tribes comprise the regional association known as Affiliated Tribes of Northwest Indians. Their lands, which formerly encompassed the whole Northwest, are now represented by reservations in the rural parts of Idaho, Oregon, Montana, and Washington (Figure 4). Legislated consultation has led many of these tribes to establish cultural programs or enlarge existing ones, both to preserve and protect heritage resources and graves on reservations as well as to consult with federal and state agencies about development projects on traditional lands ceded to the government by treaty (Figure 5). These ceded lands are usually greater in size than the existing reservations, so they tend to stretch limited financial and human resources that are available to the tribes. Wherever possible, tribes attempt to acquire ceded lands in an effort to restore their former domain, so their commitment to protection of cultural resources within former territories is substantial.

These consultation efforts with tribes have now brought federal archaeologists into routine contact with regional tribes. The process for developing this trust took place slowly over a number of years, and after much intense polarized discussion. Respect for tribal elders and good listening skills were prerequisites for common ground. The dialogue in this region was actually initiated by the Affiliated Tribes of Northwest Indians in 1986 as a series of tribally hosted annual conferences on cultural preservation. The first conference, hosted by the Oregon Governor's Office for Indian Affairs at Salem, Oregon, was a fierce confrontation of academic/ government archaeologists with representatives from 40 tribes; most left the conference feeling that they had nothing in common. In 1987, the conference was hosted at Warm Springs Reservation, Oregon. In spite of efforts by archaeologists to show the relevance of their studies to the tribes, all archaeologists were characterized by the tribes as ghouls. By 1988, when the conference was hosted by the Suquamish Tribe at Silverdale, Washington, tribes played a stronger role in the panel discussions and began to take the lead in active management of cultural resources on reservations and ceded lands. This was the beginning of some degree of mutual respect. These acquaintanceships established during the 1980s between tribal cultural staff and professional archaeologists became the basis for later working relationships leading to greater tribal participation.

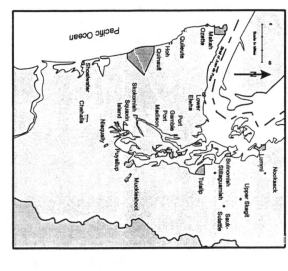

WESTERN WASHINGTON

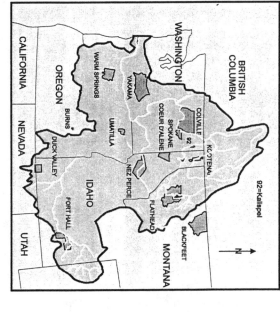

COLUMBIA RIVER BASIN

Figure 4. Indian reservations in western Washington state and the Columbia River Basin. In the mid-nineteenth century, Washington Territorial Governor Isaac Stevens called the Indian peoples to treaty councils to ward off conflict with Euroamerican settlers. He asked the people to relinquish ("cede") certain territorial and governmental rights to the United States in return for guarantees of access to crucial resources in ceded lands (customary fisheries, plant gathering areas, hunting grounds, and pastures); land set aside for tribal use as a corporation (reservations) and for individuals (allotments); and the right of self-governance for aspects of sovereignty not ceded to the United States. In 1855, Congress ratified the Hell Gate, Point Elliott, and Walla Walla treaties. The treaty process continued for the next 15 years, resulting in additional ratified treaties and occasional failures. In the early 1870s, the federal government halted the treaty process. Although it took additional Indian lands, especially in the Columbia River Basin, it created several reservations by Executive Order to provide for tribes that were unable to obtain them by treaty.

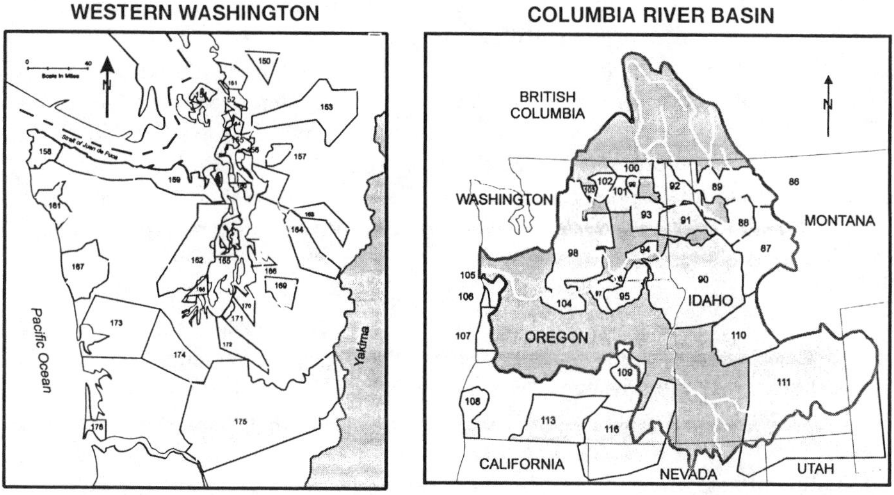

WESTERN WASHINGTON   COLUMBIA RIVER BASIN

Figure 5. Tribal ceded lands in western Washington state and the Columbia River Basin, listed by Indian Claims Commission docket number (Source: Bureau of Indian Affairs).

86 Blackfeet and Gros Ventre	104 Warm Springs	158 Makah
87 Flathead	105 Clatsop	159 S'Klallam
88 Upper Pend D'Oreille	106,	160 Snohomish
89 Kootenai	107 Tillamook	161 Quileute
90 Nez Perce	108 Coquille, Chetco,	162 Skokomish
91 Coeur d'Alene	Too-Too-To-Ney	163 Skyokmish
92 Kalispel	109 Snake	164 Snoqualmie
93 Spokane	110 Lemhi	165 Suquamish
94 Palus	111 Shoshoni	166 Duwamish
95 Cayuse	113 Klamath	167 Quinaelt
96 Walla Walla	116 Northern Paiute	168 Squaxin
97 Umatilla	150 Nooksack	169 Muckleshoot
98 Yakama	151 Lumhi	170 Puyallup
99 Colville	152 Samish	171 Steilacoom
100 Lake	153 Upper Skagit	172 Nisqually
101 Sanpoil-Nespelem	154 Swinomish	173 Lower Chehalis
102 Okanogan	155 Lower Skagit	174 Upper Chehalis
103 Methow	156 Kikiallus	175 Cowlitz
	157 Stillaguamish	176 Chinook

Governmental Efforts at Improving Relations With Tribes

President Clinton's 1994 memorandum instructing federal departments and agencies to improve relations with tribes set off numerous intensive efforts by federal agencies. The U.S. Army Corps of Engineers was directed in April 1994 by the acting assistant secretary for civil works of the U.S. Army to hold tribal workshops. The Corps of Engineers formed a Native American Intergovernmental Relations Task Force composed of 18 representatives from headquarters, division, and district offices. Only one-third of the working task force were archaeologists, but they played a strong role in shaping the format of the tribal workshops. The director of civil works at headquarters instructed 12 division offices to hold Native American workshops nationwide.

Between February and June 1995, field offices met with government representatives of 186 (47 percent) of the federally recognized tribes in the lower 48 states and reported the results of these meetings in after-action reports. The workshops emphasized listening to tribal leaders and resulted in lists of issues and concerns to be addressed by local districts and affected tribes. This experience raised the visibility of tribes within the federal bureaucracy and has led to quick resolution of many longstanding issues at the local level. The effort has also served to market Corps of Engineers programs. Within the Pacific Northwest, workshops were held in Seattle and Anchorage. The Seattle workshop invited 41 tribes, and 94 persons representing 26 tribes actually attended. Every participating tribe was left with names of specific persons to contact regarding future issues. The task force compiled a report to the Directorate of Civil Works at Corps of Engineers headquarters to summarize tribal issues and concerns and make recommendations for improving tribal relations (U.S. Army Corps of Engineers 1996).

Another regional governmental effort to improve tribal relations includes Washington Governor Spellman's Centennial Accord with federally recognized Indian tribes in August 1989. This document, signed by all but one tribe, acknowledges tribal sovereignty and commits state agencies to carry out a government-to-government relationship with tribes in conducting state business. In June 1996, the Oregon governor issued a similar proclamation to promote better tribal relations.

Funding Tribal Efforts

Funding for tribal cultural programs has been an abiding problem. Most tribes depended on funding from the Bureau of Indian Affairs and the National Park Service. The Indian Self-determination and Education Assistance Act (as amended 1994) and reduced federal budgets have shifted the monetary burden to the tribes.

The Nuclear Waste Policy Act of 1984 provided a major boost for cultural programs of the Yakama, Umatilla, and Nez Perce tribes, with a focus on the cultural program at the U.S. Department of Energy's Hanford Site. This program offered the first direct funding to tribes for cultural resources within this region.

Federal agency contracts with Native American tribes in the Northwest for technical services began in 1985 when the U.S. Army Corps of Engineers contracted with the Colville Confederated Tribes, Nespelem, Washington, for the accessioning and curation of archaeological collections from sites impacted by the pool raise at Chief Joseph Dam. The Corps of Engineers funded training for tribal staff, equipment for storage and curation, and part-time operation for each facility. The tribes provided the building, the technical staff, and the ongoing maintenance cost. The Corps of Engineers soon extended this approach to meeting its curation needs by initiating artifact accessioning and curation contracts and cooperative agreements starting in 1991 for archaeological collections from Libby Dam–Lake Koocanusa with the Confederated Salish-Kootenai Tribes of the Flathead Reservation at Pablo, Montana, and in 1993 with the Yakama Indian Nation, Toppenish, Washington, for curation of artifacts from the North Bonneville Dam archaeological project on the lower Columbia River. These accomplishments are doubly significant in view of requirements for artifact inventories under the Native American Graves Protection and Repatriation Act of 1991. Under this curation arrangement, the tribes can be contracted to produce the artifact inventories in a respectful fashion, using their own trained personnel.

Many tribes, notably the Colville, Kalispel, Nez Perce, Umatilla, Warm Springs, and Yakama, have hired professional archaeologists as part of their tribal staff. A few tribes, like the Shoshone-Bannock at Fort Hall, Idaho, have professionally trained Native American archaeological staff. All of these tribes have sought contracts with federal agencies to take over certain cultural resource management activities on federal lands within their ceded territories. The Corps of Engineers has contracted with all of these tribes for archaeological monitoring, burial issues, and oral histories on project lands.

Some Examples of Constructive Contacts With Tribes

In 1992 the Bureau of Reclamation, Bonneville Power Administration, and the Corps of Engineers invited 14 federally recognized tribes to participate in a joint agency study of Columbia River Federal Hydropower System Operation. Because of the special cultural and subsistence interest of the tribes in the Columbia River system, and because the three-agency Cultural Resources Work Group needed specific information from the tribes, contracts were issued in 1993 by the Bonneville Power Administration to six tribes for cultural resources information. Much of the information supplied by tribes concerns traditional cultural properties and is being incorporated into reservoir management plans for the protection of cultural resources. Later in 1993, the three agency study managers for the Columbia River System Operation Review met with representatives of the 14 tribes in an effort to solicit tribal participation and to improve communication. Funding was made available to tribes for their general attendance and participation in Columbia River system study meetings. Finally, five government-to-government meetings were held by the three agency study managers with tribes that requested them. Long-term agreements between the three federal agencies and the Advisory Council on Historic Preservation hold promise of continuing opportunities for active tribal participation in federal agency cultural resource management programs at Columbia River reservoirs. Current ideas advanced by the tribes include funded site erosion monitoring studies, recommendations for cultural site protection, sacred site surveys, and cultural geographies of traditional place names.

During the early 1930s, archaeological investigations were conducted by the U.S. National Museum in and around the proposed Bonneville Dam reservoir on the lower Columbia River. The artifacts and human remains ended up at the Smithsonian Institution. In addition, the ancestral human remains recovered from The Dalles reservoir at upper and lower Memaloose Island are claimed by both the Yakama and Warm Springs tribes. Unable to resolve this issue, the remains were held by the government for more than 20 years. Owing to tribal consultation efforts by the Corps of Engineers under the Native American Graves Protection and Repatriation Act, the Smithsonian collection of human remains was returned to the tribes and finally reburied along with the human remains from the reservoir.

In December 1994, the Yakama and Warm Springs tribes resolved their differences through joint reburial of the 143–173 human remains at an Indian cemetery in Washington. The Corps of Engineers in the Northwest has now established nine agreements with regional tribes for repatriation of human remains under the Native American Graves Protection and Repatriation Act.

Between 1936 and 1956, when the Corps of Engineers flooded the lower Columbia River reservoirs at Bonneville Dam, The Dalles Dam, and John Day Dam, the treaty tribes lost important usual and accustomed fishing sites established by treaty. In 1981, due to tribal efforts, Congress directed the Corps of Engineers to create 17 in-lieu treaty fishing sites to compensate for this loss. These fishing sites were acquired and access was developed for the tribes by the Corps of Engineers in November 1995. Another 6 sites are planned for acquisition for tribal treaty fishing in Bonneville Dam reservoir. These sites will be held in trust by the Bureau of Indian Affairs on behalf of four Columbia River treaty tribes, Yakama, Umatilla, Warm Springs, and Nez Perce.

Regional tribes have identified the need for professional training in field archaeology, laboratory methods, collections accessioning, and archaeological curation. Opportunities for on-the-job training in all aspects of field archaeology abound through federal agency cultural resources survey and mitigation programs. In a current example, the Corps of Engineers identified five prehistoric archaeological sites within planned highway rights-of-way on the Army's Yakama Training Center near Ellensburg, Washington. Site avoidance through project redesign eliminated potential impacts to ancestral graves pointed out by tribal elders. Excavation of the five sites, however, was approved by the Advisory Council on Historic Preservation as acceptable mitigation. Formal tribal coordination was conducted, including site visits and reviews of proposed data recovery for the contract statement of work. Tribes were reluctant to comment on the data recovery project formally. Nevertheless, the Corps of Engineers required the archaeological contractor, Eastern Washington University, to hire archaeological trainees from each of the affected tribes, Yakama and Wanapum. These tribal members, working on each field crew, reported back to their respective Indian communities daily on the archaeological work being conducted. Tribal members learned about professional archaeological techniques, and field archaeologists learned much about Native American perspectives and insights about the habitation features being unearthed. Mutual respect was achieved. Representatives of tribal governments periodically visited the field sites but never formally acknowledged the work being done. Upon conclusion of excavations, tribal members invited all the field archaeologists to participate in a traditional religious ceremony that asked the Creator for forgiveness for digging in the earth and requested protection for crew members on their homeward journey.

Cultural resource site protection at Columbia River system reservoirs has usually been accomplished by federal agency staff or through contracts with professional archaeologists. In 1995 the Corps of Engineers shifted these efforts to interested tribes whose ceded lands were affected by hydroelectric projects. Contracts have been negotiated with the Nez Perce Tribe for survey and site evaluation at Dworshak reservoir in Idaho; the Colville Confederated Tribes are conducting a preliminary archaeological reconnaissance of Chief Joseph Dam reservoir in Washington; and the Kalispel Tribe will monitor reservoir fluctuations at Albeni Falls Dam–Lake Pend Oreille, Idaho. All tribal staff meet required archaeological qualifications. These changes in tribal role from passive to active signify meaningful measures of trust, cooperation, and increased common ground shared by archaeologists and Native Americans within this region.

What Can Archaeologists Do to Promote Better Relations With Tribes?

Although some common understanding now exists between tribes and professional archaeologists, a wide gulf in cultural values still separates them. The gulf does, however, provide a potential benefit to the developing field of archaeology. This can come about if archaeologists are willing to recognize that their discipline is regarded as both a science and a humanity by the National Science Foundation and the National Endowment for the Humanities.

Professional archaeologists have developed elaborate procedures for designing and implementing sophisticated scientific methods and analyses for archaeological studies. The humanistic aspect of archaeological study has not been equally well developed by practicing archaeologists, and it has been used by academic practitioners principally to interpret scientific findings and results for the public. One of the humanistic skills includes the development of new perspectives for consultation with tribes. In addition, plans for future archaeological study should include a balance of humanistic studies such as oral histories, place name studies, and sacred site surveys to complement scientific studies such as protonmagnetometry, X-ray diffraction, and radiocarbon dating analyses. Acceptance of humanistic study means acceptance of its practitioners, including tribal elders, and their findings. The validity of humanistic data in its own right is foreign to the scientific mind and requires some accommodation. Federal archaeologists need to identify, in consultation with tribes, appropriate roles for tribal members in cultural resource management. Many of these roles may be defined through participation in humanistic studies to complement the rigor of contemporary archaeological science. This trend in Native American archaeology is reminiscent of Walter Taylor's (1948) "conjunctive approach" and supports the close association of American archaeology and anthropology, as argued by Willey and Phillips (1958). One current recommendation is for professional archaeologists to incorporate more humanistic methods of study into a truly conjunctive approach that includes the opportunity for tribal perspectives, religious values, worldview, and linguistic contributions to be expressed in cultural resource program planning and execution. The future prospect for more common ground between Native Americans and archaeologists depends on our willingness to accept broader paradigms than science as our justification for studying the past.

The opinions and conclusions expressed in this presentation do not necessarily reflect the official views or concurrence of the U.S. Army Corps of Engineers. The author is indebted to Lawr V. Salo who prepared the figures and who shared equally in these tribal accomplishments on behalf of Seattle District, Corps of Engineers. In addition, Lynda Walker, Portland District, Corps of Engineers, and John Leier, Walla Walla District, Corps of Engineers, shared information regarding tribal outreach through district cultural programs. Finally, thanks to Cheryl Lohman, Native American coordinator, North Pacific Division, Corps of Engineers, and Colonel Donald T. Wynn, Seattle district engineer, who supported this effort, and to Lynn Larson, Larson Anthropological/Archaeological Services, who presented the opportunity.

Twenty-Four

Tribal Consultation in the National Park Service
A Personal Perspective

Having spent seemingly most of my lifetime as a graduate student learning never to write in the first person, the volume editors' request for an article written from a personal perspective presented a challenge. They asked for a contribution on National Park Service approaches to tribal consultation from my perspective as a tribal-turned-federal employee. There seems no way of accomplishing this without using the dreaded first-person pronouns.

The task is also difficult because tribal consultation is conducted in the National Park Service's Southwest Office by a team of people headed by Edward Natay, American Indian trust responsibility officer, and consisting of Virginia Salazar, curation program leader, Alan Bohnert, curator, and me. I was reluctant to write this paper separately from the rest of the team because not only do the other team members handle the majority of direct consultation, but there are very few things about the subject that we don't do jointly and by consensus.

Consultation about park-specific matters is also conducted in the Southwest by many superintendents and staff members of individual parks. On a larger scale, in the Intermountain Field Area (the administrative unit of the National Park Service of which the Southwest area is one part) consultation is handled by many other individuals in other parks and park support offices, and all consultation activities are guided by a consultation coordination committee composed of superintendents, curators, American Indian liaisons, archaeologists, and anthropologists. My role is one small component of a tightly integrated team, which in turn contributes to a much larger whole. My perspective, therefore, does not necessarily represent the views of other members of the team, nor the National Park Service as a whole.

My professional life has been intertwined with the National Park Service and American Indian tribal historic preservation and cultural resource management interests for the past 12 years. In 1984 I was hired by the National Park Service as a temporary employee to research the history of Navajo occupation at Wupatki National Monument, which borders the Navajo Indian Reservation in northern Arizona. What I found was a long and unflattering history of federally sanctioned destruction of customary Navajo land use practices. Sadly, post–World War II National Park Service policies perpetuated the pattern, until by the early 1980s the long-time Navajo presence in the Wupatki Basin was almost obliterated.

After finishing the report and while beginning a doctoral dissertation on the same subject, I went to work for the Navajo Nation Historic Preservation Department. I spent four years as the program's deputy director and another two as an anthropologist researching Navajo history in the Grand Canyon for the tribe's contribution to the Glen Canyon Environmental Studies program (Roberts, Begay, and Kelley 1995).

During the late 1980s and early 1990s, the Historic Preservation Department became a strong force in bringing Indian tribal cultural preservation concerns into the national historic preservation arena, concurrently with major initiatives of the National Park Service (see Downer and Roberts [1996] for discussion). The National Park Service clarified the applicability of the National Register of Historic Places to places significant in American Indian versions of their own histories; it brought tribal consultation and substitution of tribal historic preservation programs for state programs unequivocally into the provisions of the National Historic Preservation Act (NHPA); it began making historic preservation grants to tribes and to the Keepers of the Treasures; it supported passage of the Native American Graves Protection and Repatriation Act (NAGPRA) and took the lead role in its implementation. Still, despite the National Park Service's leadership role in incorporating tribal preservation concerns into the national historic preservation program, compliance with the spirit and intent of the NHPA and National Park Service policies often did not seem to be carried out by individual parks.

For example, the Navajo Indian Reservation encompasses or is bordered by 15 national parks or monuments, and many more are within Navajo aboriginal lands. As a tribal employee, one of my main interests and duties was to ensure that parks were following legal mandates and National Park Service policies in consulting with the Navajo Nation about planning and management activities in which the tribe had an interest.

The Navajo Nation had a lot to say about how the park service should be doing things better, or at least differently. We wrote articles and gave presentations about federal agencies' seeming inability to consult in the context of undertakings subject to compliance with NHPA, to incorporate consultation into proactive planning processes, to develop systematic means of consultation through the use of agreement documents and tribal advisory committees, and to devote the financial resources necessary to conduct meaningful consultation. We commented on park planning documents and policies generated from regional and Washington offices. I wrote more than my share of vehement letters to park superintendents, the regional director, and Washington. Altogether, it must have seemed that the Navajo Nation didn't approve of much of anything that the National Park Service did.

So, several years later when the position of cultural anthropologist for the National Park Service's Southwest Region was advertised, I thought it was time to put my money where my mouth was and apply for the job. What I didn't expect was that the position would be offered to me. When I left the Navajo Nation, my friends joked that I would have to go to Santa Fe and answer all my own letters. And their jokes were not far from the truth. I was prepared for a change of perspectives, but I had no idea what that perspective was to be.

On my third day of working at the park service I was sent to a meeting involving representatives from a tribe, another federal agency, the state historic preservation office (SHPO), and the National Park Service. The meeting was about the other agency's preparation of an environmental impact statement and the involvement of the tribe in National Environmental Policy Act (NEPA) and National Historic Preservation Act compliance processes, a subject with which I was very comfortable. I knew exactly what I believed personally and professionally, but suddenly realized that I didn't know what I was supposed to believe on behalf of the park service. I did not know what the agency stood for or what kind of position it would be acceptable for me to advance. That feeling of a lack of identity consumed me for the next six months, and I began to understand why the Navajo Nation has experienced so much frustration in trying to develop a relationship with the National Park Service over the years.

As a tribal employee, even during the times when it seemed like all I was doing was governmental bureaucratic busywork, every action and duty, no matter how big or small, contributed to a larger purpose: promoting and protecting tribal sovereignty. Each individual had a place and a purpose as part of the collective whole.

We were guided by the sovereignty principle, and being part of the "we" working toward a common purpose gave each individual an identity. After joining the park service, I kept looking for the "we" and couldn't find it. I was unable to identify the collective values that provided a context for my daily activities. What was my work contributing to? What does the agency stand for? What do we believe with respect to our relationships with Indian tribes? The answers to these questions have long been well formed for the park service's preservation and conservation missions but were—and are—still in the formative stages with regard to the living communities traditionally associated with park lands.

Then, in June 1995, Ed, Virginia, Allen, and I started getting mired in coordinating preparation of the inventories of human remains and associated funerary objects required by NAGPRA. The act requires that inventories be pre-pared in consultation with tribes, partially to help determine which tribes are affiliated with the remains. Like all other federal agency and federally funded museum officials, our team's job was to consult with tribes about their affiliations with the human remains inventoried in our collections, evaluate all the lines of evidence available to us, and assist the park superintendents in making decisions about which tribes are most likely to be affiliated with the remains. Looking back, it is probably a good thing none of us knew beforehand what a monumental task the consultations would be.

Our team was working with the inventories for parks in Oklahoma, Texas, New Mexico, and part of Arizona. While some of the human remains in the park collections date to the postcontact period and are known to be affiliated with certain tribes, the great majority are precolumbian and might be considered affiliated with many contemporary tribes. In New Mexico alone, for example, more than 20 tribes claimed affiliation to remains of the precolumbian past, in addition to tribes in other states whose ancestral territories included lands in New Mexico, and the same can be said for other states. Asking questions of the tribes about their affiliations with ancestral human remains, therefore, presents a tremendously complex set of issues.

First, precolumbian culture areas defined on the basis of patterns found in the archaeological record do not carry the same meaning to tribes as they do to archaeologists. Thus, the divisions between so-called cultural groups, such as Sinagua, Mogollon, Fremont, Anasazi, and even subdivisions of each such as Kayenta Anasazi, Rio Grande Anasazi, and so forth, simply do not make sense to tribal members.

Second, and related to the first point, tribal traditional histories are based on much different concepts of time than the histories archaeologists and anthropologists have constructed of the precontact past. Reference points to periods of "prehistory" that make sense in anthropological thinking do not make sense in the context of tribal histories.

Third, many tribes have not been asked questions about their pasts requiring specialized traditional knowledge in a long time. Federal managers are asking questions that require considerable internal discussion within a tribe, and the mandated deadlines for answers are too short.

Fourth, layered among various tribes' traditional knowledge of their pasts are contemporary political issues that pit one tribal oral history against another.

From June to October 1995, the National Park Service's Southwest Office and the Intermountain Cultural Resources Center sponsored seven NAGPRA consultation meetings with various combinations of representatives from nearly 40 tribes, at a total cost of more than $60,000, not including salaries. Individual parks hosted a number of more specific meetings at their own expense, involving at least another dozen tribes. The main objective of the meetings was to communicate our process for preparing the inventories and to listen to tribal representatives' concerns about our procedures and to learn how they defined their own affiliations with the past. We regard these consultations as one of the most significant requirements of the law because we believe that oral tradition about affiliation with the past is a line of evidence equal to those derived from archaeology, anthropology, biology, linguistics, and documented history, but far more elusive and generally under-represented in agency decision making. We also believe that the results of our decisions have direct impact on living communities, and we cannot make those decisions independently of the people affected.

But the scope and the weight of what we were asking people to discuss was immense. Sometimes the meetings were incredibly tense. People cried when they spoke of their pasts and the knowledge that has been lost. They had difficulty discussing subjects in the sacred realm in such a public and clinical context. Sometimes accusations of political agendas or personal motivations were hurled from one tribe to another, from tribes to us as representatives of the federal government, and even, outside the meetings, among National Park Service employees.

I can safely speak for all the team members in saying that the NAGPRA consultations were among the most emotionally draining experiences any of us has ever gone through. Each of us spent almost every day dwelling on the implications of what we were doing, the impact on people and communities, and the weight of our ethical and professional responsibilities. What often kept us going was knowing that we were conducting our consultations honestly and responsibly and fulfilling the spirit and intent of the law to the best of our abilities. By the time the inventories were submitted in November 1995, I finally felt that a collective value was shared by the National Park Service. Since that time, I have come to see how fortunate the park service is in having preservation as its mandate and having the benefit of multidisciplinary expertise to apply to the preservation and management of resources under its stewardship. The use of an interdisciplinary cultural resource management team and a consultation team in the Southwest Office and Intermountain Cultural Resources Center is allowing us to develop a commitment to meaningful tribal consultation, and to apply what we learn from consultations to our resource management practices.

Still, we cannot relax with the thought that we are doing well. In many ways, the job we have before us is greater than ever, partly because NAGPRA has helped push the consultation doors wide open, and partly because of the current park service reorganization, which has deconstructed the old hierarchy and distributed authority to individual parks. Except for a few functions still handled out of Washington because they do not directly involve parks (e.g., tribal replacement of SHPOs under the revised NHPA provisions, the historic preservation fund grants), relationships with tribes are now directly between individual parks and the tribes with interests in those parks. Individual park superintendents represent "the United States" in the "government-to-government relationship" that President Clinton's 1994 Executive Memorandum promised and that tribes have come to expect.

This new decentralized structure can be very good for development of relationships between tribes and the National Park Service, very bad, or perhaps both. On the one hand, it means that parks and tribes can work closely together on issues that are specifically applicable to lands and resources at a particular park. Park managers and tribal representatives can get to know one another as individuals. Together, they can develop agreements for the unique situations of human remains and other discoveries, cultural and natural resource management and preservation, park planning, interpretation, and visitor services that make sense to each park and the tribes associated with it. Development of positive tribal relationships is already working well in some parks. Parks are sponsoring studies of tribal affiliations, holding their own consultation meetings, and developing memoranda of agreement with individual tribes.

On the other hand, reorganization has the potential to fragment decision making and policy setting, leaving the tribes with dozens of separate park services with which to deal. Parks can make decisions that are not consistent with other parks' decisions, leaving tribes to wonder what the National Park Service's position is. More than before, tribes are having to "start over," explaining their positions each time they consult with an individual program or park, especially when park administrations change. Park managers now have an even bigger responsibility of knowing what's happening in the larger context around them. When it comes to tribal consultation, none of us, whether in parks, park support offices, or Washington, can remain isolated. Each of us must understand the larger implications of our words and promises, know the larger contexts of our decisions, and be aware of the larger issues affecting tribal relationships with parks and the park service as a whole. We all need to know how the relationships between tribes and one park affect the tribes' relationships at another park; parks need to know how events in Washington, such as development of tribal-SHPO substitution agreements, affect relationships with the parks; and Washington programs need to know how their actions affect the ability to develop relationships with tribes at the park level.

Park managers, support offices, and Washington, now more than ever, have a responsibility to understand many complex issues. We must all understand what kinds of consultation are required for compliance, not just with NAGPRA, but with NHPA, the Archaeological Resources Protection Act, and other laws and policies. We have to know what tribal sovereignty really means, what the American Indian Religious Freedom Act does or does not do, what First Amendment issues are, and the potential legal implications of each decision. We need to consider when consultation about undertakings can more effectively be initiated in the context of compliance with NEPA rather than Section 106 of NHPA. We must understand the importance of incorporating tribal traditional history into interpretive messages, and about staying out of tribal politics. Above all, we must take a step beyond" compliance" with the requirements of law and regulation into genuine symbiotic cooperation for our common interests.

These things will not happen by decree. They must happen by example and consensus. More than ever, the National Park Service needs those commonly held guiding principles I was looking for a couple of years ago. We need to know collectively where we are going with tribal relationships as the National Park Service, not just as individual parks, offices, and programs. If we really consider tribes to be partners in the our preservation mission, then that commitment must be demonstrated collectively. It is our responsibility to communicate across boundaries and to present ourselves as the single—albeit diverse and decentralized—agency that tribes believe and expect us to be. Reorganization can be an opportunity for developing a common vision, or it can be an excuse for allowing it to disintegrate.

The editors of this volume asked the authors to consider "What can we do better?" This is what I think we can do better in the National Park Service. Reorganization is an opportunity for park service leadership to foster a corporate ethic that guides each of us as members of the larger whole, much like our corporate ethic guides us in resources management or visitor services. It would be easy to toss up our hands and say that we need more money to do a better job. But money is not the only answer to the question about how can we do a better job; to me, the answer is in a better definition of who "we" are and what we believe.

I believe that in the Intermountain Field Area we need to put a lot of effort into the Consultation Coordination Committee to coordinate discussion and resolution of issues and provide direction for the parks and programs that now function independently from one another. The committee can monitor and coordinate such activities as keeping track of consultations in individual parks and their outcomes so that consistent results can be applied from park to park, as well as provide consistent guidance on major issues such as confidentiality of records, legal consequences of decisions on repatriation of items claimed under the provisions of

NAGPRA, models of agreement documents between tribes and parks, and so forth. The committee can gather from many park experiences information on what works and what does not and can share the benefit of those experiences with others who need it. From these common experiences, it might even be able to articulate the needed common vision.

With a shared commitment to common values and consistency in the application of our policies, eventually we may be able to implement some of the procedures tribes have been asking for in consultation meetings over and over for so long. We should be consulting tribes during programmatic planning rather than waiting until the development and construction phases for individual undertakings. We should be developing tribal advisory committees and memoranda of understanding—and really make tribes partners in our preservation and resources management activities.

Thanks to Nina Swidler, Alan Downer, Roger Anyon, and Kurt Dongoske for asking for this paper and for their efforts in bringing the book together. Thanks also to June-el Piper for her excellent editing. Special thanks to Southwest Support Office Superintendent Jerry Rogers, Intermountain Field Area Director John Cook, and Navajo Nation/NPS Chaco Protection Program Manager John Stein for their very helpful comments on an earlier draft and their influence on my thinking over the years. And thanks as always to Ed Natay, Virgina Salazar, and Allen Bohnert for their professional guidance and friendship.

SECTION VI

Commentary

T.J. FERGUSON ■
JOE WATKINS
GORDON L. PULLAR

Twenty-Five

Native Americans and Archaeologists
Commentary and Personal Perspectives

Americanist archaeology is currently undergoing many intriguing changes as archaeologists respond to criticism by Native Americans whose ancestors created the archaeological record that most archaeologists study in the United States and Canada. Native Americans have challenged archaeologists to conduct their work in a manner that respects tribal cultural values and tribal authority, and to address research and management issues that are important to Native Americans. In the United States, the passage of the Native American Graves Protection and Repatriation Act of 1990 (NAGPRA) and recent amendments to the National Historic Preservation Act have given needed changes the force of law. Beyond mandatory changes, however, many archaeologists and the Native Americans they work for are committed to transforming archaeology so that it has more relevance to native populations.

Archaeology is changing in part because more archaeologists are being directly employed by Indian tribes and other Native American organizations, more Native

Americans are serving as consultants in archaeological research and educational outreach, and more Native Americans are becoming archaeologists in their own right. The chapters in this book reflect the emerging perspectives that stem from all three of these new and positive trends.

Cultural Diversity

It is hard to discuss "Native Americans" when there are more than 550 recognized tribes, Hawaiian organizations, and Alaska Native villages in the United States, additional tribes in Canada and Mexico, and even more Native American groups that are not recognized by national governments. Each of these tribes and Native American groups has unique cultural values and beliefs, and it is difficult to reduce this diversity to the singularity implied in the term "Native Americans." The ways that you can characterize one tribe don't necessarily apply to other tribes. What is true for the Navajo may not be true for the Arapaho; what is true for an urban Indian may not be true for a traditionalist living on a reservation or in a remote Alaska Native village. Anthropologists therefore need to be careful when they discuss "Native Americans" so that they don't end up with caricature rather than valid generalization. For this reason, it is often more accurate to talk about specific tribes rather than the generic "Native Americans." Given this fact, it is encouraging that most of the authors in this book grounded their observations in the context of particular tribal cultures. The marvelous and important diversity of Native Americans is therefore well represented and served.

Like Native Americans, archaeologists also exhibit diversity in their values and beliefs, and this has to be kept in mind when considering contemporary archaeology. Thus, when Tsosie writes that archaeologists have perceived ancient people as "research specimens," believing that the codes of ethical behavior that govern European burials do not govern the treatment of ancient peoples, our response is: "Sure, we know there are archaeologists who did and still do think like that. But we also know many archaeologists, especially those who work for Indian tribes, who don't think like that." This book contains many chapters by archaeologists, some of whom are also Native Americans, who view both ancient and contemporary Native Americans as people.

What Is the Relationship Between the Past and the Present?

In many of the chapters, it is clear that Native Americans and archaeologists sometimes view the relationship between the past and present in fundamentally different ways. Tsosie observes, for instance, that most Native American peoples see the past as being connected to the present, with knowledge about it being preserved in oral traditions, ceremonial practices, and beliefs. This connection also pertains in a scholarly context, as evidenced by the emotional connection that Lippert feels when she views artifacts recovered from the archaeological record.

In western culture, almost everything is categorized or put in conceptual pigeon holes or boxes. Western scientists become uncomfortable if they can't find the appropriate box to put data or information in. This is contrary to most, if not all, indigenous cultures in North America, who tend to see connections, complexities, and overlaps to everything. The "box system" thus doesn't work very well for Native Americans. As Suzuki and Knudsen (1992) observe, western scientists see time as linear, while Native Americans see time as circular. For the Koyukon Indians of Alaska, Suzuki and Knudsen (1992:35) conclude that, "Distant time is a dim but potent memory, illuminated by traditional stories and spiritual practices; it forever lies beyond precise measure or clear human understanding."

In talking about the Hopi and Zuni Indians, Dongoske and Anyon note that these Pueblo people view ancestral sites as being imbued with life, and inhabited by the spirits of the ancestors who once lived there. The Navajo, as Martin describes, have a similar view. In contrast, many archaeologists view these same sites as static sources of data to be studied in an objective and unemotional manner. As many authors in this book observe, this discrepancy in worldview makes it incumbent on archaeologists to consult with Native Americans before undertaking research that impacts the vital role archaeological sites play in Native American culture.

What Do Archaeologists Do and What Do They Value?

The contributions to this volume raise the issue of what archaeologists actually do. In this regard, it is important to note that archaeologists study the present to learn about the past: that is, archaeologists use the scientific method to study artifacts and sites in an archaeological record that exists in the present. There are many issues dealing with how the past is represented in archaeological research, but with the exception of Echo-Hawk and Begay, few of the authors explicitly address them in this book. Most of the contemporary problems discussed in the volume stem from how archaeological resources existing in the present are managed in the present. Thus, when Jemison and Tsosie question "Who owns the past?" and Tsosie frames an answer in terms of property law, the issues really revolve around who owns artifacts or controls human remains that exist in the present. Forsman points out this fact in his chapter, and Tsosie adds that "property law is in many ways completely unsuitable to address the legal rights of Indian people with regard to their ancestors."

Tsosie is correct when she notes that archaeologists consider the archaeological record formed by Native Americans as a valued object for study. It should be kept in mind, of course, that many archaeologists also consider the archaeological record of Spanish churches, slave quarters, Euroamerican ranches, urban Chinese settlements, and other non-Indian archaeological sites as valuable for study. We don't think the essence of archaeology is racist; archaeologists study their own ancestors, as well as the ancestors of other peoples.

What Does Archaeology Have to Offer Native Americans?

One of the questions addressed in this volume is "What does archaeology have to offer Native Americans?" In this regard, some Native Americans, as Tsosie notes, dispute that science can "tell" them much about their origins. These Native Americans already know where they came from according to traditional knowledge. Other Native Americans, as Lippert, Echo-Hawk, Martin, Begay, Van Pelt, and Munnell explain, do find archaeology interesting, and they suggest archaeology has the potential to contribute important historical information.

Archaeology also offers other benefits to Native Americans. Dongoske and Anyon as well as Forsman observe that archaeologists have provided supporting evidence for the litigation of land claims, and this has been important for many tribes. Moreover, as Martin and Cypress observe, when Native Americans become archaeologists they can influence how cultural resources and burials are managed and protected. Native Americans can use archaeology to promote their tribal sovereignty, or self-governance as Ravesloot calls it. The historical and political implications of archaeology with respect to tribal sovereignty are also discussed by White Deer, Forsman, and Jackson, and archaeologists should pay close attention to the points that are made in these chapters. Tribal sovereignty is an important social and political issue that archaeologists need to understand in order to work effectively with Native Americans.

Furthermore, as Martin, Begay, and Cypress discuss, archaeology can facilitate development and also provide important financial benefits for Native Americans. The Navajo Nation, for instance, employs upwards of 150 people in its historic preservation and archaeology departments, the majority of whom are tribal members. The combined budget of these two tribal programs is $7 million a year, and the economic impact of a budget of this size is substantial. Of course, with 220,000 tribal members, the Navajo Nation is a very large tribe. Even smaller tribes, however, can benefit by establishing cultural resource management programs. The

Hualapai Tribe in Arizona, for example, with a population of 2,000 members, employs 7 people in its Office of Cultural Resources, all of whom are tribal members. On a reservation with an unemployment rate of 40 percent, these 7 jobs are an important part of the tribal economy.

As Ravesloot and Carter point out, archaeology can also be used as a tool to help educate young Native Americans. The Red Earth Summer Archaeology Program sponsored by the Gila River Indian Community provides a good example.

What Do Native Americans Have to Offer Archaeology?

Another issue addressed in this book is what Native Americans have to offer archaeology. One thing Native Americans can offer archaeology, as Echo-Hawk and Anyon and his coauthors explain, is a perspective on ancient history informed by the study of traditional history. Archaeologists are gradually gaining a more sophisticated understanding of the methodological problems involved with using Native American oral traditions in historical research. As Echo-Hawk notes, much of the history contained in oral traditions is embedded in a religious context, and this needs to be respected. That is why it is essential for this type of research to be done by tribal members or by scholars working in close collaboration with tribal members. It is significant that Echo-Hawk realizes that to have scholarly credibility, academic studies of Native American oral traditions need to be subjected to "careful scrutiny and reasoned criticism." As he notes, Indians who make claims for historicity in oral traditions should expect academic treatment of the history that is extracted from those traditions. Echo-Hawk is right when he says that the successful integration of oral traditions with information from archaeology and physical anthropology has great potential for reshaping the academic construction of ancient human history. From a scholarly perspective, the combination of human osteology, archaeology, and Native American oral traditions will yield a more complete understanding of the past than can be gained by using any one of those sources by itself.

Another way that Native Americans can contribute to archaeology is by directly helping archaeologists to interpret the archaeological record. Martin, in her work for the Navajo Nation, has learned to value the perspective of traditional Navajo people, who taught her to recognize the different archaeological components in a ceremonial location rather than viewing these features as a single, massive site. The conceptualization of the archaeological record in terms of the ceremonies that created it holds great interest for archaeologists, and at the same time, it is presumably a more meaningful way of describing these sites for Navajo people who need to make decisions about how they should be managed.

A final way Native Americans are helping archaeology is by operating tribal archaeology and cultural resource management programs. Exciting things are happening in the archaeology programs operated by the Umatilla, Leech Lake, Navajo, Hopi, Zuni, and Gila River programs discussed in this book. These programs are on the cutting edge of establishing the new ethics and research protocols that our discipline needs to develop.

Experience of Native American Archaeologists

This volume presents important perspectives from Native Americans who also happen to be archaeologists. Perhaps not surprisingly, the often negative history of Native Americans with respect to archaeology has caused problems for those tribal members attempting to make use of some western concepts and methods in cultural preservation efforts. Cypress tell us that archaeology is a science that members of his tribe have expressed little interest in, pointing out that there are no Seminole archaeologists. Begay suggests there is a need for Native Americans to get into archaeology so informed decisions involving archaeology can be made at a local level. However, Begay rightly questions whether Native American archaeologists should be forced to choose between "archaeological discipline and tribal tradition." The words of Martin, Fuller, and Lippert reveal that Native Americans can become very effective archaeologists and retain a strong sense of who they are as native people. Archaeologists themselves can help this situation. As Ravesloots says, "Archaeologists can change Native American perspectives of and interest in archaeology, but we cannot expect traditional approaches to work."

To be sure, archaeology is a western science with western biases. Yet, native peoples have become part of many western sciences and are encouraged by their tribes and local communities. Why should they be made to feel as if they have done something wrong by becoming an archaeologist? Archaeology is a science developed exclusively in western culture, and western science as a whole is, more often than not, very different from native ways of knowing. Western science likes, and even demands, that everything fit into a neat category. Often these categories cause problems for Native Americans, as Begay recounts. It is sad that among his people Forsman is "often subject to teasing and sometimes distrust" because of his academic background. Tessie Naranjo, who unfortunately decided not to publish in this volume the excellent presentation she gave at the SAA meeting, also described the distrust that her tribal administration has of its own cultural preservation program because the tribal members working in it were educated in the western system. Their efforts are viewed "suspiciously," she said. Given how much Native American people who choose to bridge the gap between traditional knowledge and Western science care about preserving and protecting their culture and heritage, some of the attitudes that their own people have toward them are hurtful.

NAGPRA and State Burial Laws

NAGPRA is a theme that runs through many of the chapters in this volume. It is clearly an important and crucial law for the protection of Native American human remains. As Tsosie points out, NAGPRA is "human rights legislation." As is evident in Cypress's chapter, disturbance of graves is an issue of common concern among Native Americans. Unlike some others, however, Cypress accepts the notion that it may be necessary for archaeologists to disturb graves under some circumstances, provided there are well-defined limits on how long human remains should be studied before they are reinterred.

NAGPRA is having, and will continue to have, a profound impact on how archaeology is conducted. In part this is because, as Carter points out, NAGPRA forces archaeologists to consult with Native Americans. As described by Echo-Hawk, however, legal negotiations to determine the control of human remains and artifacts can be contentious and, in the case he wrote about, can actually work against the scholarly integration of oral traditions with archaeological data. Carter identifies other problems with how NAGPRA is being implemented. These problems are unfortunate, and we hope that over the long term, the new relationships archaeologists are building with Native Americans will transcend NAGPRA and transform the entire practice of archaeology.

One issue that needs attention is the disparities between the provisions of NAGPRA and various state burial laws. As Brooks points out for Oklahoma, the differences between NAGPRA and state burial laws can be confusing to those Native Americans who think there should be legal uniformity in protecting the dead on federal, state, and private land. Brooks suggests that NAGPRA should be extended to cover all land in the United States, and this is a proposal that should receive serious consideration.

There is some indication that NAGPRA may fundamentally change the way that archaeologists view the archaeological record. For instance, Dongoske and Anyon point out that many archaeologists perceive the archaeological record as having been "abandoned" by the Native Americans who created it. One positive impact of NAGPRA should be a change in how archaeologists think of "abandonment." Future generations of archaeologists will be trained to realize that, under NAGPRA, Native Americans may have continuing property rights to cultural patrimony contained within ancestral sites, and the logical inference is that these sites were never actually abandoned. Continuity in the cultural importance of archaeological sites for Native Americans will be recognized in discussions of changing patterns of land use, hopefully supplanting the current and often misleading notion of "abandonment."

Treatment of the Dead

One important issue raised in several chapters is how archaeologists treat the remains of the dead. Clearly, under NAGPRA, and out of human decency, archaeologists need to respect how contemporary Native Americans want their ancestors' remains treated. As several authors have noted, many Native Americans think that archaeologists have treated their ancestors in outrageous and callous ways. Some Native Americans, as well as archaeologists like Trigger (1980, 1989) and McGuire (1992), see this as an unfortunate legacy of a colonialist archaeology. To some degree in the United States, this issue has been resolved by NAGPRA, and archaeologists now have a legal requirement to handle Native American human remains with the respect and dignity they deserve. Nonetheless, as Ravesloot observed in his chapter, some archaeologists still have much to learn about the ethical behavior involved in respecting the dead.

In a historical context, however, all of us, Native Americans and archaeologists alike, have to be careful not to cast mistreatment of the dead as simply a racial issue between Indians and non-Indians. The archaeological record at La Quemada in Mexico clearly shows that some ancient Native Americans mutilated and displayed human remains with little respect for the deceased (Nelson 1995). Similar mortuary behavior also appears to have been practiced in other parts of North America during some periods (Turner 1983; Zimmerman and Bradley 1993). We think it is important for Native Americans and scholars not to fall prey to "presentism"—the uncritical and often romanticized projection of the present into the past. The past was often different than the present, and these differences are one of the things that archaeologists study.

As Lippert notes in her chapter, for some Native Americans the scientific study of human skeletons can provide a means for letting the ancestors tell their stories about the past with a "voice made from bone." As a Native American archaeologist, Lippert correctly observes that biological archaeology is a privilege that cannot be taken lightly. The proper treatment of the dead in archaeological research therefore requires close consultation with their living descendants. In this regard, archaeologists need to think about what Martin observed in discussing the Navajo people: that is, there are consequences in going too far in asking and answering research questions. Investigation of the sites and human remains we study as archaeologists has impacts on both the "others" that occupied them and on living people. Fortunately, as several authors point out, when consultation with tribal cultural advisers sets the parameters of appropriate techniques, methods, and research questions, everyone—both Native Americans and archaeologists—can benefit. Archaeologists benefit because they can do some research; Native Americans benefit because not too much unwanted research will be conducted.

Legal Mandate for Historic Preservation

As several authors in this volume point out, much of the archaeology being done by or for Native Americans in the United States is legally mandated by historic preservation laws. Tsosie, a law professor at Arizona State University, provides a useful review of these laws. A subtext in Tsosie's review, however, is disconcerting because it characterizes the legal mandate for historic preservation as pitting Euroamerican values against those of Native Americans. There is some truth in this, of course, but the real legal and ethical landscape is much more complex. Native Americans themselves face hard decisions about how to keep ancestral sites from being desecrated.

For instance, is it desecration to destroy archaeological sites within the coal mines operated or leased by tribes? Is it desecration to destroy archaeological sites impacted by the roads being constructed to develop the modern infrastructure that most Native Americans want on their reservations? Is it ethical for one tribe to destroy archaeological sites that are affiliated with another tribe? Is it ethical (even if legal) for members of a native community, though strapped for cash, to destroy their own archaeological sites in order to obtain artifacts for sale? As we all know, in the modern world there is often no way to mine coal or build roads without impacting archaeological sites. Is archaeological research in this context less of a desecration than total destruction? Both the Native American and non-Indian archaeologists contributing to this volume who work for Indian tribes think that archaeological research is warranted in this context.

It should also be kept in mind that some Indian tribes have reservations that contain ancestral sites or religious shrines affiliated with other tribes. If, as Tsosie seems to suggest, tribes should have the right to veto projects or excavations that adversely impact archaeological sites outside their reservation, should this right of veto extend to the reservations of other tribes? Will a uniform application of this principle thereby work to diminish tribal sovereignty? These are hard questions, and they go beyond a dichotimization of the issues solely in terms of Euroamericans vs. Native Americans.

As Zimmerman notes in his chapter, oppositional views are ultimately limiting. Just as oppositional views of "us vs. them" once justified imperial domination, they now serve in reverse to justify a postcolonialist "victimist history." Zimmerman argues that unless criticism seeks to replace oppositional models with dialogical frameworks that incorporate cultural differences, all we end up with is more rhetoric —and we need more than rhetoric. We need change.

In this regard, Tsosie is correct when she concludes that "federal statutes encourage controlled access to Native American ancestral sites," and that this can be problematic from a Native American perspective. Nonetheless, our present laws are better than no laws at all. Without our historic preservation legislation, the destruction and therefore the desecration of archaeological sites would be even more widespread than it is now. We therefore hope that Tsosie's legal analysis does not end with the critique presented in this book but that it serves as a point of departure for developing better legislation that more fairly represents Native American values. That is what we need if we are to improve historic preservation on Indian reservations and other lands where Native Americans have an interest.

Consultation and Compliance With the Regulatory System for Historic Preservation

As Brooks, Rice, and others observe, the regulatory system governing historic preservation compliance is being expanded to cover traditional cultural properties as well as archaeological sites. In order to accomplish this, effective consultation with Native Americans is now more essential than ever in the management of cultural resources. As Brooks and Fuller note, however, historical and political factors can make identifying the appropriate Native Americans who need to be consulted a difficult process. Brooks's experience in Oklahoma demonstrates that consultation with Native Americans needs to be based on realistic and equitable solutions to potential problems rather than simply appeasement of vocal individuals. Fuller recommends that consultation is most advantageous when it is undertaken at the earliest possible stage of a project. This gives Native Americans the greatest opportunity to influence how projects will be conducted.

The formidable challenges the federal government faces in consulting with Native Americans are described by Roberts. As Swidler and Cohen point out in describing the activities of the Navajo Nation Historic Preservation Department, the mandate to consult with Native Americans can apply to Indian tribes as well as the federal government. As tribes assume federal responsibility for historic preservation, they also become responsible for consultation with other tribes. The difficulties the Navajo Nation has experienced in this regard, and the solutions it has sought to the problems it has encountered, are instructive for everyone who needs to consult with Native Americans.

For the past decade, archaeologists who work for Indian tribes have discussed the need for legal reform in the regulatory compliance system that stems from historic preservation legislation (Nichols, Klesert, and Anyon 1989; Klesert and Downer 1990). The perspectives offered in this volume provide additional examples of why such change is needed. We think it is now time for the Society for American Archaeology to join with Native Americans to seek the changes needed to improve the regulatory system for management and preservation of tribal cultural resources.

Reconciliation of Divergent Views

Zimmerman's chapter also provides insight into the syncretism (i.e., the reconciliation of diverse views) that is occurring within the discipline of archaeology. Zimmerman thinks this reconciliation bodes well for archaeology, and we agree with him. Dongoske and Anyon, Ravesloot, Kluth, and Martin describe how this process of reconciliation works in the tribes for whom they work, with tribally employed archaeologists acting as cultural brokers. Lippert, Martin, and Forsman describe this process as it is experienced by Native Americans working as professional archaeologists.

Some thought should be given to Zimmerman's notion that archaeologists are "remythologizing" the past by accentuating the idea that they have always been strong supporters of Native Americans. Zimmerman's use of the term "remythologizing" implies this is not really the case. Zimmerman and other authors in this volume describe many aspects of archaeology that have in the past offended Native Americans and worked against their valid interests. Be that as it may, it is important that we correctly understand the history of archaeology. In the late nineteenth century, at the same time that some scholars were practicing archaeology in a colonialist manner, other archaeologists were working hard to change how the American public viewed the relationship of Native Americans to the archaeological record. As Downer says, we need to keep in mind the archaeologists who debunked the Myth of the Moundbuilders in the Midwest, or the "Aztec Theory" in the Southwest, both of which were popular explanations of ancient history that served to disenfranchise Native Americans from the legacy of their ancestors (Lekson 1988; Trigger 1989).

There are other examples of archaeologists who historically sought to strengthen the political, social, and intellectual position of Native Americans (King 1972; Johnson 1973), and these should not be forgotten when archaeologists put on a professional hair shirt and flog their discipline. We need balance and depth in our historical perspective, not a revisionist characterization that focuses only on our shortcomings.

There *are* things about archaeology that were and are wrong from a Native American perspective, and these things need to be changed. However, *all* of archaeology is not "bad." Chapters in this volume by archaeologists who are also Native Americans (Lippert, Forsman, Martin, Begay, and Van Pelt) demonstrate that Native Americans can and do find value in our profession. Other chapters by Native Americans who provide intellectual critiques of archaeology, including those by White Deer, Echo-Hawk, Carter, and Tsosie, suggest that the potential exists for archaeologists to communicate more effectively with Native Americans and, in so doing, to establish new ethics that will make the work of archaeologists both more relevant and more acceptable to Native Americans.

Personal Perspectives

T.J. Ferguson

Many archaeologists wonder whether the changes their profession is experiencing represent a clash of cultural values, an infringement of academic freedom, or a new opportunity for change and cooperation. The contributions to this volume demonstrate that the changes our discipline is undergoing in developing a new relationship with Native Americans are all of these things, and more. The personal perspectives of the Native Americans and archaeologists presented in this book indicate that the changes are sometimes exhilarating, sometimes frustrating, but always interesting. The changing role of Native Americans in cultural resource management and archaeological research augurs well for the future of archaeology.

Archaeologists who work for Native Americans act as cultural brokers. As Dongoske and Anyon point out, these archaeologists explain the alien concepts of archaeology to Native Americans, and, at the same time, articulate tribal positions to federal and state cultural resource managers. In doing so, these archaeologists have learned to use the straight talk that Carter advises is needed to build trust between Native Americans and archaeologists. This trust is sorely needed because, as Tsosie and White Deer observe, many Native Americans still regard anthropology with a fundamental distrust based on a long history of intrusive or inappropriate research. Archaeologists who work for Native Americans provide models of discourse and behavior that should be closely examined and adopted by the rest of our profession.

Joe Watkins

When I first read the session abstracts for the three linked sessions sponsored by the Society for American Archaeology, I saw points that I felt described the entire sessions. In the following, I have added emphasis to draw attention to those points.

In the abstract for the first symposium, Native Americans and Archaeology: Personal Perspectives from Both Sides, I was struck by one pertinent sentence: "What may seem to many as an *irreconcilable clash* of cultural values is seen by others as an *unparalleled opportunity* for change and cooperation."

This strikes to the heart of the matter, for most Americans and archaeologists have felt that American archaeology has reached the point where none of us touched by the discipline remains unaffected. We have each been affected by the *clash of cultural values* to which Kurt Dongoske and Roger Anyon call our attention, whether as a full-blown protest of our researches or a polite but firm reminder of our shortcomings. But we should also remember that our discipline is what we make it, not what it has always been. We have the *opportunity* to change the ways things are, but also the responsibility to affect that change through cooperation with those whose culture we study, regardless of their status.

The session abstract for the symposium, Roles and Relevancy: Native American Perspectives on Archaeology, offers a path archaeology must take if it wishes to survive through the next century. Nina Swidler and Alan Downer wrote: "This symposium will address whether or not the discipline is *relevant* to Native Americans and what Native Americans' *role* should be in the future of American Archaeology."

By discussing tribal perspectives on American archaeology, the symposium presenters focused on the ways that archaeologists can make the management of cultural resources *relevant* to American Indians and their tribal members. If we listen to those around us, we will not forget why we became archaeologists—to learn more about ourselves. If we provide a relevant reason for American Indians to become partners, we will remain relevant to society in general.

Finally, Lynn Larson and I wrote: "The *consultation process* may be a *stepping stone* to the development of *productive relationships* between tribes and archaeologists, and it can prove *beneficial* to the *preservation* of cultural resources and to the respective *communities* served by both groups."

Six points need emphasizing in this one sentence. I've chosen more from this abstract partly because I remembered the importance Lynn and I placed on word choice. We wanted to focus on the *process*, the *relationships*, and the *benefits* our efforts bring to the Native American and academic *communities* in which we live. We chose the image of *stepping stones* because we know we need solid places on which to make our tentative steps through a possible mire. And we chose *preservation* because we know that what we do is important, that the past is relevant to the future, and that the future is nothing but what we make it.

The presenters were the stars of the sessions, and their papers are the body of this volume, but I thought it necessary to be reminded of the foundations, the ideas, that brought them all together.

Gordon L. Pullar

My first glimpse into archaeology came nearly three decades ago when, as a young undergraduate cultural anthropology student, I enrolled in an archaeology seminar. The class took place in an archaeology lab and was a basic classroom introduction to archaeology. I found the information mildly interesting, but had trouble concentrating because lining the shelves on the side of the room were rows of Indian skulls set up like bowling trophies. I couldn't help but stare at them during class and wonder who these people had been, what they were like, and how sad it seemed that they would end up as they were. Despite my discomfort, I didn't become an anti-archaeology activist or do anything else to express my concerns. I just avoided archaeology and archaeologists for a number of years.

Jumping ahead nearly a decade and a half, a scene at a meeting appears that is still vivid in my mind. An Indian in the audience stated flatly, "All archaeologists should be executed!" I was attending a National Congress of American Indians (NCAI) Annual Conference, and a separate meeting was held for those people who had interests in developing cultural preservation programs. At the time I was president of the Kodiak Area Native Association in my home area of Kodiak Island, Alaska, where we had recently begun a series of programs focused on cultural preservation and revitalization. Bryn Mawr College had offered an opportunity for us to collaborate on an archaeology project that included youth from our villages in the actual excavations. After discussions among ourselves, we decided this could be one of the cornerstones of our cultural program. My old misgivings about archaeology seemed to fade. Many of our cultural practices had been displaced, and most people had little knowledge of the distant past of our homelands. Archaeology, it seemed, had presented an opportunity for young people to learn the richness of their past. But as the NCAI meeting began to focus on the misdeeds of archaeologists and the issue of repatriation I felt a bit uncomfortable. I told of our project, of its successes and challenges, and to some, we seemed to be taking a bizarre course. The young man who had advocated the execution of all archaeologists approached me during a break. He very sincerely advised me to be very careful in any interactions I had with archaeologists. "You can't trust them," he said.

Not long after the incident at NCAI, I hired a full-time archaeologist to work at coordinating all of our cultural programs, to help educate and preserve archaeological sites near our villages, and to do excavations that included native people. We all learned a lot from these projects as archaeology provided a focal point for our cultural revitalization efforts. We agreed that we could not hope to know who we were and where we were going if we did not know where we had been. This was not a claim that archaeological views of the past were superior to other ways of seeing. It was just that due to our circumstances our oral histories were not as complete as they might have been. This is not an either/or situation. Both ways of looking at the past are legitimate, and by using both there is much we can learn. British archaeologist Stephen Shennen (1989:2) describes it well, saying, "As far as reconstructing the past is concerned, traditional origin myths are as good as archaeology, which is, in fact, simply a way of producing origin myths which are congenial to the way of thinking of a particular kind of society. It is all a question of upbringing."

The fact that considerable native/archaeologist collaboration has taken place on Kodiak Island does not mean that Kodiak natives are apologists for archaeology, as some have privately suggested. In fact, we held firm on the issue of repatriation of the remains of more than 1,000 of our ancestors that had been stored in the

Smithsonian Institution for more than 50 years. Negotiations with the Smithsonian involved a number of native/archaeologist adversarial confrontations that took place before any federal repatriation laws were in place. We were successful with the remains being returned to the village of Larsen Bay for reburial in 1991 (Bray and Killion 1994). But that is a separate issue from whether archaeology has value to Native Americans. We believed it was a useful tool and conducted archaeological projects throughout the period we were working on the repatriation case.

The 1980s brought special focus to the issue of Native American relationships to archaeologists and who had the right to decide what. The emotion of protecting graves of ancestors was central to this debate. I was in many meetings where the debate raged, usually framed as a conflict between the needs of scientific research against the rights of native people to protect their burials. So when Pete Jemison described the symposium he organized in 1989 I felt like I had been there even though I hadn't. While we like to feel that we are beyond that point in Native American/archaeologist relations, remnants of these attitudes remain.

As the 1980s came to a close, Native Americans across the country were exerting their influence in getting state laws passed that began to shift the power between them and archaeologists. These laws had to do with burial protection and repatriation and were natural outgrowths of what was happening on a national level. In my area, we were facing an unusual challenge. We wanted to continue performing archaeology but, at the same time, wanted archaeologists from outside to recognize that we, as native people, should have the authority to decide what should be researched, how the research should be conducted, and above all, that our ancestors' graves should be protected. We were therefore very active in proposing a bill to the Alaska State Legislature that would accomplish these important things. The opposition was intense. The archaeological community "circled their wagons" and fought hard against the legislation. In the public comment process, archaeologists called our proposed legislation "racist," "protectionist," and "pandering to public opinion," among other things. Despite two legislative sessions of effort, no state Alaska Native burial protection law was passed. From a native perspective, this is very unfortunate.

Few can argue that profound changes have taken place in the relationship between Native Americans and archaeologists in recent years. There is no doubt that some of the change has been forced, as a number of authors point out, but it has been positive change just the same. There are, however, some people, both native nonarchaeologists and nonnative archaeologists, who are resistant to a change in this relationship. It seems unfortunate that this volume shows that some of the oppositional positions between Native Americans and archaeologists remain. I am hopeful that the extremes on both sides of this issue who seem to be unmovable in their positions can drift toward the center. This spirit of cooperation is prevalent in most of the papers presented here.

Conclusion

We have now arrived at a point where a series of symposiums endorsed by one of the largest and most prestigious archaeology associations in the land, the Society for American Archaeology, is providing a forum for constructive discussion and dialogue on the relationships between Native Americans and archaeologists. The uniqueness of the session is that it focused on Native American points of view. It is important to note that the emphasis is on the plural, points of view, as there are many Native Americans with varying views on this topic. As Cypress states quite clearly, and correctly, "Archaeology is neither good nor bad." It is a fact that archaeology is a western science and one that began foreign to virtually all Native American cultures. But like other western sciences, it can find its useful place among Native Americans.

In conclusion, we'd like to end by reaffirming the anthropological perspective of Dorothy Lippert, who succeeds in overcoming the oppositional thinking that characterizes the world in terms of indigenous vs. scientific values. In observing that there should be room in our discipline for a variety of viewpoints, Lippert wrote, "After all, we are all still human. We all share genetic characteristics and fundamental concerns and when we look in the mirror we all see basically the same thing: our very human selves." We need to recognize and act on our common humanity to recreate the archaeological discipline and imbue scientific archaeology with a humanistic and anthropological perspective that makes it more acceptable to Native Americans. In so doing, we will create the common ground that is needed between archaeologists and Native Americans. The papers in this volume give us hope that this goal will be attained.

References

Anaya, S. James
1996   *Indigenous Peoples in International Law*. Oxford University Press, New York.
Anyon, Roger
1996   Zuni Protection of Cultural Resources and Religious Freedom. *Cultural Survival* 19(4):46–49.
Anyon, Roger, and T. J. Ferguson
1995   Cultural Resources Management at the Pueblo of Zuni, New Mexico, USA. *Antiquity* 69:913–930.
Anyon, Roger, T. J. Ferguson, Loretta Jackson, and Lillie Lane
1996   Native American Oral Traditions and Archaeology. *SAA Bulletin* 14(2): 14–16.
Ayau, Edward Halealoha
1992   Restoring the Ancestral Foundation of Native Hawaiians: Implementation of the Native American Graves Protection and Repatriation Act. *Arizona State Law Journal* 24:193–216.

Bacon, Willard S.
1993   Factors in Siting a Middle Woodland Enclosure in Middle Tennessee. *Midcontinental Journal of Archaeology* 18(2):245–281.

Bahr, Donald M., Juan Smith, William Smith Allison, and Julian Hayden
1994   *The Short, Swift Time of Gods on Earth: The Hohokam Chronicles.* University of California Press, Berkeley.

Barrett, S. A.
1908   The Geography and Dialects of the Mi wok Indians. *University of California Publications in American Archaeology and Ethnology* 6:333–368.
1919   Myths of the Southern Sierra Mi wok. *University of California Publications in American Archaeology and Ethnology* 16:1–28.

Barrett, S. A., and E. W. Gifford
1933   Miwok Material Culture. *Public Museum of the City of Milwaukee Bulletin* 2: 117–376.

Begay, Daryl
1991   Navajo Preservation: The Success of the Navajo Nation Historic Preservation Department. *CRM* 14(4):1–4. National Park Service, Washington, D.C.

Billeck, William T., Erica B. Jones, Stephanie A. Makseyn-Kelley, and John W. Verano
1995   Inventory and Assessment of Human Remains and Associated Funerary Objects Potentially Affiliated with the Pawnee in the National Museum of Natural History, Case Report No. 88–007. Submitted to Repatriation Office, National Museum of Natural History, Smithsonian Institution, Washington, D.C.

Bowman, Margaret B.
1989   The Reburial of Native American Skeletal Remains: Approaches to the Resolution of a Conflict. *Harvard Environmental Law Review* 13:147–208.

Bozell, John R.
1995a   Culture, Environment, and Bison Populations on the Late Prehistoric and Early Historic Central Plains. *Plains Anthropologist* 40:145–163.
1995b   Nebraska State Historical Society NAGPRA Implementation. In *Native American Graves Protection and Repatriation Act of 1990 (NAGPRA) Compliance Workshop Proceedings*, edited by Myra J. Giesen, Haskell Indian Nations University, pp. 29–33.

Bray, Tamara L., and Thomas W. Killion, editors
1994   *Reckoning with the Dead: The Larsen Bay Repatriation and the Smithsonian Institution.* Smithsonian Institution Press, Washington, D.C.

Brinkley-Rogers, Paul, and Richard Robertson
1993   Stealing the Hopi Soul. *Arizona Republic*, March 14, pp. A16–A17.

Buikstra, Jane E., and Claire C. Gordon
1981   The Study and Restudy of Human Skeletal Series: The Importance of Long-Term Curation. *Annals of the New York Academy of Sciences* 31:449–466.

Carr, Robert S., and Willard Steele
   1993   Seminole Heritage Survey: Seminole Sites of Florida. Archaeological and Historical Conservancy, Miami. AHC Technical Report 74. Submitted to Seminole Tribe of Florida and U.S. Department of the Interior. Funded by a grant provided by the U.S. Department of Interior National Park Service Tribe Preservation Program. Copies available from National Park Service.

Center for the Study of the First Americans
   1995   Clarification Is Sought Regarding Status of Hair. *Mammoth Trumpet* 10(1): 3, 7.

Cordell, Linda, and Fred Plog
   1979   Escaping the Confines of Normative Thought: A Reevaluation of Puebloan Prehistory. *American Antiquity* 44:405–429.

Crawford, O. G. S.
   1953   *Archaeology in the Field.* Phoenix House, London.

Deloria, V.
   1995   *Red Earth, White Lies, Native Americans and the Myth of Scientific Fact.* Scribners, New York.

Dongoske, Kurt, T. J. Ferguson, and Leigh Jenkins
   1993   Understanding the Past through Hopi Oral History. *Native Peoples* 6(2):24–31.

Dongoske, Kurt, Michael Yeatts, T. J. Ferguson, and Leigh Jenkins
   1995   Letter to the Editor. In Point/Counterpoint: Historic Preservation and Native American Sites. *SAA Bulletin* 13(4):13.

Dorsey, George A. [and James R. Murie]
   1906   *The Pawnee: Mythology.* Carnegie Institution of Washington, Washington, D.C.

Downer, Alan S.
   1989   Anthropology, Historic Preservation and the Navajo: A Case Study in Historic Preservation on Indian Lands. Unpublished Ph.D. dissertation, Department of Anthropology, University of Missouri-Columbia.

   1990   Tribal Sovereignty and Historic Preservation: Native American Participation in Cultural Resources Management on Indian Lands. In *Preservation on the Reservation: Native Americans, Native American Lands and Archaeology*, edited by Anthony L. Klesert and Alan S. Downer, pp. 67–100. Navajo Nation Papers in Anthropology 24. Window Rock, Arizona.

Downer, Alan S., and Anthony L. Klesert
   1990   Introduction. In *Preservation on the Reservation: Native Americans, Native American Lands and Archaeology*, edited by Anthony L. Klesert and Alan S. Downer, pp. 1–8. Navajo Nation Papers in Anthropology No. 26. Navajo Nation Archaeology Department and Navajo Nation Historic Preservation Department, Window Rock, Arizona.

Downer, Alan S., and Alexandra Roberts
   1996   The Navajo Nation Experience with the Federal Historic Preservation Program. *Natural Resources & Environment* 10(3):39–42, 78–79.

Echo-Hawk, Roger C.
1990   Ancient Pawnee History: A Brief Survey of Caddoan Traditional Evidence Regarding Pawnee Ancestry in the Central Plains. Submitted to Native American Rights Fund, Boulder, Colorado.
1992   Discovering Ancient Worlds: Final Report of the Archeological Monitor for the New Denver Airport Office. Submitted to New Denver Airport Office, City and County of Denver, Denver, Colorado.
1994   Kara Katit Pakutu: Exploring the Origins of Native America in Anthropology and Oral Traditions. Unpublished M.A. thesis, Department of History, University of Colorado, Boulder.

Eggan, Fred
1967   From History to Myth: A Hopi Example. In *Studies in Southwestern Ethnolinguistics,* edited by Dell Hymes, pp. 33–53. Mouton, The Hague.

Ferguson, T. J.
1995a   Zuni Archaeology and Culture History. In *Zuni and the Courts: A Struggle for Sovereign Land Rights,* edited by E. Richard Hart, pp. 3–7. University Press of Kansas, Lawrence.
1995b   An Anthropological Perspective on Zuni Land Use. In *Zuni and the Courts: A Struggle for Sovereign Land Rights,* edited by E. Richard Hart, pp. 103–120. University Press of Kansas, Lawrence.

Ferguson, T. J., Kurt Dongoske, Leigh Jenkins, Mike Yeatts, and Eric Polingyouma
1993   Working Together: The Roles of Archaeology and Ethnohistory in Hopi Cultural Preservation. *CRM* 16:27–37.

Ferguson, T. J., Kurt Dongoske, Mike Yeatts, and Leigh Jenkins
1995   Hopi Oral History and Archaeology, Part I: The Consultation Process. *SAA Bulletin* 13(2):13–15.

Fowler, Andrew P., John R. Stein, and Roger Anyon
1987   An Archaeological Reconnaissance of West-Central New Mexico: The Anasazi Monuments Project. Unpublished ms. on file, New Mexico State Historic Preservation Division, Santa Fe.

Fox, Richard A., Jr.
1993   *Archaeology, History, and Custer's Last Battle: The Little Bighorn Reexamined.* University of Oklahoma Press, Norman.

Gifford, E. W.
1916   Miwok Moieties. *University of California Publications in American Archaeology and Ethnology* 12:139–194.
1917   Miwok Myths. *University of California Publications in American Archaeology and Ethnology* 12:283–338.
1926   Miwok Lineages and the Political Unit in Aboriginal California. *American Anthropologist,* n.s. 28:389–401.
1944   Miwok Lineages. *American Anthropologist,* n.s. 46:376–381.
1955   Central Mi wok Ceremonies. *Anthropological Records* 14:261–318.

Goldstein, Lynne
1992 The Potential for Future Relationships between Archaeologists and Native Americans. In *Quandaries and Quests: Visions of Archaeology's Future,* edited by LuAnn Wandsnider, pp. 59–71. Center for Archaeological Investigations, Southern Illinois University at Carbondale.

Goldstein, Lynne, and Keith Kintigh
1990 Ethics and the Reburial Controversy. *American Antiquity* 55:585–591.

Goss, James A.
1995 Usual and Customary Use and Occupancy by the Muccosukee and Seminole Indians in Big Cypress National Preserve, Florida. Texas Tech University. Submitted to Southeast Region National Park Service under Subagreement No. CA-5000-2-9025/2 of Cooperative Agreement CA-5000-2-9016. Copies available from Southeast Region National Park Service.

Graff, James A.
1994 Human Rights, Peoples, and the Right to Self-determination. In *Group Rights,* edited by Judith Baker, pp. 186–214. University of Toronto Press, Toronto.

Greaves, Tom, editor
1994 *Intellectual Property Rights for Indigenous Peoples, A Sourcebook.* Society for Applied Anthropology, Norman, Oklahoma.

Grossman, Anita Sue
1993 Digging the Grave of Archaeology. *Heterodoxy* (Spring 1993):9–12.

Hall, Robert L.
1983 A Pan-Continental Perspective on Red Ocher and Glacial Kame Ceremonialism. In *Lulu Linear Punctated: Essays in Honor of George Irving Quimby,* pp. 74–107. Museum of Anthropology, University of Michigan, Ann Arbor.
1989 The Cultural Background of Mississippian Symbolism. In *The Southeastern Ceremonial Complex: Artifacts and Analysis,* edited by Patricia Galloway, pp. 239–278, University of Nebraska Press, Lincoln.

Hancock, Graham
1995 *Fingerprints of the Gods.* Crown, New York.

Harjo, Suzan Shown
1992 Native Peoples' Cultural and Human Rights: An Unfinished Agenda. *Arizona State Law Journal* 24:321–328.

Hart, E. Richard, editor
1995 *Zuni and the Courts: A Struggle for Sovereign Land Rights.* University Press of Kansas, Lawrence.

Hart, E. Richard, and T. J. Ferguson
1993 The Fence Lake Mine Project: Conclusions. In *Traditional Cultural Properties of Four Tribes: The Fence Lake Mine Project,* Vol. II, pp. 1–33. Institute of the NorthAmerican West, Seattle.

Hart, E. Richard, and Andrew L. Othole
1993   The Zuni Salt Lake Area: Potential Impacts to Zuni Traditional Cultural Prop-
       erties by the Proposed Fence Lake Mine. In *Traditional Cultural Properties of
       Four Tribes: The Fence Lake Mine Project,* Vol. 1, pp. 1–185. Institute of the
       NorthAmerican West, Seattle.

Haury, E. W.
1976   *The Hohokam: Desert Farmers and Craftsmen.* University of Arizona Press,
       Tucson.

Holt, H. Barry
1990   Tribal Sovereignty over Archaeology: A Practical and Legal Fact. on Indian
       Lands. In *Preservation on the Reservation: Native Americans, Native American
       Lands and Archaeology,* edited by Anthony L. Klesert and Alan S. Downer, pp.
       9–14. Navajo Nation Papers in Anthropology 24. Window Rock, Arizona.

Hualapai Tribe
1993   Hualapai Tribe Ethnographic and Oral Historical Survey for Glen Canyon
       Environmental Studies and the Glen Canyon Dam Environmental Impact
       Statement. In *Glen Canyon Dam Environmental Impact Statement.* Submitted
       to the U.S. Department of the Interior, Bureau of Reclamation, Glen Canyon
       Environmental Studies, Flagstaff, Arizona.

Hualapai Tribe Office of Cultural Resources
1995a Hualapai Tribe Ethnographic Surveys for Milkweed Springs, Diamond
       Creek and Youth Camp on the Walapai Indian Reservation, Mohave and
       Coconino Counties, Arizona. Submitted to the National Park Service,
       Washington D.C.
1995b Hualapai Tribe Office of Cultural Resources Native American Graves Protection
       and Repatriation Act (NAGPRA) Repatriation Project Draft Report. On file,
       Hualapai Tribe Office of Cultural Resources, Peach Springs, Arizona.
1996   *Hualapai Tribe's Traditional Cultural Properties on and along the Colorado
       through the Grand Canyon: A Hualapai Tribe Research Report to the United
       States Department of Interior Bureau of Reclamation, for Glen Canyon
       Environmental Studies and Glen Canyon Dam Environmental Impact
       Statement.* On file, Hualapai Tribe Office of Cultural Resources, Peach
       Springs, Arizona.

Hubert, Jane
1989a First World Archaeological Congress Inter-Congress, Vermillion, South Dakota,
       USA. *World Archaeological Congress Bulletin* 4:18–20.
1989b A Proper Place for the Dead. In *Conflict in the Archaeology of Living Tradi-
       tions,* edited by R. Layton, pp. 131-266. Unwin Hyman, London.

Hughes, Robert
1992   Art, Morals, and Politics. *The New York Review* (April 23):21–27.

Hutt, Sherry, Elwood W. Jones, and Martin E. McAllister
1992   *Archeological Resource Protection.* The Preservation Press, National Trust for
       Historic Preservation.

Jantz, Richard L.
1993   *Pawnee-Central Plains Relationships: The Craniometric Evidence.* Submitted to Repatriation Office, National Museum of Natural History, Smithsonian Institution, Washington, D.C.

Johnson, Elden
1973   Professional Responsibilities and the American Indian. *American Antiquity* 38: 129–130.

Joukowsky, Martha
1980   *A Complete Manual of Field Archaeology.* Prentice-Hall, Englewood Cliffs, New Jersey.

Kelley, Klara B., and Harris Francis
1994   *Navajo Sacred Places.* Indiana University Press, Bloomington.

King, Thomas F.
1972   Archaeological Law and the American Indian. *The Indian Historian* 5(3):31–35.
1993   Beyond Bulletin 38: Comments on the Traditional Cultural Properties Symposium. *CRM* 16:60–64. U.S. Department of the Interior, National Park Service, Washington, D.C.

Klesert, Anthony L., and Alan S. Downer, editors
1990   *Preservation on the Reservation: Native Americans, Native American Lands, and Archaeology.* Navajo Nation Papers in Anthropology No. 26. Window Rock, Arizona.

Klesert, A. L., and S. Powell
1993   A Perspective on Ethics and the Reburial Controversy. *American Antiquity* 58:348–354.

Knecht, R. A., and P. Hausler-Knecht
1992   The Smithsonian Response to the Larsen Bay Repatriation Request: Research, Rhetoric, and Recrimination. Paper presented at the symposium on Kodiak Island Archaeology and the Larsen Bay Repatriation at the Ninety-First Annual Meeting of the American Anthropological Association, San Francisco.

Kroeber, A. L.
1907   Indian Myths of South Central California. *University of California Publications in American Archaeology and Ethnology* 4:167–250.
1908   On the Evidences of the Occupation of Certain Regions by the Miwok Indians. *University of California Publications in American Archaeology and Ethnology* 6:369–380.
1917   California Kinship Systems. *University of California Publications in American Archaeology and Ethnology* 12:356–358.

Krupat, A.
1992   *Ethnocriticism: Ethnography, History, Literature.* University of California Press, Berkeley.

Lankford, George E.
1987   *Native American Legends, Southeastern Legends: Tales from the Natchez, Caddo, Biloxi, Chickasaw, and Other Nations.* August House, Little Rock.

Layton, Robert, editor
1989   *Conflict in the Archaeology of Living Traditions.* Unwin Hyman, London.

LeBlanc, Steven A.
1996   The Impact of Warfare on Southwestern Regional Systems after A.D. 1250. Paper presented at the Southwest Symposium, Arizona State University, Tempe.

Lekson, Steve
1988   The Idea of the Kiva in Anasazi Archaeology. *Kiva* 53:213–234.

Linton, Ralph, editor
1923   *Annual Ceremony of the Pawnee Medicine Men.* Leaflet No. 8, Field Museum of Natural History, Chicago.

Lippert, Dorothy
1992   Skeletons in Our Closets: Archaeology and the Issue of Reburial. Unpublished M.A. thesis, Department of Anthropology, University of Texas, Austin.

Ludwickson, John, Terry L. Steinacher, John R. Bozell, and Gayle F. Carlson
1991   Nebraska State Historical Society Position Statement: Section B. Submitted to Nebraska Office of Public Counsel, Lincoln.

Marsh, Gene A.
1992   Walking the Spirit Trail: Repatriation and Protection of Native American Remains and Sacred Cultural Items. *Arizona State Law Journal* 24:79–133.

Matunga, H.
1991   The Maori Delegation to WAC 2: Presentation and Reports. *World Archaeological Bulletin* 5:43–54.

McGimsey, Charles R., III
1980   *Mariana Mesa: Seven Prehistoric Settlements in West-Central New Mexico.* Papers of the Peabody Museum of Archaeology and Ethnology 72. Peabody Museum, Cambridge.

McGuire, Randall H.
1992   Archaeology and the First Americans. *American Anthropologist* 94:816–836.

Meighan, Clement W.
1992   Some Scholars' Views on Reburial. *American Antiquity* 57:704–710.
1993   The Burial of American Archaeology. *Academic Questions* 6(3):9–19.
1996   Disowning the Past. *Social Facts* (online version) URL http://www.nas.org/newsletters/socfacts/meighan.html

Merriam, C. H.
1907   Distribution and Classification of the Mewan Stock. *American Anthropologist,* n.s. 9:338–357.

1957   The Hang-e or Ceremonial House of the Northern Miwok near Railroad Flat,
         Calaveras County, California. *University of California Archaeological Survey
         Records* 38:34–35.

Moodie, D. Wayne, A. J. W. Catchpole, and Kerry Abel
1992   Northern Athapaskan Oral Traditions and the White River Volcano. *Ethno-
         history* 39(2):148–171.

Morris, Glenn T.
1992   International Law and Politics: Toward a Right to Self-Determination for
         Indigenous Peoples. In *The State of Native America: Genocide, Colonization
         and Resistance,* edited by M. Annette Jaimes, pp. 55–86. South End Press,
         Boston.

Morris, John W., Charles R. Goins, and Edwin C. McReynolds
1976   *Historic Atlas of Oklahoma.* University of Oklahoma Press, Norman.

Murie, James R.
1981   *Ceremonies of the Pawnee,* 2 vols., edited by Douglas R. Parks. Smithsonian
         Contributions to Anthropology No. 27. Smithsonian Institution Press,
         Washington, D.C.

Naranjo, Tesse
1995   Thoughts on Migration by Santa Clara Pueblo. *Journal of Anthropological
         Archaeology* 14:247–250.

Navajo Nation
1986   Navajo Nation Cultural Resources Protection Act. Tribal Council Resolution
         CMY-19-88. Window Rock, Arizona.
1991   Navajo Nation Policy to Protect Traditional Cultural Properties. On file, Navajo
         Nation Historic Preservation Department, Window Rock, Arizona.

Navajo Nation Historic Preservation Department, Roads Planning Program (NNHPD-RPP)
1994a   A Programmatic Agreement Among the Navajo Nation, the Bureau of
         Indian Affairs–Navajo Area Office, the Advisory Council on Historic
         Preservation, the Arizona State Historic Preservation Officer, the New
         Mexico State Historic Preservation Officer, and the Utah State Historic
         Preservation Officer for Cultural Resource Management Projects Conducted
         Under the Auspices of the Navajo Nation Historic Preservation Department,
         Roads Planning Section within the Boundaries of the Navajo Nation. On
         file, Navajo Nation Historic Preservation Department, Window Rock,
         Arizona.
1994b   Consultation Procedures for Interested Persons, January 21, 1994. FLG–
         94.026. Memorandum on file, NNHPD, Roads Planning Program, Flagstaff
         Office.
1994c   Preliminary Guidelines for Identification of Cultural and Historic Properties on
         Federally-Funded Road Improvement Projects Throughout the Navajo Nation,
         September 16, 1994. FLG-94.329. On file, NNHPD, Roads Planning Program,
         Flagstaff Office.

Nelson, Ben
  1995   Complexity, Hierarchy, and Scale: A Controlled Comparison between Chaco
          Canyon, New Mexico, and La Quemada, Zacatecas. *American Antiquity* 60:
          597–618.

Nicholas, George P. and Thomas D. Andrews, editors
  1997   *At a Crossroads: Archaeology and First Peoples in Canada.* Archaeology Press,
          Simon Fraser University, Burnaby, British Columbia.

Nichols, Deborah L., Anthony L. Klesert, and Roger Anyon
  1989   Ancestral Sites, Shrines, and Graves: Native American Perspectives on the
          Ethics of Collecting Cultural Properties. In *The Ethics of Collecting Cultural
          Properties*, edited by Phyllis M. Messenger, pp. 27–38. University of New
          Mexico Press, Albuquerque.

Othole, Andrew L.
  1993   *Zuni Traditional Cultural Properties Assessment for the Cibola National Forest,
          Forest Roads 49 and 50 in the Zuni Mountains, McKinley and Cibola Counties,
          New Mexico.* Zuni Heritage and Historic Preservation Office, Zuni.

Othole, Andrew L., and Roger Anyon
  1993   A Tribal Perspective on Traditional Cultural Property Consultation. *CRM* 16:
          42–45.

Parker, Patricia L., and Thomas F. King
  1990   *Guidelines for Evaluating and Documenting Traditional Cultural Properties.*
          National Register Bulletin No. 38. U.S. Department of the Interior, National
          Park Service.

Pendergast, David M., and Clement W. Meighan
  1959   Folk Traditions as Historical Fact: A Paiute Example. *Journal of American
          Folklore* 72(284):128–133.

Peregoy, R. M.
  1992   Nebraska's Landmark Repatriation Law: A Study of Cross-Cultural Conflict
          Resolution. *American Indian Culture and Research Journal* 16(2):139–195.

Powell, John W.
  1894   *12th Annual Report of the Bureau of Ethnology.* Smithsonian Institution,
          Washington, D.C.

Powell, S., C. E. Garza, and A. Hendricks
  1993   Ethics and Ownership of the Past: The Reburial and Repatriation Controversy.
          Archaeological Method and Theory 5:1–42.

Pueblo of Zuni
  1992   Policy Statement Regarding the Protection and Treatment of Human Remains
          and Associated Funerary Objects, November 1992. Pueblo of Zuni, Zuni, New
          Mexico.

Ravesloot, J. C.
  1989   Communication and Cooperation Between the Arizona State Museum and
          Native Americans. *Museum Anthropology* 13(3):7–10.

1990   On the Treatment and Reburial of Human Remains: The San Xavier Bridge Project. *American Indian Quarterly* 14(1):35–50.

1995   The Road to Common Ground. *Federal Archeology* 7(3):36–40.

Raymond, Anan
1992   Who Were the Ancient People of Stillwater National Wildlife Refuge, Nevada? U.S. Department of the Interior, Fish and Wildlife Service, Stillwater Wildlife Refuge, Fallon, Nevada.

Reddy, Marlita A., editor
1993   *Statistical Record of Native North Americans.* Gale, Detroit.

Red Elk Hardman, Rose
1995   Presentation at the 1995 Conference on Indian Education in Texas, San Antonio.

Reid, J. J.
1992   Editor's Corner: Recent Findings on North American Prehistory. *American Antiquity* 57:195.

Riding-In, James
1992   Without Ethics and Morality: A Historical Overview of Imperial Archaeology and American Indians. *Arizona State Law Journal* 24:11–34.

Roberts, Alexa, Richard M. Begay, and Klara Kelley
1995   *Bis'íís Nínéézi (The River of Neverending Life): Navajo History and Cultural Resources of the Grand Canyon and the Colorado River.* Navajo Nation Historic Preservation Department, Window Rock, Arizona.

Roper, Donna C.
1993   *Historical Processes and the Development of Social Identity: An Evaluation of Pawnee Ancestry.* Submitted to Repatriation Office, National Museum of Natural History, Smithsonian Institution, Washington, D.C.

1995   Spatial Dynamics and Historical Process in the Central Plains Tradition. *Plains Anthropologist* 40:203–221.

Sebastian, Lynne
1995a   Letter to the Editor. *SAA Bulletin* 13(3):3.

1995b   Letter to the Editor. Point/Counterpoint: Historic Preservation and Native American Sites. *SAA Bulletin* 13(4):13.

Shennan, Stephen
1989   Introduction: Archaeological Approaches to Cultural Identity. In *Archaeological Approaches to Cultural Identity*, edited by S. J. Shennan, pp. 1–32. Unwin Hyman, London.

Silverberg, Robert
1968   *Moundbuilders of Ancient America.* New York Graphic Society, Greenwich, Connecticut.

Society of Professional Archaeologists
1981   Code of Ethics and Standards of Performance. *Directory of Professional Archaeologists* pp. 3–6. Society of Professional Archaeologists, St. Louis.

Stevens, Robert Henry ("Hank")
1992   Cultural Interpretation through Oral History. Ms. on file, Hualapai Tribe Office of Cultural Resources, Peach Springs, Arizona.
1995   American Indian Cultural Studies Using Ethnographic Methods: A Research Handbook for Cultural Continuity, Cultural Resource Management and Historic Preservation in Accordance with Tribal Sovereignty. Submitted to the Department of the Interior, Bureau of Reclamation, Glen Canyon Environmental Studies, Flagstaff, Arizona.

Strickland, Rennard, and Kathy Supernaw
1993   Back to the Future: A Proposed Model Tribal Act to Protect Native Cultural Heritage. *Arkansas Law Review* 46:161–201.

Suzuki, David, and Peter Knudsen
1992   *Wisdom of the Elders: Honoring Sacred Native Visions of Nature.* Bantam, New York.

Taylor, Walter W.
1948   *A Study of Archaeology.* American Anthropological Association Memoir No. 69. Menasha, Wisconsin.

Teague, Lynn S.
1993   Prehistory and the Traditions of the O'Odham and Hopi. *Kiva* 58(4):435–454.

Theodoratus, Dorothea J.
1993   A Perspective on Traditional Sites. *Society for California Archaeology* 6:45–48. San Diego.

Thomas, Cyrus
1894   Report on the Mound Explorations of the Bureau of American Ethnology. In *12th Annual Report of the Bureau of Ethnology,* edited by John W. Powell, pp. 1–730. Smithsonian Institution, Washington, D.C.

Thompson, Stith
1966   *Tales of the North American Indians.* Indiana University Press, Bloomington. Originally published in 1927.

Thornton, Russell, Andrea A. Hunter, Roger Anyon, Lynne Goldstein, and Christy G. Turner, II
1995   Recommendations Regarding the Dispute between the Pawnee Tribe of Oklahoma and the National Museum of Natural History Repatriation Office over the Steed-Kisker Phase Human Remains and Funerary Objects. Submitted to Secretary I. Michael Heyman, Smithsonian Institution, Washington, D.C.

Trigger, Bruce
1980   Archaeology and the Image of the American Indian. *American Antiquity* 45:662–676.
1989   *A History of Archaeological Thought.* Cambridge University Press, Cambridge.

Trope, Jack F., and Walter R. Echo-Hawk
1992   The Native American Graves Protection and Repatriation Act: Background and Legislative History. *Arizona State Law Journal* 24:35–77.

Turner, Christy
1983   Taphonomic Reconstructions of Human Violence and Cannibalism Based on Mass Burials in the American Southwest. In *Carnivores, Human Scavengers, and Predators: A Question of Bone Taphonomy,* edited by G. M. LeMoine and A. S. Maceachern, pp. 219–240. Archaeology Association, University of Calgary, Alberta, Canada.

U.S. Army Corps of Engineers
1996   Assessment of Corps/Tribal Intergovernmental Relations. Water Resources Support Center, Institute for Water Resources, IWR Report 96–R–6A. Fort Belvoir, Virginia.

United States Department of the Interior (USDI)
1993   Traditional Cultural Properties. *CRM* 16. National Park Service, Washington, D.C.

United States Senate
1936   *Walapai Papers: Historical Reports, Documents, and Extracts from Publications Relating to the Walapai Indians of Arizona.* United States Senate Document No. 273. Washington, D.C.

Vansina, Jan
1985   *Oral Tradition as History.* University of Wisconsin Press, Madison.

Watahomigie, Lucille J., Philbert Watahomigie, Sr., and Josie Uqualla
1989   *Project Tradition and Technology (Project TNT): The Hualapai Bilingual Academic Excellence Program.* Peach Springs Elementary School, District 8. Peach Springs, Arizona.

Watkins, J., L. Goldstein, K. Vitelli, and L. Jenkins
1995   Accountability: Responsibilities of Archaeologists to Other Interest Groups. In *Ethics in American Archaeology: Challenges for the 1990s,* edited by M. Lynott and A. Wylie, pp. 33–37. Society for American Archaeology, Washington, D.C.

Whitely, Peter
1988   *Deliberate Acts.* University of Arizona Press, Tucson.

Wiget, Andrew
1982   Truth and the Hopi: An Histiographic Study of Documented Oral Tradition Regarding the Coming of the Spanish. *Ethnohistory* 29:181–199.
1985   *Native American Literature.* Twayne, Boston.

Willey, Gordon R., and Philip Phillips
1958   *Method and Theory in American Archaeology.* University of Chicago Press, Chicago.

Willey, Gordon, and Jeremy Sabloff
  1980   *A History of American Archaeology,* second edition. W. H. Freeman, San Francisco.

Williams, Stephen
  1991   *Fantastic Archaeology: The Wild Side of North American Prehistory.* Philadelphia: University of Pennsylvania Press.

Zedeno, M. Nieves, and Richard W. Stoffle
  1995   Casa Grande Ruins National Monument: Foundations for Cultural Affiliation. Unpublished ms. on file, National Park Service, Western Archaeological and Conservation Center, Tucson, Arizona.

Zimmerman, Larry J.
  1989   Made Radical by My Own: An Archaeologist Learns to Accept Reburial. In *Conflict in the Archaeology of Living Traditions,* edited by R. Layton, pp. 60–67. Unwin Hyman, London.

Zimmerman, Larry, and Lawrence E. Bradley
  1993   The Crow Creek Massacre: Initial Coalescent Warfare and Speculations about the Genesis of Extended Coalescence. *Plains Anthropologist* 38(145):215–227.

About the Authors

ROGER ANYON has spent the past 20 years in various aspects of cultural resources management in the southwestern United States. His archaeological fieldwork has focused primarily in the Mimbres Valley of southwest New Mexico and the Zuni area of west-central New Mexico. Between 1985 and 1996 Anyon was director of the Zuni Archaeology Program and Zuni Heritage and Historic Preservation Office. He served as a member of the Society for American Archaeology Executive Board from 1992 to 1995 and has been a member of the Smithsonian Institution's Native American Repatriation Review Committee since 1990. His M.A. is from the University of New Mexico. Anyon is a cultural resources consultant based in Tucson. His address is 3227 N. Walnut, Tucson, AZ 85712 (e-mail: ranyon@worldnet.att.net).

THOMAS BAILOR received his B.A. in anthropology/sociology at St. Mary's College of Maryland in 1988. He worked as a technician for small contractors and then for the USDA Forest Service on Winema National Forest. At that time he was trained by members of the Klamath Tribe and exposed to Native American cultural resource issues. He later had a two-year appointment as an archaeologist for the Prairie City Ranger District on Malheur National Forest. He was hired by the Confederated Tribes of the Umatilla Indian Reservation (CTUIR) as an archaeologist with the Department of Economic and Community Development and currently works as a cultural resources technician for the CTUIR's Cultural Resources Protection Program. The program's address is P.O. Box 638, Pendleton, OR 97801.

RICHARD BEGAY is a member of the Navajo Nation and hails from Crystal, New Mexico. He has worked in the Navajo Nation's cultural preservation program for the past nine years as both an archaeologist and an ethnographer. He is very active in traditional Navajo practices, particularly the Nightway (Yei Bichei) and Blessingway ceremonies. Begay has a B.A. in anthropology from Dartmouth College and has done graduate work in anthropology at Northern Arizona University. He began a master's program in education at Harvard University in the fall of 1996 and intends to return home to teach in the cultural and historic preservation field. His address is P.O. Box 3025, Gallup, NM 87305 (e-mail: begayri@hugsel.harvard.edu).

ROBERT L. BROOKS is the state archaeologist with the Oklahoma Archaeological Survey. During his 15 years at the survey he has published on a variety of research, management, and education issues. Brooks has also worked to enhance communication and preservation efforts with tribal people. The Oklahoma Archaeological Survey's address is 111 Chesapeake, Norman, OK 73019–0575.

MICHAEL S. BURNEY received his B.A. in anthropology from the University of Idaho and his M.A. in Western American prehistory from the University of Colorado. He has been an archaeological and historical consultant since 1976 and established a consulting firm in 1978. In 1987 he began assisting the Confederated Tribes of the Umatilla Indian Reservation in building a tribal cultural resource protection program. He is currently the CTUIR tribal archaeologist and historic preservation officer. Burney also assists the Rosebud Sioux and the Northern Cheyenne tribes, and others, in cultural resource issues as a consulting archaeologist. His address is P.O. Box 7063, Boulder, CO 80306.

CECILE ELKINS CARTER chairs the Heritage Committee of the Caddo Indian Tribe of Oklahoma. She is the author of *Caddo Indians: Where We Came From* (University of Oklahoma Press, 1995). The book, a narrative history of the three branches of the Caddo nation, has received the Oklahoma History Book of the Year award. Her address is Caddo Tribe of Oklahoma, Route 1, Box 365, Mead, OK 73449 (e-mail: carterc@isc-durant.com).

JANET COHEN received her M.A. in applied anthropology in 1989 from the University of Maryland. She is currently employed by the Navajo Nation Historic Preservation Department–Roads Planning Program, where she specializes in the ethnographic component of cultural resource investigations and intertribal consultation. Prior to her work with the Navajo Nation, Cohen worked for the state of Alaska on a project aimed at assessing the impact of the *Exxon Valdez* oil spill on the traditional subsistence practices of Kodiak Island villagers. Her office address is P.O. Box 4950, Window Rock, AZ 86515.

BILLY L. CYPRESS is a member of the Seminole Tribe of Florida. He is the executive director of the Seminole Tribal Museum Authority. Primarily an educator, he is currently developing the official Seminole museum. This work has been challenging and it has offered him many related issues to address, such as the role of archaeology in the Seminole Tribe of Florida. His address at the Seminole Tribal Museum Authority is HC 61, Box 21-A, Clewiston, FL 33440.

KURT E. DONGOSKE has 19 years of professional experience in archaeology and cultural resource management, and 12 years experience in human osteological analysis. He has an M.A. degree in anthropology from the University of Arizona and a B.A. in anthropology from the University of Minnesota. From 1977 to 1989 he worked in varying capacities as a field archaeologist, crew chief, and field director throughout Arizona, Minnesota, and Idaho. Between 1989 and 1991, he was employed by the Navajo Nation Archaeology Department as a supervisory archaeologist and project director. Since 1991 he has been the tribal archaeologist with the Hopi Tribe. Dongoske is a member of SAA's Native American Relations Committee and is the associate editor for the "Working Together" column that appears in the *SAA Bulletin*, the newsletter of the Society for American Archaeology. He is also a member of the Society of Professional Archeologists' Committee on Native American Issues and the American Association of Physical Anthropologists' Career Development Committee. In 1994, during his term as an Executive Council Representative for the Arizona Archaeological Council, Dongoske organized and chaired a workshop on Native Americans and archaeology, which was funded through the inaugural granting cycle of the National Center for Preservation Training and Technology. He is also an adjunct faculty member in the Anthropology Department at Northern Arizona University, where he is assisting in the development of a Hopi educational program in the field of anthropology. His address at the Hopi Cultural Preservation Office is P.O. Box 123, Kykotsmovi, AZ 86039.

ALAN S. DOWNER received a B.A. in geology, an M.A. in anthropological archaeology, and a Ph.D. in anthropology from the University of Missouri at Columbia. From 1978 to 1983 he was employed in the Historic Sites Division of the Illinois Department of Conservation, during which time he served as the staff archaeologist for the Illinois State Historic Preservation Office. From 1983 to 1986 he was a historic preservation specialist with the Advisory Council on Historic Preservation and served as the senior archaeologist in the council's Western Division of Project Review in Denver. In 1986 he was appointed historic preservation officer for the Navajo Nation. During the next years he established the first tribal historic preservation office in the United States, developing it into the largest such agency in the country. Downer has published widely on archaeology, historic preservation, cultural resources management, and Native American preservation concerns. In 1990 he helped organize the Keepers of the Treasures and represented the Navajo Area on the organization's first Board of Directors. He has been a member of the National Trust for Historic Preservation's Preservation Forum for the past seven years. His address at the Navajo Nation Historic Preservation Department is P.O. Box 4950, Window Rock, AZ 86515.

ROGER ECHO-HAWK serves as repatriation coordinator for the Denver Art Museum and the Colorado Historical Society. His address at the Denver Art Museum is 100 W. 14th Avenue Parkway, Denver, CO 80204.

T.J. FERGUSON conducts anthropological research in Tucson, Arizona, as an independent consultant specializing in the archaeology and ethnohistory of the southwestern United States. Dr. Ferguson has worked on a variety of projects implemented by southwestern tribes to apply anthropological research in the preservation and management of tribal cultural resources. His address is 5000 W. Placita de los Vientos, Tucson, AZ 85745.

LEONARD A. FORSMAN is a member of the Suquamish Indian Tribe and an elected member for the past nine years of the seven-person Suquamish Tribal Council. He received his B.A. in anthropology from the University of Washington and has been the director of the Suquamish Tribal Cultural Center and Museum. He currently works for a private cultural resource consulting firm. His address is Larson Anthropological/Archaeological Services, P.O. Box 70106, Seattle, WA 98107.

REBA FULLER is a member of the Tuolumne Band of Me-Wuk Indians in central California. She currently serves as the NAGPRA project director of the Central Sierra Me-Wuk Cultural and Historic Preservation Committee, a consortium of two federally recognized and three nonfederally recognized Me-Wuk tribes or councils. Fuller directs the NAGPRA Compliance Project, which conducts research in archaeological collections on behalf of these five Me-Wuk tribes in four California counties. She was a recipient of the 1994–1995 National Park Service NAGPRA grant to tribes and, with the Phoebe Hearst Museum of Anthropology, University of California–Berkeley, a recipient of a 1996–1997 NAGPRA grant to museums. Fuller is actively involved with Native American issues in California. Her address at the Central Sierra Me-Wuk Cultural and Historic Preservation Committee is P.O. Box 699, Tuolumne, CA 95379. She can also be reached at the Phoebe Hearst Museum, 103 Kroeber Hall, University of California–Berkeley, CA 94720.

LORETTA JACKSON is a member of the Hualapai Tribe, whose traditional and contemporary homeland is located in northwestern Arizona. Jackson is program manager at the Hualapai Tribe Office of Cultural Resources (she has worked there since 1991). She, her family, and all her relatives reside at Peach Springs on the Hualapai Reservation. She is affiliated with Pine Springs Band through her father and Milkweed Springs Band through her mother. Loretta was raised in the Colorado and Hualapai plateau country among the juniper and ponderosa pines, as her family maintained their practices of Hualapai traditions and subsistence lifeways. With this as a context, members of Jackson's family committed themselves to incorporating Hualapai language, traditional cultural knowledge and social values into the Peach Springs Public Elementary School, resulting in the internationally acclaimed Hualapai Bilingual Education Program. These influences reinforce Jackson's dedication to work for the Hualapai Tribe. Her address at the Cultural Resources Division is P.O. Box 310, Peach Springs, AZ 86434.

G. PETER JEMISON is an enrolled member of the Seneca Nation of Indians. He is the site manager for Ganondagan State Historic Site, a seventeenth-century Seneca town located in Victor, New York. Jemison is the chairman of the Haudenosaunee Standing Committee on Burial Rules and Regulations and the NAGPRA representative for the Seneca Nation. His address at the Seneca Nation is P.O. Box 239, Victor, NY 14564.

ROSE A. KLUTH is the tribal historic preservation officer and heritage sites program director for the Leech Lake Band of Chippewa. She received her B.A. in anthropology from Northern Kentucky University and her M.A. in anthropology from the University of Wisconsin–Madison. She has been involved in archaeological fieldwork, management, and project review for 10 years. Her address at the Leech Lake Heritage Sites Program is Route 3, Box 100, Cass Lake, MN 56633 (e-mail: Rkluth@aol.com).

LILLIE LANE is a Navajo woman who belongs to the To'baahi (Near the Water) clan and was born for the Tł'ízílání (Manygoats) clan. She is from the westernmost end of the reservation, from around Dził Łichii (Shinumo Altar). Her formal education was at the University of Arizona. For three years she was a cultural specialist with the Navajo Nation Historic Preservation Department in Window Rock, Arizona. Her work included incorporating Navajo cultural values in the repatriation of ceremonial objects from museums, educational institutions, and federal agencies pursuant to the Native American Graves Protection Act. She has accepted an appointment as the McCune Curator at the Museum of Indian Arts and Culture, P. O. Box 2087, Santa Fe, NM 87504.

DOROTHY LIPPERT (Choctaw) is currently finishing a doctorate in anthropology at the University of Texas at Austin. She received a B.A. from Rice University in 1989 and an M.A. from the University of Texas at Austin in 1992. Her interests within archaeology include bioarchaeology, native tribes of the southeastern United States, and the moral and ethical issues surrounding repatriation. Her address is 10719 Burr Oak, San Antonio, TX 78230 (e-mail: d.lippert@mail.utexas.edu).

RENA MARTIN belongs to the Nashashidine'é and was born for Hooghan aní. Her maternal grandfather is Naakai Dine'é and her paternal grandfather is Tódich'ii'nii. She is from Bloomfield, New Mexico. Martin has worked in cultural resources management and historic preservation since 1978. Her B.A. is from Fort Lewis College. She plans to go back to school to earn a master's degree in American studies and then return home to teach Navajo students. She has been employed as an archaeologist but her favorite work has been as an ethnographer working in her own language with her Navajo people. Martin is the manager of the Traditional Culture Program in the Navajo Nation's Historic Preservation Department. She is also the secretary for the Keepers of the Treasures and is one of the Native American advisors for Crow Canyon Archaeological Research Center. Her office address is P.O. Box 4950, Window Rock, AZ 86515.

KATHY MUNNELL, a member of the Leech Lake Band of Chippewa in northern Minnesota, is currently employed by the Leech Lake Health Division. She has worked with the Leech Lake Tribal Council as a NAGPRA representative, as well as a liaison to the Leech Lake Elder Council. Munnell has dealt with a wide variety of cultural issues on the reservation involving burial sites, NAGPRA, and heritage sites protection. She has a strong background in social services and is certified as a chemical dependency counselor, a home heath aide, and a special education assistant. Munnell has also served as a family skills coordinator, a foster care worker, and an Ojibwe Cultural Arts assistant teacher. Her address at the Health Division is Route 3, Box 100, Cass Lake, MN 56633.

GORDON L. PULLAR, a Supiaq (Alutiiq), is the director of the Department of Alaska Native and Rural Development in the College of Rural Alaska, University of Alaska–Fairbanks. He is the Alaska representative to, and past president of,

Keepers of the Treasures: Cultural Council of American Indians, Alaska Natives, and Native Hawaiians and has represented the organization at the United Nations in Geneva. Pullar has been involved in tribal self-determination and cultural revitalization efforts for the past two decades, including six years as president of the Kodiak Area Native Association, the regional tribal organization for his home area of Kodiak Island, Alaska. He is currently the chairman of the Steering Committee for the Arctic Studies Center at the Smithsonian Institution and a member of the advisory board of "Dig Afognak," an Alaska Native–owned and controlled archaeological project. Pullar has published articles on cultural identity, cultural revitalization movements, repatriation, and other issues related to Native Americans. His address at the Department of Alaska Native and Rural Development is 2221 E. Northern Lights Blvd., Suite 213, Anchorage, AK 99508 (e-mail: ANGLP1@uaa.alaska.edu).

JOHN C. RAVESLOOT is the cultural resources coordinator for the Gila River Indian Community, Sacaton, Arizona. He also holds the position of adjunct professor in the Department of Anthropology at Arizona State University. Previously he held positions as research assistant professor in the department and assistant curator at Arizona State Museum, University of Arizona. Ravesloot received his Ph.D. in anthropology in 1984 from Southern Illinois University, Carbondale. His address at the Cultural Resource Management Program, Gila River Indian Community, is P.O. Box E, Sacaton, AZ 85247.

DAVID RICE is the Native American coordinator at the U.S. Corps of Engineers, Seattle District. His address is P.O. Box 3755, Seattle, WA 98124-2255.

ALEXA ROBERTS is a native of New Mexico and has been involved in cultural resource management in the Southwest since 1980. She conducted research on the history of Navajo occupation of Wupatki National Monument for the National Park Service and for her doctoral dissertation. Roberts earned her Ph.D. in anthropology from the University of New Mexico in 1992, and served as the assistant director of the Navajo Nation Historic Preservation Department in Window Rock, Arizona, from 1988 to 1992. From then until 1994 she was coprincipal investigator on the Glen Canyon Environmental Studies–Navajo Cultural Resources Project, researching Navajo history in the Grand Canyon. Currently, she and her five dogs live near Santa Fe, where she supports them by working as the cultural anthropologist for the Southwest System Support Office of the National Park Service. Her office address is P.O. Box 728, Santa Fe, NM 87504 (e-mail: alexa_roberts@nps.gov).

ROBERT HENRY ("HANK") STEVENS is a member of Osage Nation of northern Oklahoma. Stevens was born, raised, and educated in small towns on the southern

California coast. He received his higher education in Washington, Oregon, and California. He holds an interdisciplinary M.A. in social science and is an advanced doctoral candidate at the School of Social Sciences, University of California–Irvine, where he teaches American Indian studies, cultural anthropology, and geography. Since 1991 he has been an ethnographic consultant for the Hualapai Tribe, specializing in research designs, researcher training, and social scientific writing for the Hualapai Tribe's Office of Cultural Resources. His address is P.O. Box 627–4960, Irvine, CA 92716.

NINA SWIDLER has been involved in archaeology for more than 20 years. Between 1975 and 1989 she was employed by various state and federal agencies, private consultants, and universities in California, the Great Basin, and the Southwest. Her tenure as an archaeologist with the Navajo Nation began in 1989. Currently, Swidler manages the Flagstaff Office of the Navajo Nation Historic Preservation Department's Roads Planning Program, administers cultural resource management contracts, and is involved in compliance and intertribal consultation issues. She received her bachelor's degree in anthropology from the University of California–Santa Barbara and a master's degree in anthropology from Arizona State University, Tempe. Swidler serves on the Society for American Archaeology's Native American Relations Committee and is the treasurer for the Arizona Archaeological Council. Her office address is 124 N. San Francisco, Suite E, Flagstaff, AZ 96001 (e-mail: hpdroads@azaccess.com).

REBECCA TSOSIE (Pascua Yaqui) is an associate professor at the Arizona State University College of Law. Tsosie received her J.D. and B.A. degrees from the University of California–Los Angeles. She currently teaches on federal Indian law, property law, and seminars on cultural property and tribal environmental policy. She is the author of several articles dealing with tribal rights, and she has given numerous public lectures on tribal sovereignty and tribal cultural preservation. Her address at ASU College of Law is P.O. Box 877906, Tempe, AZ 85287–7906 (e-mail: rebecca.tsosie@asu.edu).

JEFFREY VAN PELT is a member of the Cayuse Tribe and manager of the Cultural Resource Program for the Confederated Tribes of the Umatilla Indian Reservation. He has been actively involved with asserting Umatilla tribal preservation concerns in the Pacific Northwest and is an advocate for the development of cultural preservation strategies in common with other Pacific Northwest tribes. Van Pelt has presented numerous lectures on management and protection of cultural resources from a tribal perspective. The program's address is P.O. Box 638, Pendleton, OR 97801.

PHILIP VICENTI is a member of the Zuni Tribe and currently holds several key leader positions in Zuni religious societies. His maternal clan is the Deer Clan and his paternal clan is the Eagle Clan. He holds the leader position in the Ahayuta (War God) Society and an interim leader position in the Katchina Society (Komosoma). Vicenti is presently employed by the Department of Human Services, Indian Health Service, Zuni Service Unit, as a computer system specialist. He attended several United States Air Force Technical Schools and the University of New Mexico. Vicenti is a Vietnam Veteran who served in Southeast Asia as a sergeant. His address is P.O. Box 1046, Zuni, NM 87327.

JOE WATKINS, a Choctaw Indian, is agency archeologist for the Bureau of Indian Affairs–Anadarko Agency and an adjunct professor of anthropology at the University of Oklahoma. His primary interests are ethics in archaeology and relationships between archaeologists and aboriginal populations. Dr. Watkins's address at the BIA Anadarko Agency is P.O. Box 309, Anadarko, OK 73005.

GARY WHITE DEER is one of Native America's best-known artists, who has exhibited both nationally and internationally and whose venues have included the American Embassy in Dublin and a private showing for the president of Ireland, Her Excellency Mary Robinson. A former tribal historic preservation officer and cultural resources department director, White Deer now serves as a regional director for the Keepers of the Treasures, where his focus is international repatriation. He also serves as an adviser to the National Museum of the American Indian and as a leader at Kullihoma, his tribal dance ground. He is executive director of CAIT, Inc., an internationally funded organization dedicated to humanitarian relief, reconciliation, and human rights education. White Deer is a member of the Choctaw Nation of Oklahoma. His address is Route 5, Box 308P, Ada, OK 74820.

LARRY J. ZIMMERMAN is adjunct professor of anthropology at the University of Iowa and research associate in the Office of the State Archaeologist of Iowa. He has served as executive secretary of the World Archaeological Congress, editor of *Plains Anthropologist, South Dakota Archaeology,* and the *World Archaeological Bulletin,* and associate editor of *American Antiquity.* Dr. Zimmerman's research interests and publications focus on Plains archaeology, public education, and computer applications. His address is 1840 Friendship Street, Iowa City, IA 52245 (e-mail: larry-zimmerman@uiowa.edu).

Index